To Harry:

Great fan of a
great game — and of the
Cardinals, f...

Bob Blow

Rookies of the Year

Jeff Bagwell, Houston Astros, 1991

ROOKIES
OF THE
YEAR

Bob Bloss

TEMPLE UNIVERSITY PRESS
Philadelphia

Temple University Press
1601 North Broad Street
Philadelphia PA 19122
www.temple.edu/tempress

Text design by Lynne Frost

Library of Congress Cataloging-in-Publication Data

Bloss, Bob, 1935–
    Rookies of the year / Robert Bloss.
        p.   cm.
    Includes index.
    ISBN 1-59213-164-6 (cloth : alk. paper)
        1. Rookie baseball players—Biography.   I. Title.

GV865.A1B589 2005
796.357′092′273—dc22
[B]
                                                    2004062086

2 4 6 8 9 7 5 3 1

To our own rookie, Alexandra Jill.

May you have a long lifetime filled with as many joys
as you bring to your four grandparents.

Contents

Acknowledgments ix

Introduction 1
One and Done

1. The Jackie Robinson Award 5
A Jewel in the Legacy of Baseball's First Rookie of the Year

Chronological Listing of Rookies of the Year
(1947–2004) 11

2. First Steps toward Cooperstown 13
Rookies of the Year in the Hall of Fame

3. A Double Helping of Hardware 40
Rookies of the Year Who Became Most Valuable Players

4. Dugout Directors 59
Rookies of the Year Who Became Managers

Rookies of the Year by Franchise (1947–2004) 75

5. The Short Timers 78
Rookies of the Year with Short Careers

6. Available Only Once 96
Other Rookies of the Year

7. Ready for 21st-Century Action   158
Rookies of the Year Still Active in the Major Leagues

**List of *The Sporting News* Rookies of the Year
(1946–2004)**   196

Summary   200
Saluting So Few

Index   205

Acknowledgments

The author gratefully acknowledges the cheerful assistance and professional expertise offered by numerous interested parties, including the following:

Jay Alves, Robbin Barnes, Baseball Solutions Info, Kevin Behan, Greg Casterioto, Richard Cerrone, Matt Charbonneau, Murray Chass, Bob DiBiasio;

And Andrew Feirstein, Jennifer French, Debbie Gallas, Molly Gallatin, Mary Ann Gettis, Paul Hagen, Elrod Hendricks, Tim Hevly, Steve Hoem, Jay Horwitz, editor Micah Kleit, Adam Liebermann, P. J. Loyello;

And Jim Luker, Debbie Matson, Christine Negley, John Olguin, Sharon Pannozzo, Johnny Pesky, Lisa Ramsperger, Scott Reifert, Peter Reinhart, the Jackie Robinson Foundation, Mitchell Rose, Jim Schultz;

And Nancy Score, Marty Sewell, Kevin Shea, Larry Shenk, Chris Stathos, Leigh Tobin, Rich Westcott, Dave Wilson, Dave Witty, and Don Zimmer.

Rookies of the Year

Introduction

One and Done

A rookie, according to a dictionary definition, is "one who is in his first year of participation in a major professional sport" (*Webster's New Collegiate Dictionary*, 1975).

It seems reasonable to expand that definition now by adding a "her" to "his," and to assume the subject is a first-year participant in any endeavor . . . major, minor, amateur, anything. Not just a big league sport.

However, for the purpose of what follows on these pages, we arbitrarily revert to the original, narrower description, and focus entirely on major league baseball rookies.

Not just some of them, but all of the 116 talented men officially saluted as Rookies of the Year.

This prestigious award is unique because a player has only one opportunity to win it. Cy Young awards, Manager of the Year, and MVP honors can be achieved multiple times, as can individual "best" years in all offensive and defensive categories. In quotes from the profiles that follow, several players remind us just how distinctive the Rookie of the Year honor is.

THE AWARD'S HISTORY

Professional baseball was in business for the better part of a century before official Rookie of the Year recognition was instituted. One could wonder if, say, young George H. Ruth would have outpolled George H. Sisler for the honor if the award had been presented back in 1915. Or, in 1932, might Arky Vaughan have won out over Dizzy Dean? We'll never know.

It was 1940 when something resembling the current Rookie of the Year citation was first bestowed. The Chicago chapter of the Baseball Writers' Association of America (BBWAA) initiated it. For seven years—1940 through 1946—the Chicago writers selected one player, from among all 16 major league teams, as Rookie of the Year.

The first honoree was Cleveland shortstop Lou Boudreau, an eventual Hall of Famer. Pistol Pete Reiser of the pennant-winning Brooklyn Dodgers was the 1941 choice. He was followed by Cardinal pitcher Johnny Beazley, Yankee third baseman Billy Johnson, New York Giants right-hander Bill Voiselle, Red Sox pitcher Boo Ferriss, and, in 1946, by Cubs first baseman Eddie Waitkus.

In late '46, following baseball's first post–World War II full season, *The Sporting News,* the so-called bible of baseball, inaugurated its own Rookie of the Year choices. Phillies slugger Del Ennis was its initial RoY selection. Experimenting with a number of different formats over the years, *The Sporting News* has continued to name top rookies ever since. Its complete listing of honorees appears later in the book.

Whether the Baseball Writers' Association of America felt that *The Sporting News* was intruding on the Chicago chapter's notoriety, or whether the BBWAA simply chose to expand its program, is no longer clear. Whatever its motives, the BBWAA went national. In other words, it decided to have its members in all major league cities choose Rookies of the Year.

So, beginning in 1947, the writers have been Major League Baseball's authorized voting body. It is this national BBWAA group's 116 honorees who are recognized in this book as baseball's official Rookies of the Year.

As an added distinction, since 1987 the annual prize has officially been the Jackie Robinson Award in honor of the national BBWAA's first recipient in 1947.

ROOKIE OF THE YEAR CRITERIA AND QUALIFICATIONS

A player shall be considered a rookie *unless,* during a previous season or seasons, he had (a) exceeded 130 at bats—or 50 innings pitched—in the major leagues; or (b) accumulated more than 45 days on the active roster of a major league club or clubs during the period of a 25-player limit (typically opening day through August 31). Military service time and time on the disabled list are not charged as time on active rosters.

In connection with the player profiles that will follow you'll frequently find that a man's career start technically preceded his official Rookie of the Year season. That's because he participated in big league action earlier, but not enough of it to disqualify him from rookie status.

Scott Rolen is the foremost example. A 1997 Rookie of the Year, Rolen joined the Philadelphia Phillies in August 1996. By mid-September he had recorded precisely 130 at bats. During his next plate appearance he was injured by a pitched ball and removed from the lineup, and was unable to play again that year. "Hit by pitch" is not an official time at bat. He was therefore still eligible for the rookie award. And, indeed, he won it the following season.

Various selection formulas, sometimes altered from season to season, guided the writers in the early years. During the 1960s players weren't considered if they had more than 75 at bats, registered more than 45 innings pitched, or were rostered between May 15 and September 1 in a previous season. The current criteria were established in the early 1970s.

CASTING THE BALLOTS

Two BBWAA members who regularly cover each major league team are selected to vote for Rookie of the Year. Thus, 28 journalists covering the 14 American League teams cast ballots; 32 writers, two for each club, vote for the National League's top freshman.

Each writer can vote for three players under a ranking system that awards five points for a first-place vote, three points for second, and one point for third.

Example: When Eric Hinske was chosen American League Rookie of the Year in 2002, he received 19 first-place votes (a 95-point total). He placed second on nine ballots (27 points). Hinske's overall score: 122 ballot points. Two Baltimore pitchers were runners-up. Rodrigo Lopez, the only American Leaguer other than Hinske with first-place votes, totaled 97 points. His Oriole teammate, Jorge Julio, earned one second-place pick and 11 thirds ... 14 points.

Most Valuable Player voters are permitted to cast ballots for up to 10 players. But for the other major award categories—Manager of the Year, Cy Young, and of course Rookie of the Year—BBWAA writers can submit no more than three names.

A CELEBRATED ROLL OF HONOR

On the following pages each of the 116 Rookies of the Year, since 1947, is profiled. You'll see that pitcher Bob Grim is the only RoY to record 20 victories in his rookie season. That Pittsburgh, of the 16 franchises in business from 1947 on, did not have its first Rookie of the Year until 2004. That the Boston Braves had two in the award's first four years, but the All-Star-laden Milwaukee Braves never had any. That the Dodgers have 16 Rookies of the Year, by far the most of any franchise, and feature an unprecedented five consecutive selections from 1992 through '96. That Joe Charboneau appeared in fewer games than any of the other RoY position players.

And that such top-shelf luminaries as Mickey Mantle, Hank Aaron, Ernie Banks, Mike Schmidt, Steve Carlton, Brooks Robinson, Roberto Clemente, Greg Maddux, Sandy Koufax, Al Kaline, Barry Bonds, and Bob Gibson were not selected as Rookies of the Year.

Each Rookie of the Year's up-or-down career following his breakthrough first season is reviewed, as are the post-baseball ventures of those RoY who are no longer active major leaguers. Be they current or former players, we raise a toast to every one of them.

1 The Jackie Robinson Award

A Jewel in the Legacy of Baseball's First Rookie of the Year

JACKIE ROBINSON
1947   Brooklyn Dodgers, Major League Rookie of the Year

Personal Data: B. January 31, 1919, at Cairo, GA. D. October 24, 1972.
Physical Attributes: 5'11½", playing weight 195 lbs. Bats right, throws right.
Rookie Year, 1947:   Primary position first base. Led league with 29 stolen bases.
Total Career, 10 years: Dodgers 1947–56.

	BA	G	H	2B	3B	HR	RBI
1947	.297	151	175	31	5	12	48
Lifetime	.311	1,382	1,518	273	54	137	734

The Baseball Writers' Association of America could not have picked a better time to inaugurate its national organization's annual Rookie of the Year selections.

Nineteen forty-seven was perfect.

Because never in history has a rookie been more scrutinized, more publicized, and more a subject of controversy than 1947 Brooklyn Dodger newcomer Jackie Robinson.

It is indeed fitting that this pioneer—for whom babies are named, postage stamps issued, and monuments cast—was crowned the BBWAA's first Rookie of the Year.

Appropriate, too, was Commissioner Peter Ueberroth's 1987 announcement that, thenceforth, the prestigious accolade would be known officially as the Jackie Robinson Award.

Jackie Robinson, Brooklyn Dodgers, 1947
The famous pathfinder, major league baseball's first African American player in the 20th century, was the national Baseball Writers' Association of America's first Rookie of the Year. Since 1987, the trophy, presented to the honored freshmen in both the American and National leagues, has been officially known as the Jackie Robinson Rookie of the Year Award.
(Courtesy of Los Angeles Dodgers)

Voters usually have a relatively easy time choosing Rookie of the Year winners. Many times the honoree is a clear-cut unanimous choice. Yes, occasionally decision-making can be difficult, as we see with two pairs of cowinners over the years, as well as a few other tight elections. Invariably, though, the Jackie Robinson Award goes to men who've started their big league careers with season-long excellence. Selectors base their voting on the performances turned in during *that first year*, with no regard for what the players' future production might be.

The majority of those futures, as you'd figure, are relatively lengthy—about 12 seasons on average. With few exceptions, the outstanding freshman years chalked up by Rookies of the Year usually predict fulfilling careers. As Jackie Robinson's was.

His career lasted only 10 years. But it featured appearances in six World Series, a Most Valuable Player award, six seasons hitting more than .300, one batting championship, two stolen base titles, and an incredible 20 thefts of home plate. It's a career forever memorialized at baseball's Hall of Fame.

Numerous players' uniform numbers have been retired by their principal teams. During 1997 ceremonies recognizing the 50-year anniversary of Jackie

Robinson's first big league season, his number 42 was retired by Major League Baseball. No player on any team (excepting those men then currently assigned that numeral) will ever again wear number 42.

A second baseman in midcareer, Robinson's initial season was spent entirely at first base for Brooklyn. His numbers were solid that first year, yet not spectacular: 12 homers, only 48 RBI, and a .297 average. But he was an intimidating base runner. Jack stole 29 bases to lead the National League, hit 31 doubles, and scored 125 runs as the Dodgers won the pennant. Creditable enough stats, and worthy of his rookie award. That season and the next the BBWAA presented only one Major League Rookie of the Year award. Voters ranked New York Giants pitcher Larry Jansen second to Robinson. Other legitimate contenders in 1947 were Yankees pitcher Frank Shea, Giants outfielder Bobby Thomson, and two first basemen—Earl Torgeson of the Boston Braves and the Philadelphia Athletics' Ferris Fain.

Jackie Robinson's statistics, the rings and trophies he earned, and the honors—beginning with Rookie of the Year—are much less remembered than the way he entered the big leagues. And how he brilliantly managed to pave a path for the hundreds of other African Americans who have followed him into professional baseball.

The story of Brooklyn baseball executive Branch Rickey's successful effort to shatter the game's so-called color barrier has been retold for nearly 60 years now. Jackie Robinson is the principal character.

Organized baseball—the two major leagues and their minor league affiliates—unofficially but firmly prevented black athletes from participating. So talented black youngsters displayed their baseball skills in a variety of Negro leagues where spectator attendance was sometimes thin but where competition was always spirited. Many Negro Major Leaguers were judged to have talent equal—and frequently superior—to organized baseball standouts. (Recent research indicates that a handful of African Americans briefly made their way into 19th-century lineups during professional baseball's unstable formative years.)

Eventually, in 1971—a quarter century after Jackie Robinson's Organized Baseball debut—Negro league players became eligible for Hall of Fame installation. Satchel Paige, Judy Johnson, Buck Leonard, Josh Gibson, Martin Dihigo, Ray Dandridge, and "Cool Papa" Bell are among the more than one dozen now enshrined at Cooperstown.

Branch Rickey was certain that somewhere in the Negro leagues was a player with the desire, baseball talent, and emotional stability to handle his "noble experiment"—opening organized baseball to black players. Rickey's scouts pinpointed Jackie Robinson, a first-year shortstop with the Kansas City Monarchs. He was a U.S. Army veteran and a former UCLA scholar-athlete. Rickey invited Robinson to a Brooklyn meeting purportedly to discuss a new Negro league. Upon Jackie's arrival Rickey explained his actual plan.

Robinson, then 26, understood the necessity to "turn the other cheek." If he did not, warned Rickey, the experiment would not work. Jackie agreed to a contract. When the 1946 season opened he was the first black in a professional baseball uniform in the 20th century. Jackie played for the Dodgers' Triple-A Montreal Royals farm club that year. Enduring recurring taunts and inside pitches all year, Robinson simply won the International League batting title with a .349 mark. He was as ready as he'd ever be. For Brooklyn.

April 15, 1947. Boston Braves at Brooklyn's Ebbets Field. Surprisingly only 25,623 fans showed up, 9,000 short of capacity, to witness the game's most significant event of the century and a civil rights happening of monumental proportions:

A black man playing major league baseball.

Robinson happened to go 0-for-3 that afternoon, but his season-long exploits clearly warranted his Rookie of the Year selection, not only for his box score performances, but also for what he had to do between pitches, during pregame warm-ups, entering and exiting ball parks, and interfacing at the workplace with teammates and opponents. Sometimes friends and foes were indistinguishable.

Degrading racial comments were regularly issued from opposition dugouts, especially Philadelphia's and St. Louis's in the early years. National League president Ford Frick proclaimed that any player who would boycott a game against the Dodgers would be suspended. "This is the United States of America," he said. "One citizen has as much right to play as any other." The rebels backed down.

In his biography, Robinson wrote, "Sometimes I felt tortured. I just tried to play ball and ignore the insults. It was getting to me. What was I doing turning the other cheek?" But turn it he did. "The haters almost won that round."

Jackie's confrontations with profane bigots were tougher than his challenges from baseball's day-to-day complexities. After his fine rookie season, followed by .296 hitting and 85 RBI in 1948, Robinson registered his career year that was capped off with the 1949 MVP award. Its highlights: a league-leading .342 batting average, 124 runs batted in, 203 hits, 38 doubles, and a league-best and career-high 37 stolen bases. His achievements led the Dodgers to another World Series (and, yes, another defeat by New York).

He was 30 by then, and still delivering prime-of-career quality. Having transferred to second base in 1948, then to third, and eventually the outfield, his game showed no significant signs of slowing down until 1955. Injuries limited him to 105 games that year, and a .256 average. Jack improved to .275 over 117 games in '56. Fans were not aware of it at the time, but the 1956 World Series was Jackie's baseball farewell. He homered once and hit .250 in the seven-game set against the Yankees. In his last at bat Jackie struck out. Then he retired from baseball.

His knees were sore, he was then 38, and he wasn't particularly chummy with manager Walt Alston or the Dodgers front office. *Look Magazine* offered him $50,000 for the story of his baseball career and retirement. But before the magazine was distributed, Brooklyn surprisingly traded him across town to the New York Giants, who offered him a good salary. What to do? Following his conscience he fulfilled his deal with *Look* and upheld his decision to retire. Journalist Roger Kahn said Jackie was disturbed about that until the next season's opening day. When Robinson awakened that morning, his knee hurt so badly he could not get out of bed. He never again regretted his decision.

Out of baseball for good, Jack was employed by commercial firms, worked with political campaigns, and lent his time and talents to civil rights issues. His first post-baseball job was with the Chock Full o' Nuts coffee company as personnel manager and unofficial public relations representative. He later was a founder of the Freedom National Bank in Harlem and a low-cost housing project in Brooklyn.

Robinson also worked for the 1960 campaign committee of Richard M. Nixon, and in 1964 was deputy director for Nelson Rockefeller's presidential campaign. Soon after joining Chock Full o' Nuts, Jackie became cochairman of the NAACP's Freedom Fund Drive.

While still with the Dodgers, Jackie and his wife Rachel moved to the Stamford, Connecticut, area, where they resided throughout the remainder of Jack's life. Their three children—Jackie, Jr., Sharon, and David—grew up there.

Sadly, Jackie, Jr., became addicted to drugs while serving in Vietnam. At age 24 and recovering, he was a fatal car accident victim just one year prior to his father's death. David, now in his 50s, has owned a coffee farm in Tanzania. Sharon, the middle Robinson child, is a certified nurse-midwife who now has a position in Major League Baseball's marketing department. Her son accepted a football scholarship to UCLA, where his grandfather had once played football, basketball, and a little baseball, and ran track.

Rachel Robinson, a former nursing professional, is as energetic and involved today as she was 50 years ago. Now in her 80s, she is the founder and active leader of the Jackie Robinson Foundation. Headquartered in midtown Manhattan, the foundation awards four-year college scholarships to academically gifted students of color with financial need. Students are encouraged to continue the Robinson family's legacy of commitment to social causes and community concerns. Since Rachel Robinson founded it in 1973, JRF has issued more than 800 scholarships.

As the 50th anniversary of Jackie's major league debut neared, Rachel wrote a book about the Robinson family. It included numerous memories of that 1947 Rookie of the Year season—its shameful incidents but its triumphs too, and what those meant for the hundreds whose careers followed Jackie's.

"I remember 1947 as a relief and not an accomplishment," wrote Mrs. Robinson. "After all we had gone through to get there, all I can remember is feeling relieved."

By the late 1960s Jack's health had begun to deteriorate. Diabetes sapped his strength. His gait was slowed, a sad sign to those who had watched him run with determination and resolve just 20 years earlier. Cardiac concerns also surfaced. Eventually his eyesight was severely impaired. In October 1972, in commemoration of Jackie's first big league game, he threw out the first pitch prior to World Series Game Two in Cincinnati.

Nine days later, stricken with a heart attack, Jackie Robinson died. He was 53.

His funeral service in New York was attended by more than 3,000 persons. The Reverend Jesse Jackson spoke there: "[Jackie] didn't integrate baseball for himself. This man turned the stumbling block into a stepping-stone."

Jack Roosevelt Robinson would have turned 86 in early 2005. In the 58 years since he first entered the Brooklyn Dodgers lineup, thousands of examples of his courage, tenacity, talent, and contributions have been commemorated—nowhere more appropriately than on the facing of the handsome trophy presented annually to baseball's Rookies of the Year: The Jackie Robinson Award.

Chronological Listing of Rookies of the Year (1947–2004)

Major League

1947	Jackie Robinson, Brooklyn Dodgers
1948	Alvin Dark, Boston Braves

	American League	National League
1949	Roy Sievers, St. Louis	Don Newcombe, Brooklyn
1950	Walt Dropo, Boston	Sam Jethroe, Boston
1951	Gil McDougald, New York	Willie Mays, New York
1952	Harry Byrd, Philadelphia	Joe Black, Brooklyn
1953	Harvey Kuenn, Detroit	Jim Gilliam, Brooklyn
1954	Bob Grim, New York	Wally Moon, St. Louis
1955	Herb Score, Cleveland	Bill Virdon, St. Louis
1956	Luis Aparicio, Chicago	Frank Robinson, Cincinnati
1957	Tony Kubek, New York	Jack Sanford, Philadelphia
1958	Albie Pearson, Washington	Orlando Cepeda, San Francisco
1959	Bob Allison, Washington	Willie McCovey, San Francisco
1960	Ron Hansen, Baltimore	Frank Howard, Los Angeles
1961	Don Schwall, Boston	Billy Williams, Chicago
1962	Tom Tresh, New York	Ken Hubbs, Chicago
1963	Gary Peters, Chicago	Pete Rose, Cincinnati
1964	Tony Oliva, Minnesota	Dick Allen, Philadelphia
1965	Curt Blefary, Baltimore	Jim Lefebvre, Los Angeles
1966	Tommie Agee, Chicago	Tommy Helms, Cincinnati
1967	Rod Carew, Minnesota	Tom Seaver, New York
1968	Stan Bahnsen, New York	Johnny Bench, Cincinnati
1969	Lou Piniella, Kansas City	Ted Sizemore, Los Angeles
1970	Thurman Munson, New York	Carl Morton, Montreal
1971	Chris Chambliss, Cleveland	Earl Williams, Atlanta
1972	Carlton Fisk, Boston	Jon Matlack, New York
1973	Al Bumbry, Baltimore	Gary Matthews, San Francisco
1974	Mike Hargrove, Texas	Bake McBride, St. Louis

Chronological Listing of Rookies of the Year (1947–2004) (continued)

	American League	National League
1975	Fred Lynn, Boston	John Montefusco, San Francisco
1976	Mark Fidrych, Detroit	Butch Metzger, San Diego . . . and Pat Zachry, Cincinnati
1977	Eddie Murray, Baltimore	Andre Dawson, Montreal
1978	Lou Whitaker, Detroit	Bob Horner, Atlanta
1979	John Castino, Minnesota . . . and Alfredo Griffin, Toronto	Rick Sutcliffe, Los Angeles
1980	Joe Charboneau, Cleveland	Steve Howe, Los Angeles
1981	Dave Righetti, New York	Fernando Valenzuela, Los Angeles
1982	Cal Ripken, Jr., Baltimore	Steve Sax, Los Angeles
1983	Ron Kittle, Chicago	Darryl Strawberry, New York
1984	Alvin Davis, Seattle	Dwight Gooden, New York
1985	Ozzie Guillen, Chicago	Vince Coleman, St. Louis
1986	Jose Canseco, Oakland	Todd Worrell, St. Louis
1987	Mark McGwire, Oakland	Benito Santiago, San Diego
1988	Walt Weiss, Oakland	Chris Sabo, Cincinnati
1989	Gregg Olson, Baltimore	Jerome Walton, Chicago
1990	Sandy Alomar, Jr., Cleveland	David Justice, Atlanta
1991	Chuck Knoblauch, Minnesota	Jeff Bagwell, Houston
1992	Pat Listach, Milwaukee	Eric Karros, Los Angeles
1993	Tim Salmon, California	Mike Piazza, Los Angeles
1994	Bob Hamelin, Kansas City	Raul Mondesi, Los Angeles
1995	Marty Cordova, Minnesota	Hideo Nomo, Los Angeles
1996	Derek Jeter, New York	Todd Hollandsworth, Los Angeles
1997	Nomar Garciaparra, Boston	Scott Rolen, Philadelphia
1998	Ben Grieve, Oakland	Kerry Wood, Chicago
1999	Carlos Beltran, Kansas City	Scott Williamson, Cincinnati
2000	Kazuhiro Sasaki, Seattle	Rafael Furcal, Atlanta
2001	Ichiro Suzuki, Seattle	Albert Pujols, St. Louis
2002	Eric Hinske, Toronto	Jason Jennings, Colorado
2003	Angel Berroa, Kansas City	Dontrelle Willis, Florida
2004	Bobby Crosby, Oakland	Jason Bay, Pittsburgh

2 First Steps toward Cooperstown

Rookies of the Year in the Hall of Fame

Their Rookie of the Year seasons were springboards to baseball immortality for an even one dozen players now enshrined at the Hall of Fame.

Arbitrarily added to their profiles that follow are two other men—Mark McGwire and Cal Ripken, Jr.—who most assuredly will join their Rookie of the Year brethren in Cooperstown when their five-year waiting period ends in 2006.

It's likely that others, who more recently received Rookie of the Year honors, will themselves eventually complete careers worthy of Hall of Fame consideration. As Rookies of the Year they're clearly off to a head start.

Rookies of the Year in the Hall of Fame	
Rookie, Year	Induction Year
Luis Aparicio, 1956	1984
Johnny Bench, 1968	1989
Rod Carew, 1967	1991
Orlando Cepeda, 1958	1999
Carlton Fisk, 1972	2000
Willie Mays, 1951	1979
Willie McCovey, 1959	1986
Eddie Murray, 1977	2003
Frank Robinson, 1956	1982
Jackie Robinson, 1947	1962
Tom Seaver, 1967	1992
Billy Williams, 1961	1987

LUIS APARICIO
1956   Chicago White Sox, American League

Personal Data: B. April 29, 1934, at Maracaibo, Venezuela.
Physical Attributes: 5′ 9″, playing weight 160 lbs. Bats right, throws right.
Rookie Year, 1956:   Primary position shortstop. 21 stolen bases to lead AL for first of nine consecutive seasons.
Total Career, 18 years: White Sox 1956–62; Orioles ʼ63–67; White Sox ʼ68–70; Red Sox ʼ71–73.

	BA	G	H	2B	3B	HR	RBI
1956	.266	152	142	19	6	3	56
Lifetime	.262	2,599	2,677	394	92	83	791

When Luis Aparicio was enshrined at the Hall of Fame, a few skeptics raised their eyebrows about his qualifications. After all, they observed, he achieved only a modest .262 lifetime batting average and hit over .300 only once in his 18-year major league career.

However, the handful of doubters were corrected when reminded that the Hall of Fame can acknowledge skills other than offensive prowess. The composite of Aparicio's credentials more than certified his Hall admittance.

His talent was apparent at the very start of Luis's career, his 1956 Rookie of the Year season in Chicago. Not only did he lead the American League with 21 steals that season, but he would go on to pace the league in stolen bases for a record nine consecutive years.

Luis Aparicio, the first Venezuela native to be inducted at Cooperstown, is widely credited with returning the stolen base to its former role as a major offensive weapon.

Base-path speed was just one of Aparicio's key assets. The wide-ranging shortstop with the strong arm was a nine-time Gold Glove winner. He's among all-time leaders in putouts and total chances, and is fondly remembered as part of the Aparicio–Nelson Fox double-play combination that helped spark the Go-Go White Sox to their 1959—and most recent—World Series appearance.

Later in Luis's career he was an important part of the Baltimore Orioles' first American League—and World Series—championship. He paced the league in at bats that season and fielded flawlessly as Baltimore swept Los Angeles in the 1966 World Series.

After five solid seasons as an Oriole, Luis was traded back to Chicago, where he put together his two best batting averages—.280 in 1969 and .313 the next year. In 1971, approaching age 37, he was dealt to the Red Sox, for whom he played three years and completed his active career.

Little Looie, as he was often called, was one of the most durable, injury-free middle infielders of all time. He played in more than 100 games in each of his 18 seasons. Only four times did he miss more than a dozen games. Aparicio was also a perennial participant in the All-Star Game. He was chosen for the AL squad on 10 occasions, including seven consecutive years from 1958 through 1964.

When Luis Aparicio's lifetime accomplishments were collectively put in full view, skeptics were won over. His Hall of Fame induction was cheerfully hailed. And nowhere more than in his native Venezuela, where he still resides. As his selection was announced during a January 1984 winter league game in Caracas, 10,000 fans applauded for several minutes.

Two decades later there was clear-cut proof that the baseball public continues to hold Luis in high esteem. It was nearly a half century after his exciting Rookie of the Year season. Yet, when he was introduced as the American League's honorary captain during the 2003 All-Star Game hosted by the White Sox, Chicago fans heartily remembered him with another lengthy hats-off salute.

JOHNNY BENCH
1968   Cincinnati Reds, National League

Personal Data: B. December 7, 1947, at Oklahoma City, OK.
Physical Attributes: 6′ 1″, playing weight 197 lbs. Bats right, throws right.
Rookie Year, 1968:   Primary position catcher.
Total Career, 17 years: Reds 1967–83.

	BA	G	H	2B	3B	HR	RBI
1968	.275	154	155	40	2	15	82
Lifetime	.267	2,158	2,040	381	24	389	1,376

Once every two or three years there comes to baseball a man whose skills and charisma are so magnetic that fans will say they'd buy a ticket just to see him display his craftsmanship—regardless of what else might happen in that day's game.

Names such as DiMaggio, Bonds, Gehringer, several Robinsons, Rose, Ruth, and many All-Star pitchers are among those that come to mind.

And, of course, Johnny Bench.

The National League's 1968 Rookie of the Year was hailed as a "sure thing" even before he first donned a Cincinnati Reds uniform. In 1966, before his 19th birthday, Bench had already been named Minor League Player of the Year. His jersey number had been retired by his Carolina League club. At the outset of the 1968 season, Bench's first full big league campaign, Ted Williams presented him with a baseball signed to "a Hall of Famer for sure."

It took just one time through the National League to convince opponents and patrons alike that this young Oklahoman was something special. No surprise then—in fact it was soon expected—that he would be Rookie of the Year. Prior to the season Johnny himself was privately confident that he would win that honor.

When the 1968 campaign ended, Bench had hit .275 with respectable but not spectacular power numbers.

He rapidly increased both his average and long-ball totals. He hit .293 in both 1969 and '70. If his 1970 season were categorized as a career year, that might be an understatement. Bench, en route to his first NL Most Valuable Player award (the other came in 1972), combined that .293 batting average with a league-leading 45 home runs and 148 runs batted in. That year Cincinnati, under rookie manager Sparky Anderson, won its first of four pennants during the decade of the 1970s when the aptly labeled Big Red Machine was baseball's most prolific team.

Bench's leadership—with the Reds pitching staff, with the examples he set through on-field offensive and defensive excellence, and in the clubhouse—was a major factor in the ball club's decade-long successes. Of course, such All-Star-caliber teammates as Pete Rose, Joe Morgan, Tony Perez, Dave Concepcion, and George Foster had something to do with the championships, too.

In 1972, another NL flag-winning summer, Bench again led the league in homers (40) and RBI (125). He was the runs batted-in leader once more after that, with 129 in 1974.

All the while, game after game, Bench conducted a virtual clinic on the art of catching. His style behind the plate was fluid and graceful. His arm was one of the strongest ever displayed by a catcher. He regularly blocked base runners with intimidating resolve. And his one-handed receiving style—at first criticized—was soon adopted as standard.

His brilliant fielding average, over the course of his 17 seasons, was .987. Strictly as a catcher, his mark was even better because his final three years found him playing first base or third (and erring there too often). By then his knees were feeling the wear of more than 15 years of major and minor league crouching. Reds managers placed him at those infield slots to keep his bat in the lineup. No designated hitter, you know, in the National League!

Bench's fielding excellence, as a catcher, was spotlighted nationally in 45 postseason games—league championship contests and World Series. He committed only two errors in those 45 games. He recorded 264 putouts and was credited with 36 assists. Johnny's probably remembered more for his 1976 World Series hitting, though, than for his defensive contributions. His .533 average, featuring a double, triple, two homers, and six RBI, led Cincinnati to a four-game sweep of the Yankees. He was the Series MVP.

That World Series was Bench's last. He played seven more years, but called it quits in 1983 after his productivity ebbed and his knees continued to ache.

A brief summary of his career quickly explains his first-ballot admission to the Hall of Fame:

Selection to 14 All-Star teams ... two MVP awards ... 100 or more games caught 13 times ... all-time Cincinnati leader in home runs (389) and RBI

(1,376)... among Reds' top four career hitters in at bats, games, runs scored, hits, total bases, extra-base hits.

Shortly after Bench's final season, Cincinnati officials retired his number 5 uniform.

Today Johnny Bench looks as if he could still go nine innings—if he were able to crouch behind a big league plate. He works out regularly and is a frequent and good golfer. In fact, he once considered joining the PGA's Senior Tour. He's a perennial golf-outing champ at Cooperstown when Hall of Famers convene there for Induction Weekend each summer.

You still get a glimpse of him in television commercials, and he represents major league All-Stars in connection with MLB marketing and public relations at sponsors' trade shows and seminars.

When not golfing or appearing officially in behalf of baseball, the 1968 Rookie of the Year and two-time MVP is still officially a Cincinnati Red. Not in uniform, of course, but as a special consultant to the general manager.

ROD CAREW
1967   Minnesota Twins, American League

Personal Data: B. October 1, 1945, at Gatun, Canal Zone.
Physical Attributes: 6′ 0″, playing weight 170 lbs. Bats left, throws right.
Rookie Year, 1967:   Primary position second base.
Total Career, 19 years: Twins 1967–78; Angels '79–85.

	BA	G	H	2B	3B	HR	RBI
1967	.292	137	150	22	7	8	51
Lifetime	.328	2,469	3,053	445	112	92	1,015

If all Rookies of the Year had improved their careers year after nearly every year the way Rod Carew did, significantly more of them would have their images engraved at Cooperstown.

All of them start off well, of course. But more than half of the position players who were Rookies of the Year finished their careers with lifetime figures that failed to match their great starts.

Rod Carew is a shining exception.

The Canal Zone native, who as a teenager moved with his mother to his grandmother's New York City home, started out with a solid .292 average for the 1967 Minnesota Twins. After 19 seasons, when he closed out his career as a California Angel, Carew's lifetime batting average proudly stood at .328.

No other Rookie of the Year ever finished that much better, 36 percentage points higher, than his first year's performance.

Of course only four other Rookies of the Year—Messrs. Mays, Murray, Ripken, and Rose—earned admittance to the prestigious 3,000-hit circle. Rod

Rod Carew, Minnesota Twins, 1967
Hall of Famer was five-time AL batting
champion. Totaled 3,053 hits and registered a
.328 batting average over 19 seasons with
Twins and Angels.
(Courtesy of Minnesota Twins)

Carew totaled 3,053 base hits. Only 12 Rookies of the Year are Hall of Fame members. Carew was a 1991 inductee. Relatively few Rookies of the Year had uniform numbers retired. Carew was so honored by *two* teams. No future Minnesota Twin or Anaheim Angel will ever again don number 29.

About the only significant achievement that eluded him during his distinguished career was a World Series appearance. Rod did, however, play for four division winners—two each at Minnesota and California. In nine ALCS games with the Angels he totaled five home runs. Against Baltimore in 1979, when he hit .412 for California in the postseason, all seven of his hits went for extra bases.

Rod Carew is the only man who ever legged out two triples in an All-Star Game. He was chosen to play in 18 of the midseason classics.

His rookie season's .292 was followed with a bit of a letdown when he batted a career-low .273 with only 42 runs batted in. But then the Carew we learned to admire took over. His .332 in 1969 was the first of a brilliant 15-season run of .300-plus batting averages. In 1972 he won the first of four straight American League hitting titles. In so doing he tied Ty Cobb as the only American Leaguers to accomplish that feat. Two more batting crowns followed, including a .388 average in 1977, when he flirted all year with the .400 level.

Carew twice was a league leader in triples, including 1977 when he hit 16. His 128 runs scored were also tops in the league that season.

He was involved in two major moves in the late 1970s. Originally a second baseman with somewhat limited fielding range, he was shifted to first base for the 1976 season. He played that position for the remainder of his career. Then, after the 1978 campaign when he and Twins owner Calvin Griffith engaged in a dispute over some public ethnic remarks made by Griffith, Rod was traded away from Minnesota. California sent four players, including Ken Landreaux, to the Twins. Carew spent his final seven seasons with the Angels, for whom he hit over .300 five years in a row before "winding down" to .295 and .280 in his closing seasons of 1984 and '85.

No wonder, then, that this Rookie of the Year, MVP, and multiple-season batting champ was an obvious selection in his first year of Hall of Fame eligibility.

Nearly 20 years have passed since Rod left the active playing field. But many of the standards he set remain in the archives of both of his teams. His .314 is the Angels' all-time-best individual career batting average. His .334 is the Twins' all-time best. No Minnesota player has come close yet to Carew's 90 triples. He still ranks second there, behind Kirby Puckett, in base hits (2,085) and is third on the Twins' runs-scored list.

Even though he played only seven seasons for California, he is the franchise's eighth best of all time in terms of hits, with 968.

Following his playing days, Rod served as an Angels coach for several years. And, as a father whose daughter succumbed to leukemia at age 19, he is an energetic promoter of research to find a cure for the disease. Carew also spends countless hours visiting and cheering up gravely ill youngsters.

Now, after 25 years away from the Twins, Rod has rejoined the Minnesota organization as a community relations and marketing official while continuing to reside full-time in Southern California.

ORLANDO CEPEDA
1958   San Francisco Giants, National League

Personal Data: B. September 17, 1937, at Ponce, Puerto Rico.
Physical Attributes: 6′ 2″, playing weight 210 lbs. Bats right, throws right.
Rookie Year, 1958:   Primary position first base. Led league with 38 doubles.
Total Career, 17 years: Giants 1958–66; Cardinals '66–68; Braves '69–72; A's '72; Red Sox '73; Royals '74.

	BA	G	H	2B	3B	HR	RBI
1958	.312	148	188	38	4	25	96
Lifetime	.297	2,124	2,351	417	27	379	1,365

Aside from the fact that he broke in as a first baseman, several other "firsts" highlight the Hall of Fame career of Orlando Cepeda, the National League's 1958 Rookie of the Year.

He was the first *San Francisco* Giant honored as the league's top rookie. By chance it was his team's first season in California following the franchise's transfer from the Polo Grounds in New York. In his very first major league game Cepeda homered against Los Angeles. Later, with St. Louis in 1966, Orlando would be the National League's first unanimous Most Valuable Player selection in 30 years. And he was the regular first baseman in 1969 when the Braves won Atlanta's first division crown. As his career wound down, he became the Boston Red Sox's first principal designated hitter and won the American League Outstanding Designated Hitter Award in 1973, the inaugural DH season.

Orlando Cepeda, San Francisco Giants, 1958
First San Francisco Rookie of the Year. Became Hall of Famer, MVP, and eventually the first outstanding designated hitter in the American League. *(Temple University Libraries, Urban Archives, Philadelphia, PA)*

During his celebrated career Cepeda, nicknamed the Baby Bull, often ranked first in major statistical categories. The first time was in his rookie season. His 38 doubles paced the National League. The next year outfielder Willie McCovey became the Giants' second successive Rookie of the Year. McCovey, however, was often placed in the lineup as a first baseman. So for the next few years he and Cepeda alternated between first and right field. In 1961, evenly dividing time between those two posts, Cepeda delivered 46 home runs and 142 RBI—both league-leading figures.

After an early-season trade to St. Louis for pitcher Ray Sadecki in 1966, Orlando returned to first base full-time. The 1967 MVP season soon followed. Two years later, after St. Louis traded for Joe Torre by sending Cepeda to Atlanta, the Baby Bull hit .455 for the Braves in the NL Championship Series. It didn't help, though, as the 1969 Miracle Mets swept the three-game set.

The 1970 season was Orlando's last National League hurrah. He hit over .300 for the final time (.305), slugged 34 homers, and drove home 111 runs. The next two years saw him relegated to part-time duty because of knee problems that inhibited his mobility.

Suddenly there was new hope for Orlando. A resuscitated baseball life. The novel (some call it the dreaded) designated hitter role was created by the American League in 1973. Boston, figuring accurately that Cepeda could forgo defensive assignments, signed him as their first DH. The 35-year-old veteran responded with 159 hits, including 20 home runs, and 86 RBI.

But after nearly 2,100 games, many of them in later seasons on aching knees, the Baby Bull's active days were about finished. He signed a contract with Kansas City for 1974, played only 33 games for the Royals, hit just one homer in 107 at bats, and called it quits.

Cepeda was out of baseball less than a year before he made headlines again—this time in the news section. He was convicted of smuggling marijuana and sentenced to 10 months in a Puerto Rican prison. Multitudes of his countrymen looked upon their former hero with disdain, feeling he had disgraced them. In time, a contrite Cepeda returned to solid citizen status, and he has subsequently been enthusiastically inducted into the Puerto Rico Sports Hall of Fame.

One of the proudest moments of his life occurred at Cooperstown on Hall of Fame Induction Day, 1999, when his bronze plaque joined those of former teammates Willie Mays and Willie McCovey. Earlier that year he was honored by the Giants, who retired his number 30 uniform, and by the Missouri Sports Hall of Fame in recognition of his excellence with the St. Louis Cardinals.

The man who produced those numerous "firsts" on the ball field stays active with baseball-related assignments to this day. He is a community representative with the San Francisco Giants. One of his prime duties is speaking to "at risk" youngsters about the dangers of drugs and alcohol. The Baby Bull also serves as honorary spokesman for the Crohn's and Colitis Foundation of America.

Orlando Cepeda and his wife, Miriam, reside in Fairfield, California. They're the parents of four sons—Orlando, Jr., Hector, Malcolm, and Ali Manuel.

CARLTON FISK
1972   Boston Red Sox, American League

Personal Data: B. December 26, 1947, at Bellows Falls, VT.
Physical Attributes: 6′ 3″, playing weight 200 lbs. Bats right, throws right.
Rookie Year, 1972:   Primary position catcher. Led league with 9 triples.
Total Career, 24 years: Red Sox 1969, '71–80; White Sox '81–93.

	BA	G	H	2B	3B	HR	RBI
1972	.293	131	134	28	9	22	61
Lifetime	.269	2,499	2,356	421	47	376	1,330

Not many catchers earn Rookie of the Year honors. One hundred sixteen players have won the esteemed award, but only seven of them were primarily catchers. Of those, Carlton Fisk is the lone American League backstop to have been both Rookie of the Year *and* a Hall of Fame inductee. Johnny Bench is his only National League counterpart.

A ballplayer must be something special in order to attain both of those distinctive recognitions. Carlton Fisk qualifies on each count.

At 21 he had a brief trial with Boston in 1969. Fisk rejoined the "big" team for another "cup of coffee" in '71, then came to stay for a decade of excellence beginning in 1972. He made headlines immediately. His '72 season featured a .293 batting average, a league-leading nine triples, and an exceptionally strong performance behind the plate (.984 fielding average), which merited his winning a Gold Glove. His Rookie of the Year selection was no surprise. In fact, it was an accurate preview of accomplishments to come.

Even though he never again paced the AL in major offensive categories, Fisk was a team leader and model of consistency who would average 25 or so home runs a year. At Boston in 1977 he hit .315, a career high except for a .331 mark when injuries limited him to less than a half season in 1975. He returned to the lineup in time to help the '75 Red Sox win the American League pennant. Then he hit one of the most famous home runs in World Series history. The extra-inning blast, flying over Fenway Park's famous left-field wall just inches inside the fair/foul pole, sparked a Game Six victory. Visuals of the dramatic homer are still replayed whenever momentous baseball achievements are televised.

A proud New Englander by birth and rearing, Carlton left the Red Sox in the 1980–81 winter. Due to a business-office filing error, Fisk's contract was not issued before the required official deadline. Miffed also by previous contentious contractual matters, he filed for free agency. The Chicago White Sox promptly signed him.

For the next 13 seasons "Pudge," as he was nicknamed, added impressive power statistics to his already sound résumé. In 1985 he recorded career highs with 37 home runs and 107 RBI. En route to Cooperstown he was named to 11 American League All-Star teams. At age 42 he was able to match his rookie season's .293 batting average. He wasn't finished yet. And wouldn't be until he was 45 at the end of a troubled 1993 season.

Fisk and White Sox owner Jerry Reinsdorf were reported to have feuded frequently. The animosity probably stemmed from Fisk's strong belief that Reinsdorf spearheaded an alleged conspiracy by baseball owners to block free agents from moving to other teams, thus limiting salaries. Some say that when Fisk was close to breaking the record for most games caught, Chicago manage-ment began to curtail his playing time. He eventually achieved the new record, 2,226 games behind the plate, but was released shortly thereafter. At season's end, according to some insiders, Fisk was not permitted in the Sox clubhouse to congratulate his erstwhile teammates upon their AL West championship.

When the time came for him to specify which team cap to display on his Hall of Fame plaque, Carlton chose the one with Boston's distinctive *B*.

He took an interesting position on his choice of uniform numbers, too. After joining the White Sox he opted for 72, unusual numerals for a certified veteran. Carlton's reasoning: since his longtime Red Sox number, 27, had already been assigned to a Chicago player, he'd go with 72 because it was simply the reverse of the Boston 2 and 7, and it signified his Rookie of the Year summer of . . . '72.

Despite the acrimonious Fisk/front office quarrels in both Boston and Chicago, his excellent all-around career is celebrated for posterity by both his former employers. Carlton Fisk's Boston number 27 and the 72 he wore at Chicago were both retired by the respective ball clubs in recognition of his for-midable on-field contributions for two dozen American League seasons.

WILLIE MAYS
1951   New York Giants, National League

Personal Data: B. May 6, 1931, at Westfield, AL.
Physical Attributes: 5′ 10″, playing weight 173 lbs. Bats right, throws right.
Rookie Year, 1951:   Primary position outfield.
Total Career, 22 years: Giants 1951–52, '54–72; Mets '72–73.

	BA	G	H	2B	3B	HR	RBI
1951	.274	121	127	22	5	20	68
Lifetime	.302	2,992	3,283	523	140	660	1,903

Media veterans and other so-called baseball experts confidently predicted that New York City would house the next Rookie of the Year. Setting their sights on a promising phenom not yet 21 years old, they figured the talented youngster a sure bet as the new season's top newcomer. The year was 1951.

The prognosticators were right . . . about New York. But they'd targeted the wrong guy!

Oh yes, in 1951, Mickey Mantle, whom they prematurely anointed, embarked on his successful journey toward the Hall of Fame. But freshman honors went to others instead. One was Mantle's teammate, Gil McDougald, the American League's honored rookie.

Embarrassed predictors had been too quick to pick a winner. With most of their printer's ink on Mantle, many had overlooked Willie Howard Mays—fleet power-hitting outfielder, age 20—also soon to arrive in New York. Mays, an extraordinary talent, became the '51 National League Rookie of the Year. He and Mantle shared the Bronx-Manhattan spotlight until 1958 when Mays and his New York Giant teammates packed up for San Francisco. Old-timers still argue the merits of the two.

Mays, the Say Hey Kid, wasn't promoted to the Polo Grounds until May 25, 1951. Twenty-two years later, with dozens of trophies and records in tow, Willie Mays finally stopped playing baseball. His Hall of Fame admission ticket had long since been stamped.

Of the fabled Negro League players to advance to the majors, Mays, Hank Aaron, and Ernie Banks were some of the youngest. Older veterans—Sam Jethroe, Satchel Paige, and Monte Irvin, for example—exceeded Mays' age by several years and realistically could not foresee lengthy big league careers. The Negro leagues would go out of business in the middle 1950s. Organized baseball, by then, was attracting talented young African Americans. Mays was one of them. And he capitalized on his opportunity right from the start.

Well, almost from the beginning. Willie Mays was never more forlorn than he was in May 1951 after he went hitless in his first 22 major league at bats. He asked to be returned to Minneapolis, the Giants' Triple-A farm team where he'd

Willie Mays, New York Giants, 1951
Known as the Say Hey Kid for his infectious enthusiasm, he's considered by many as baseball's best all-around player. One of just four men to surpass 600 career home runs.
(George Brace Collection)

torn up the American Association with a .477 batting average. .477. It's not a misprint. Giants manager Leo Durocher had insisted that New York's front office promote Mays immediately.

It did. And the 0-for-22 followed. Then Willie Mays smacked his first hit, a home run, off Boston Braves southpaw Warren Spahn. One Hall of Famer, say hello to another!

The Rookie of the Year was on his way to Cooperstown. And the '51 New York Giants embarked on their miraculous pennant drive culminated by Bobby Thomson's historic home run. On their way to the World Series the Giants considered rookie Mays' 20-home-run performance a key factor. The newcomer added 22 doubles and hit .274.

Neither he nor his team fared well in the World Series, won by the neighboring Yankees in six games. Seldom has a World Series featured three outfielders of the remarkable caliber that this one did—fellas named Willie Mays, Mickey Mantle, and, in his baseball farewell, Joe DiMaggio.

It would be three more years, though, before Mays could fully resume his Hall of Fame career. After just 34 games in 1952 he entered the U.S. military and did not return to the Giants until 1954. Over the next 20 seasons his accomplishments, accented by a verve and excitement rarely matched before or since, fashioned a career that is often called unparalleled for its overall character and style.

In the book *My 60 Years in Baseball,* Hall of Fame broadcaster Ernie Harwell, a New York Giants announcer during Mays' rookie season, said, "Willie Mays is the greatest player I ever saw. His joy of playing impressed me more than anything. He had so much ability, and could beat you so many different ways. He knew exactly what to do, and was completely natural with it."

Mays' records, honors, and statistics are legendary. Among them: NL home run leader four times; hit over 50 home runs twice . . . 1954 batting champ (.345); lifetime .302 hitter; surpassed .300 10 times . . . MVP 1954 and 1965 . . . led league in stolen bases four straight years, 1956–59; 338 career steals . . . 12 consecutive Gold Glove awards . . . Hall of Fame inductee, 1979 . . . 1971 Roberto Clemente Award winner . . . Giants all-time career leader in nine batting categories; runner-up in two others . . . one of only four players to hit more than 600 career home runs (660).

Willie was an All-Star Game fixture, appearing in the classic 24 times, and often leading the NL to victory.

When Mays' spectacular run inevitably began to ebb, arrangements were made for him to finish his career in the city where it began in 1951. Willie was traded in mid-1972 to the New York Mets. His last official base hit was a single against Oakland in the 1973 World Series.

After his retirement Mays joined Bally's Resorts as a public relations executive, a position he still holds. For a short while he and Mantle—two storied names forever linked—were banned from participating in official baseball functions because of their gaming industry positions. Mantle, too, was a casino representative. The Office of the Commissioner of Baseball eventually lifted the restriction.

Willie and his wife, Mae, live in Atherton, California. For 18 years now he has been a special assistant to the San Francisco Giants president. He represents the ball club in various emissary capacities and has a lifetime contract with the team. In addition to retiring Willie's number 24, the Giants accorded him another special recognition. The address of San Francisco's new SBC Park is 24 Willie Mays Plaza.

More than a half century ago the timid youngster entered the national baseball stage batting 0-for-22. Now Willie Mays has stepped into the 21st century duly honored as one of baseball's most popular and admired icons.

WILLIE MCCOVEY
1959   San Francisco Giants, National League

Personal Data: B. January 10, 1938, at Mobile, AL.
Physical Attributes: 6′ 4″, playing weight 210 lbs. Bats left, throws left.
Rookie Year, 1959:   Primary position first base. Two triples in first game.
Total Career, 22 years: Giants 1959–73; Padres '74–76; A's '76; Giants '77–80.

	BA	G	H	2B	3B	HR	RBI
1959	.354	52	68	9	5	13	38
Lifetime	.270	2,588	2,211	353	46	521	1,555

Based on the way he set off fireworks in his very first big league game, fans at old Seals Stadium in San Francisco figured they might be witnessing the debut of a future Hall of Famer or Most Valuable Player. Right on both counts. But the honors for Willie Lee McCovey didn't end there.

When his first season ended, Willie was the 1959 National League Rookie of the Year. Long after his playing career was over, a prominent section of San Francisco Bay was named for him. He was to achieve and enjoy many milestones along the way.

McCovey's first day on the job loomed as quite a challenge. He faced Phillies All-Star pitcher Robin Roberts. All the newcomer did was stroke a pair of triples that afternoon. Willie didn't get many more of those; he averaged only about two triples a year over his 22-year career. But the Giants couldn't have cared less. He hit 469 home runs for them and accounted for 1,388 runs batted in.

Willie's personal totals exceed these San Francisco homer and RBI numbers because he played three years for the Padres and Athletics before wrapping up his active career from 1977 through 1980 back at Candlestick Park where, as you'd expect, he holds that arena's all-time home run record.

But it was at windy, chilly Candlestick where one of his most famous hard-hit drives resulted in a Giants loss. Review the seventh game of the 1962 World Series. Giants trail the Yankees by one run. Ninth inning. Two out and two runners on base. Ralph Terry pitching. McCovey swings. Explosive crack of the bat. Sharp line drive . . . right at New York second baseman Bobby Richardson. Yankees 1, Giants 0. Had Richardson been positioned two feet to either the right or left, San Francisco would have a World Series pennant over its ballpark, probably with Willie McCovey's features adorning it. Alas, the Giants most recent world title came at New York a half century ago.

Despite the '62 Series disappointment, Willie continually lived up to the expectations formed in his Rookie of the Year season. He was an NL leader in slugging average three times, in RBI twice, and in attracting bases on balls once. His lifetime home runs totaled 521, deadlocking him with Ted Williams for 14th on the all-time major league list. Of those 521 dingers, 18 were grand slams.

That's a National League record, and second only to Lou Gehrig in big league history. He was a three-time NL home run leader. "Stretch," as he was widely known, represented the Giants at six All-Star games. He homered twice in Washington for the 1969 National League team.

Since departing as an active player, McCovey has continued to be a popular figure at ball games, and he often played in pro-am golf outings before knee problems reduced his appearances there. Now in his fourth year as a senior adviser employed by the team, he has made public appearances in behalf of the Giants for many years.

Willie is especially proud of an annual honor presented by the ball club in his name. It's the Willie Mac Award, and it goes to the San Francisco player who best exemplifies the spirit and leadership consistently shown by McCovey during his playing days.

His name will also forever be linked to baseball archives whenever a batter at SBC Park launches a home run into the water just beyond the right-field stands. That little finger of San Francisco Bay has officially been christened McCovey Cove.

Willie McCovey and Robin Roberts frequently chat with each other during annual Hall of Fame induction weekends. There can be little doubt that one or the other revisits that two-triple afternoon of long ago when Rookie of the Year "Stretch" McCovey was propelled toward Cooperstown.

MARK McGWIRE
1987   Oakland Athletics, American League

Personal Data: B. October 1, 1963, at Claremont, CA.
Physical Attributes: 6′ 5″, playing weight 225 lbs. Bats right, throws right.
Rookie Year, 1987:   Primary position first base. League-leading 49 home runs.
Total Career, 16 years: A's 1986–97; Cardinals '97–2001.

	BA	G	H	2B	3B	HR	RBI
1987	.289	151	161	28	4	49	118
Lifetime	.263	1,874	1,626	252	6	583	1,414

A double, three home runs, and six singles in 53 at bats during a September call-up with the 1986 Oakland A's did not prophesy what the baseball world would witness over the next decade-plus from Mark McGwire—especially the very next season.

Mark's 1987 Rookie of the Year statistics clearly tell the tale. His long-ball performance resulted in a new home run record for rookies: 49 dingers. That milestone marked the first of Mark's two homer titles at Oakland. A pair of National League home run crowns would eventually follow . . . his magical 70 at St. Louis in 1998, then 65 a year later.

Mark McGwire, Oakland Athletics, 1987
First, he set a rookie record with 49 home runs for the '87 A's. Then, as a Cardinal, he became the first of only two men in history to hit 70 homers.
(Michael Zagaris, Oakland Athletics)

Of his 583 career home runs, 9.4 were slugged per every 100 at bats . . . a phenomenal frequency.

Mark McGwire was an all-around high school athlete before entering the University of Southern California, where he hoped to land a spot on the pitching staff. However, legendary coach Rod Dedeaux recognized Mark's potential as a batsman. So McGwire spent his sophomore and junior seasons at both first and third base instead.

Then Oakland drafted him. But before joining the A's, Mark gained national recognition with the 1984 U.S. Olympic baseball team. After the Olympics he played both first and third in the A's minor league system before advancing to Oakland for 18 late-season games in '86. He hit .189 without exceptional power. Hardly the kind of performance to suggest his marvelous rookie season that followed.

Playing mostly at first, with occasional time at third base and the outfield, Mark combined a .289 average with 49 homers and 118 RBI to land the Athletics a second of three consecutive Rookie of the Year awards. Jose Canseco preceded Mark; Walt Weiss followed.

"I didn't give the rookie award much thought until late July," recalls McGwire. "Then the media began mentioning it. I thought I might have a shot, but honestly figured that Kevin Seitzer at Kansas City had a good chance, too."

Seitzer delivered an AL-leading 207 hits, 15 homers, eight triples, and 83 runs, and batted .323 to rank second for the rookie award.

McGwire recently reflected on the Rookie of the Year honor. "With all the publicity about long-ball hitting, and then the injuries during my career, no one talks about the rookie award anymore. Compared with today, when the honored guy does commercials and maybe earns bonuses, there was none of that back in 1987. There were two key benefits, though. One was the satisfaction of being recognized for a pretty good season's work. The other was gaining the confidence to build a baseball future."

That future, of course, will eventually peak in Cooperstown.

Back in '87, Mark could not have foreseen the highlights and detours that followed—his trade to another league, for example. Mark considered vetoing that transaction until he was assured that, yes, the A's were clearly rebuilding for the future, and that the Cardinals were annual pennant contenders with a large base of loyal fans.

Injuries, before and after the trade, continually derailed him. Wrist problems, shoulder injuries, and knee and ankle maladies sent him to the disabled list: two weeks in 1989 and '92, mid-May to season's end in '93, 115 games in 1994. He totaled a month away from the A's in 1995 and three weeks the following year. His luck turned, though, and he played in nearly every game during the record-setting home run seasons of 1998 and '99. But injuries limited McGwire to just 89 games in 2000 and 97 in '01.

As a conservative estimate, disabilities prevented his appearing in roughly 345 games, most of them during his prime years. On average, a healthy McGwire would likely have hit another 110 or so homers. That's in the 700-plus career range of Hank Aaron, Babe Ruth, and Barry Bonds.

After missing 105 games in 2001, Mark realized that, at 38, healing takes more time than it once did. So he retired. And would forgo several million guaranteed dollars. Regretting that he could no longer satisfactorily contribute, he left with justifiable pride in his productive 16 big league seasons.

No longer beset with continuing injuries, McGwire resides with his second wife in Long Beach, where the Southern California climate permits him to indulge his fondness for a favorite new pastime. Golf. Any guesses on who's favored in the long-drive contest?

EDDIE MURRAY
1977   Baltimore Orioles, American League

Personal Data: B. February 24, 1956, at Los Angeles, CA.
Physical Attributes: 6' 2", playing weight 190 lbs. Bats both, throws right.
Rookie Year, 1977:   Primary position first base/DH.
Total Career, 21 years: Orioles 1977–88; Dodgers '89–91; Mets '92–93; Indians '94–96; Orioles '96; Angels '97; Dodgers '97.

	BA	G	H	2B	3B	HR	RBI
1977	.283	160	173	29	2	27	88
Lifetime	.287	3,026	3,255	560	35	504	1,917

As the Baltimore Orioles media information guide appropriately observes, Eddie Murray's election to the National Baseball Hall of Fame was a foregone conclusion. When the July 2003 induction program took place in Cooperstown, his unveiled plaque displayed Murray's engraved visage wearing an Orioles cap.

That, too, was appropriate and expected. For Eddie had played more than half of his 21 big league seasons with Baltimore and, as a young Oriole more than a quarter century earlier, received his first national recognition: the American League's 1977 Rookie of the Year Award.

While the Cooperstown salute had been widely anticipated for a decade or more, Eddie's spectacular rookie season was something of a surprise. Because, based on four reasonably good but unspectacular minor league seasons, Murray did not arrive at Baltimore's 1977 spring training camp with any special pedigree in his background. Murray had not impressed Oriole farm-system brass with long-ball power, averaging only 10 home runs and 63 RBI per minor league year. But all that changed quickly when he went to bat for Baltimore's "big club." Twenty-seven homers, 88 RBI, 29 doubles, and a .283 batting average earned Eddie the baseball writers' Rookie of the Year salute.

Three teams—Los Angeles, the Mets, and Cleveland—were sandwiched between his two Orioles stints. Everywhere he played Eddie generally set an offensive pace of 75 or more runs batted in a year. In fact he set a record in that category with those 75-plus RBI for 20 straight seasons. His 1,917 career RBI total is the most by any switch-hitter in history. Only Murray, Hank Aaron, and 1951 NL Rookie of the Year Willie Mays have recorded 3,000 hits *and* 500 home runs. Eddie reached or surpassed a .300 batting average seven times, posting a career-high .330 with the 1990 Dodgers.

The only time Murray led his league in any offensive category over a full season was 1984. He drew 107 walks that year. His 22 homers and 78 RBI were AL bests in the strike-shortened 1981 season. Eddie's 504 lifetime home runs rank second to Mickey Mantle among switch-hitters.

Murray helped lead teams into four League Championship Series and three World Series. His two home runs in Game Five at Philadelphia sparked Baltimore to the 1983 World Championship. He was an American League representative in seven All-Star games, a National Leaguer in another.

Eddie was also a three-time Gold Glove winner and the big league record holder of games played and career assists by a first baseman. He displayed that defensive prowess *after* his freshman year. The Orioles played veteran Lee May at first base during Eddie's debut year, so the future Rookie of the Year and Hall of Famer was primarily a designated hitter that first season.

It was apparent by 1996 that Murray, then with Cleveland, would soon be wrapping up his career. So Baltimore arranged to trade for him, anticipating that Eddie might hit his 500th home run in an Oriole uniform. He did. He recorded numbers 500 and 501 before brief finales with Anaheim and Los Angeles in 1997.

Murray's number 33 baseball shirt was un-retired by the Orioles when he returned to Baltimore as a coach from 1998 through 2001. Then, beginning in 2002, he has served as Cleveland's batting coach.

Eddie Murray was the 38th Hall of Famer chosen in his first year of eligibility. Never one to welcome media intrusion, at the ballpark or elsewhere, Murray was charmingly loquacious at the Hall's 2003 induction ceremonies. He proudly saluted several teammates, opponents, and employers, and paid tribute to his family—wife Janice and daughters Jordan and Jessica.

The Murrays maintain their full-time residence in Eddie's hometown of Los Angeles.

CAL RIPKEN, JR.
1982   Baltimore Orioles, American League

Personal Data: B. August 24, 1960, at Havre de Grace, MD.
Physical Attributes: 6′ 4″, playing weight 220 lbs. Bats right, throws right.
Rookie Year, 1982:   Primary position third base/shortstop.
Total Career, 21 years: Orioles 1981–2001.

	BA	G	H	2B	3B	HR	RBI
1982	.264	160	158	32	5	28	93
Lifetime	.276	3,001	3,184	603	44	431	1,695

Rookie of the Year. Most Valuable Player. Member of a World Championship team. Owner of several prestigious records. Is there any doubt, readers, that Cal Ripken, Jr., will enter baseball's Hall of Fame?

Players must be retired for a minimum of five years to meet a key eligibility requirement. Cal Ripken's final big league appearance was in 2001. You can be certain he will be welcomed to Cooperstown in 2007. By all odds he'll be a co-inductee that day. Popular Mark McGwire, another Rookie of the Year, also completed his distinguished career in 2001.

Ripken will be immortalized for his "iron man" durability: his streak of 2,632 consecutive games played. That astonishing accomplishment broke the successive-game record that Lou Gehrig set from 1925 to 1939. By the time Ripken finally sat out a 1998 outing, he had eclipsed Gehrig's honored record by more than 500 games.

In October 2001, as Ripken concluded his brilliant 21-season career, Commissioner Bud Selig announced a new award to commemorate Cal's famous record. Starting in 2002, the Cal Ripken, Jr., Award has been presented annually to each major leaguer who appears in all of his team's scheduled games. Ripken did not miss an Orioles contest for 15—that's right—15 years!

Of the roughly 90 Rookies of the Year now retired, he had the longest career with a single team. Cal played in 23 games for the 1981 Orioles before making the regular lineup the following spring. It was 20 seasons later, and a total of 3,001 regular-season Baltimore games, before his active playing days were over.

Cal Ripken, Jr., Baltimore Orioles, 1982
After completing his 21-year career with
just one team, the "iron man" record holder
became a minor league owner and an
activist for youth baseball and other
character-building programs for young
people.
(George Brace Collection)

Cal was 38 years old before he ever joined the disabled list. That was nearly 17 years from the start of his consecutive games run. During that stretch other big leaguers made 5,045 trips to the DL.

Primarily a shortstop, although he began and ended his career as a third baseman, Ripken was a major offensive force in the Orioles lineup. His batting average surpassed .300 five times, including his two Most Valuable Player seasons of 1983 and 1991. Four times he drove in more than 100 runs. Cal's seasonal home run total was often in the mid-20s, as his 21-year career average of 20.5 homers will attest.

Some of his special feats were performed before gigantic national television audiences. The night he equaled the Gehrig record he hit a home run. The next evening, September 6, 1995, at Baltimore's Camden Yards, Ripken homered again. In 28 postseason games, including the 1983 World Series, he hit safely 37 times in 110 at bats—a .336 average.

From his very first full season, 1982, it was obvious that the Orioles had drafted a special talent. In fact, on opening day, he was 3-for-5 with a home run and double.

En route to the Rookie of the Year citation Cal led all 1982 AL rookies in doubles, home runs, RBI, total bases, and runs scored.

Playing third base then, before switching to shortstop at midseason, he was errorless in 44 straight outings. That's a good example of Ripken's defensive ability, which was often overshadowed by his offensive headlines. He was twice a Gold Glove winner. Committing only three errors in 680 total chances in 1990, Cal posted the best fielding percentage in history among major league shortstops—.996.

During the 21 years in which Cal donned an Orioles uniform, the 1991 MVP season was probably his best overall. It was the team's final year before moving downtown to its new ballpark. It was one of Ripken's Gold Glove seasons, and a summer in which he was also the All-Star Game MVP. He led the majors with 73 multihit games and 368 total bases, and was second in baseball with 210 hits. Cal blasted 34 home runs, the most by a shortstop in 22 years. And he became only the 10th player in American League history to hit 30 or more homers with fewer than 50 strikeouts. The man who first gained notoriety playing at Memorial Stadium was, ironically, the very last batter there.

Ten years later he chalked up his final major league at bat. But before that last trip to the plate he added several 2001 achievements to his notable accomplishments. Among them: oldest man to homer and be chosen All-Star Game MVP . . . became 15th major leaguer to register 5,000 total bases . . . passed Brooks Robinson for most career games by an Oriole . . . batted .316 with runners in scoring position.

Yes, 2001 was Cal's swan song as an active player. But not as a continuing force in myriad baseball activities. Cal, Jr., was instrumental in creating the Cal Ripken, Sr., Foundation. Cal, Sr., was a one-time Orioles manager and a popular Baltimore coach for many years, and was duly credited with developing dozens of Orioles farmhands into accomplished professionals.

During his playing career Cal, Jr., and his wife Kelly had formed the Cal Ripken, Jr., Foundation, which continues to support community adult and family literacy, and youth recreational and health-related programs in the greater Baltimore area. The Cal Ripken, Sr., Foundation seemed a natural extension.

Former infielder Bill Ripken, Cal's brother, who played over 800 games with the Orioles and three other American League clubs, assists with the foundation's programs. Currently the foundation is focused on constructing a youth baseball facility to serve at-risk youngsters and to provide training for youth coaches. Recently the Cal Ripken, Sr., Foundation donated nearly a half million dollars' worth of baseball and softball equipment to youth organizations in Baltimore and several other communities throughout the nation.

Outgrowths of the Ripken family ventures are the Aberdeen Project and the Aberdeen IronBirds. The latter enterprise is the Ripken-owned Orioles affiliate in the short-season New York–Penn League. It plays in the new Ripken Stadium adjacent to Interstate 95 near the Ripken brothers' boyhood home in Aberdeen, Maryland. Centerpiece of the Aberdeen Project is the Ripken Youth

Baseball Academy and the instructional opportunities it offers. Recently Cal, Jr., and Bill authored a book featuring baseball instruction for boys and girls.

Thanks to that young 1982 Rookie of the Year, the new millennium's youth is also to be served. Baseball, he's convinced, is one way to do just that.

It figures to be another Ripken family success story. Surely you'll hear more about it some 2007 summer afternoon in Cooperstown, New York.

FRANK ROBINSON
1956   Cincinnati Reds, National League

Personal Data: B. August 31, 1935, at Beaumont, TX.
Physical Attributes: 6′ 1″, playing weight 183 lbs. Bats right, throws right.
Rookie Year, 1956:   Primary position outfield. 38 home runs tied league's rookie record. 83 RBI, 122 runs led league.
Total Career, 21 years: Reds 1956–65; Orioles '66–71; Dodgers '72; Angels '73–74; Indians '74–76.

	BA	G	H	2B	3B	HR	RBI
1956	.290	152	166	27	6	38	83
Lifetime	.294	2,808	2,943	528	72	586	1,812

If any baseball headliner personifies "first shall be last; last first, etc.," Frank Robinson's your man. He carries an impressive list of "firsts" on his résumé, and some important "lasts," or "most recents," on his long list of accomplishments.

In 1956 he became the very *first* of Cincinnati's seven Rookies of the Year. His spectacular debut was a key factor in the Reds' surprising charge toward a title that eluded them by only two games.

Ten years later, after being dealt to Baltimore in a trade that set off fan revolts in Cincinnati, Frank won the American League's Triple Crown, a difficult feat accomplished by only 12 players in the 20th century. Nearly a decade after that he was introduced as major league baseball's *first* African American manager. As the Indians' player-manager he slugged a home run in his *first* Cleveland at bat. And when the Giants sought a new pilot in 1981, Frank Robinson stepped in as the National League's *first* black manager.

At age 68 and in his third season running the Expos' dugout, Robinson became Montreal's *last* manager. The franchise was transferred to Washington, DC, for the 2005 season—and presumably beyond.

His first and lasts go on. With *firsts* far outnumbering the latter.

Frank's 21-year active career featured numerous record-setting accomplishments. Three times at Cincinnati and once at Baltimore he led his league in slugging percentage. His 51 doubles were an NL high in 1962. He scored the most runs in his league three times. His 1966 Triple Crown season at Baltimore sparkled with a .316 batting average, 49 home runs, and 122 RBI. In that fall's World Series his two homers helped the Orioles to a sweep of Los Angeles. In

26 World Series games over five seasons Robinson hit eight homers and accounted for 14 RBI.

Now, nearly 40 years after he left Cincinnati, Frank still ranks among the top five Reds' leaders in runs scored, extra-base hits, and home runs (324, second to Johnny Bench's 389). At Baltimore, where he played six seasons (four pennant winners), Frank remains number two in career slugging percentage and third in Orioles batting average (.300).

Regardless of his Hall of Fame induction, MVP honors, and other accolades along the way, Frank hails his *first* season, that Rookie of the Year summer, as the propellant toward the other successes. Details have not escaped him.

Frank Robinson, Cincinnati Reds, 1956
Only player to win MVP honors in both major leagues, he also holds distinction as first African American manager in AL (Cleveland, 1975) and later in NL (San Francisco, 1981).
(Courtesy of Cincinnati Reds)

You don't start out thinking you'll be the best rookie. You just try to fit in. To contribute. I did have a chuckle, though. In spring training the Topps gum card people took photos of the rookies they figured were best prospects. They picked Charlie Neal and Luis Aparicio as the top two. Never even took my picture. Luis won in the American League, but I guess I spoiled their party!

After the season there was no big deal. The league phoned to say I was Rookie of the Year. That was it. No citation or anything. But there was a fan club in Cincinnati—some people who got to know me that summer. They chipped in, bought a trophy with all the statistics and so forth, and presented it to me at an informal neighborhood get-together. I still cherish that trophy. It's the only one I got that signifies Rookie of the Year.

You know, looking back, that photo slight by Topps kinda motivated me. I tried to be seen but not heard. Our manager, Birdie Tebbetts, was terrific in understanding young players.

Here's an example. I went 2-for-3 in an early game. Figured pitching wasn't much different from the minors. All of a sudden I'm in an 0-for-23 slump. Then we played the Dodgers, and Don Newcombe was pitching. Birdie sat me down. "Just watch Newk," I was told. "Relax, but pay close attention to what's happening." I noticed Birdie kept the bench men thinking—always had their heads in the game. I seemed to take off after that game. I credit Birdie fully for being the key to my success.

Birdie and the veterans made me feel part of that club right from the start. It's different today. Some of these kids carry themselves and act like they've been around 20 years. And the vets accept them. In my day the vets wouldn't let you carry on. You had to earn respect. To win the rookie award you have to be on the right team...at the right time. The fact that the Reds had a good year in '56 certainly helped me.

It's fascinating to hear Frank Robinson touch on highlights of his extraordinary Hall of Fame career. And to see the extreme importance he places on rookie seasons as a springboard to success.

TOM SEAVER
1967   New York Mets, National League

Personal Data: B. November 17, 1944, at Fresno, CA.
Physical Attributes: 6' 1", playing weight 195 lbs. Throws right, bats right.
Rookie Year, 1967:   Primary position pitcher. Recorded a save in 15-inning All-Star Game.
Total Career, 20 years: Mets 1967–77; Reds '77–82; Mets '83; White Sox '84–86; Red Sox '86.

	Record	ERA	G	GS	SO	IP
1967	16–13	2.76	35	34	170	251
Lifetime	311–205	2.86	656	647	3,640	4,782$\frac{2}{3}$

Twenty-nine pitchers are among baseball's Rookies of the Year. Outstanding as their debuts were, 28 of them failed to win as many as 200 games in their careers. Some are primarily relief pitchers, and thus unlikely to post large numbers of wins or losses. Others are still active.

Tom Seaver is the lone Rookie of the Year to reach the 200-victory level. He is among only 21 pitchers in baseball history to notch 300-plus wins (311 in all). Elected in 1992, Seaver is one of the dozen Rookies of the Year, so far, to have entered the Baseball Hall of Fame. By only his seventh season, and perhaps even earlier, his Hall admittance was a foregone conclusion.

But at the outset of his spectacular career there was a question about where he'd be employed. In 1966 the Braves jumped the draft-date gun and lost their claim on the University of Southern California star. The Commissioner's Office ruled that any team willing to match Atlanta's $40,000 offer could claim Seaver. Cleveland, Philadelphia, and the Mets entered the bidding. New York won out in the subsequent drawing, and Seaver soon reigned as Shea Stadium's first superstar.

He spent the first 10½ years of his big league career with the Mets. His imposing achievements over that span would have been more than enough for Hall of Fame selection even then. Some highlights:

Three Cy Young awards...led NL in strikeouts five times; exceeded 200 strikeouts nine straight years...posted ERA under 3.00 in first seven years; a 1.76 in 1971 was Tom's career and all-time Mets' best...

Tom Seaver, New York Mets, 1967
He's the only Rookie of the Year pitcher
in the Hall of Fame. Also, the only one to
have reached not only 200 career
victories, but a total of 311 wins.
(Courtesy of New York Mets)

291 innings pitched in 1970 and 21 complete games in '71 are still
Mets records . . . staff ace in World Series seasons of 1969 (win over
Baltimore) and 1973 (loss to Oakland); 1–2 World Series record with
2.70 cumulative Series ERA.

During the summer of 1977, when the Mets were rebuilding, Seaver went
to Cincinnati in a controversial trade for Doug Flynn, Dan Norman, Steve
Henderson, and another ex–Rookie of the Year, pitcher Pat Zachry. Tom's combined Mets-Reds record was 21–6. And he turned in another sub-3.00 ERA.

Seaver would never have another 20-victory season, but he pitched extremely
well for Cincinnati. His 75–45 six-season record there included a 14–2 log with a
2.55 earned run average in the strike-shortened 1981 season. Tom was a member
of the Reds for his only no-hit game, a 4–0 win over St. Louis in 1978.

After 15 seasons Seaver finally suffered a losing year, 5–13 for the '82 Reds.
He was traded back to the Mets for the 1983 season (9 wins, 14 losses), then
transferred to the American League for his final three active campaigns.

He won 15 games for Chicago in 1984, then 16 the following year. He was
still with the White Sox when he posted his 300th victory. Tom recorded it at
Yankee Stadium, not far from the scene of his New York Mets heroics of earlier
days. Seaver finished his career the following year. Chicago traded him to Boston
for Steve Lyons at midseason.

Tom's brilliant career was highlighted by his 311–205 record . . . 3,640 strikeouts, history's fourth best at the time . . . 61 shutouts, seventh all-time . . . 231
complete games, by today's standards an incredible figure. As you would figure,

Tom was a frequent All-Star Game participant. He was named to the National League squad 12 times.

When total careers of Rookie of the Year pitchers are compared and analyzed, Tom Seaver ranks in a "league of his own."

His Mets' number 41 is long retired, but Tom continues on baseball's periphery. He's been at network microphones from time to time, he announced Yankees games for several years, and he now commutes from his native Southern California to handle selected Mets telecasts.

BILLY WILLIAMS
1961   Chicago Cubs, National League

Personal Data: B. June 15, 1938, at Whistler, AL.
Physical Attributes: 6' 1", playing weight 175 lbs. Bats left, throws right.
Rookie Year, 1961:   Primary position outfield.
Total Career, 18 years: Cubs 1959–74; A's '75–76.

	BA	G	H	2B	3B	HR	RBI
1961	.278	146	147	20	7	25	86
Lifetime	.290	2,488	2,711	434	88	426	1,475

"Sweet Swingin'," consistent Billy Williams is among the relatively few Rookies of the Year to produce a career-long batting average that surpassed his fine first season's Rookie of the Year output.

Statisticians could almost fill in Williams' season-long numbers back in midwinter. Rarely would they be far off when October arrived. Mr. Dependability would have been an apt moniker for Williams, or perhaps Old Reliable if the Yankees' old-time right fielder Tommy Henrich had not been so christened a few decades earlier.

His 1961 Rookie of the Year campaign was actually Williams' third trial with the Cubs, who had auditioned him for a few games in 1959 and 1960. Williams' 1961 numbers were not particularly spectacular, although his 25 home runs and 86 RBI were Cubs' rookie records. But the sweet-swinging newcomer from Alabama was flexible and consistently productive. In his 14 full seasons at Wrigley Field, his batting average never fell below .276 or exceeded .322 . . . except once.

That was his league-leading .333 in 1972 when he chipped in with in 37 home runs and a career-high 122 runs batted in. His top home run season (42) was 1970 when he led the NL in hits (205) and runs scored (137). Billy's runs batted in usually topped out in the high 80s to high 90s; home runs totaled between 21 and 34 for his first nine full years. And Billy was virtually injury free. In this latter regard Williams was the National League's version of Lou Gehrig or Cal Ripken for a while. From September 1963 to September 1970 he appeared in a then–NL record 1,117 consecutive games. He pinch-hit in only four of them.

Popular and well respected among teammates and opponents, Williams was a six-time National League All-Star. His eight grand-slam home runs rank ninth best in NL history. Only two Chicago Cubs are honored with retired uniforms— Billy Williams and Ernie Banks. Billy's number 26 is framed and affixed to the right-field pole at Wrigley as a constant reminder of the club's affection for him.

Unfortunately for Billy, and for the Cubs of his day, the team never advanced to postseason competition. Chicago came close in 1969, but lengthy losing streaks in August and September derailed its NL East title drive. The famous Amazin' Mets came from well behind to win the division, then the World Series.

In the mid-1960s Williams and Chicago third baseman Ron Santo combined to set a special Cubs standard. For the only time in team history, teammates recorded consecutive 30-homer seasons. In 1964, Williams led the club with 33; Santo hit 30. The next summer Billy edged Ron again, this time by 34 to 33.

When their popular outfielder had reached age 36, the Cubs traded him to Oakland, where he played his final two major league seasons and finally appeared in the postseason (a 1975 ALCS loss to Boston). Billy, primarily a designated hitter after the trade, would play one more year in Oakland before retiring after the 1976 campaign. There was still punch in his bat those final two seasons. He totaled 34 home runs for the A's.

Williams donned his Cubs uniform again a few years later. He joined the Chicago coaching staff for three separate terms that started in 1980 and concluded in 2001. His 15 seasons as a Cubs coach tied a club record. During his second coaching stint he received his highest baseball honor—inauguration to the Hall of Fame in 1987.

Even though he's no longer on the field, Billy Williams continues in the employ of the Chicago Cubs as a special assistant to the team president. He's held that post since November 1, 2001.

Billy and his wife, Shirley, live in Glen Ellyn, Illinois, just west of Chicago. They have four daughters and six grandchildren.

A 3 Double Helping of Hardware

Rookies of the Year Who Became Most Valuable Players

On the one hand, it seems reasonable to expect some Rookies of the Year to be candidates for Most Valuable Player consideration somewhere down the line. After all, their first-year achievements reflected special talent. On the other hand, the law of averages is likely to consign a small portion of first-year wonders to short-term careers.

Continuing to build on their special freshman seasons, 17 men—nearly 15 percent of the 116 Rookies of the Year—have earned MVP accolades. Four of them—Johnny Bench, Willie Mays, Cal Ripken, and Frank Robinson—each were two-time MVP winners. Those four, along with Hall of Famers Rod Carew, Orlando Cepeda, Willie McCovey, and Jackie Robinson, have been profiled in Chapters 1 and 2.

Frank Robinson is the only one of these distinguished players to have been honored as MVP with two different franchises, Cincinnati and Baltimore.

Boston's Fred Lynn, in 1975, and Ichiro Suzuki of the 2001 Mariners, enjoy a special distinction among the group of 17. Their Rookie of the Year seasons were so spectacular that they were voted MVP the very same year.

Rookies of the Year Who Became Most Valuable Players	
Rookie of the Year	MVP Year(s), Team(s)
Dick Allen, 1964	1972, Chicago White Sox
Jeff Bagwell, 1991	1994, Houston Astros
Johnny Bench, 1968	1970, '72, Cincinnati Reds
Jose Canseco, 1986	1988, Oakland Athletics

Rookies of the Year Who Became MVPs (continued)	
Rookie of the Year	MVP Year(s), Team(s)
Rod Carew, 1967	1977, Minnesota Twins
Orlando Cepeda, 1958	1967, St. Louis Cardinals
Andre Dawson, 1977	1987, Chicago Cubs
Fred Lynn, 1975	1975, Boston Red Sox
Willie Mays, 1951	1954, New York Giants
	1965, San Francisco Giants
Willie McCovey, 1959	1969, San Francisco Giants
Thurman Munson, 1970	1976, New York Yankees
Don Newcombe, 1949	1956, Brooklyn Dodgers
Cal Ripken, Jr., 1982	1983, '91, Baltimore Orioles
Frank Robinson, 1956	1961, Cincinnati Reds
	1966, Baltimore Orioles
Jackie Robinson, 1947	1949, Brooklyn Dodgers
Pete Rose, 1963	1973, Cincinnati Reds
Ichiro Suzuki, 2001	2001, Seattle Mariners

DICK ALLEN
1964   Philadelphia Phillies, National League

Personal Data: B. March 8, 1942, at Wampum, PA.
Physical Attributes: 5' 11 ", playing weight 187 lbs. Bats right, throws right.
Rookie Year, 1964:   Primary position third base. Led league with 13 triples and 125 runs scored.
Total Career, 15 years: Phillies 1963–69; Cardinals '70; Dodgers '71; White Sox '72–74; Phillies '75–76; A's '77.

	BA	G	H	2B	3B	HR	RBI
1964	.318	162	201	38	13	29	91
Lifetime	.292	1,749	1,848	320	79	351	1,119

Maybe you remember him as Rich. Or Crash. Probably Richie, as he was known during his marvelous National League Rookie of the Year season. Later, with other teams and in a different league, this enigmatic young man with a wealth of athletic talent preferred to be called Dick Allen.

Whatever his name, Allen quickly became a fan favorite when his career-high .318 batting average and league-leading 125 runs scored nearly carried Philadelphia to the 1964 pennant. The team fizzled during the final two weeks, just missing out on the title. But with Allen and his great potential on board, the Phillies' future looked bright. It darkened instead.

Dick Allen, Philadelphia Phillies, 1964
As a rookie, Allen led the National League in triples and runs scored. Eight years later, with the Chicago White Sox, he was named American League MVP.
(The Rich Westcott Collection)

In mid-1965 he and teammate Frank Thomas quarreled in the dugout. With bat in hand, Thomas, who was released the following day, took a swing at Allen. Many fans, who had come to value Thomas's offensive contributions, blamed Allen for the disagreement. A love-hate relationship between Allen and the public resulted. Some of it was stirred by the media; much of it was fostered by Allen himself.

His clubhouse arrivals were increasingly tardy. He disappeared for several days at least twice. He seriously injured his right hand in 1967 when it was reported to have smashed through his car's headlamp. Still, while frequently emotionally troubled, he continued to lead the Phillies with near-.300 batting and power hitting.

It has been suggested that his discontent stemmed from a wariness about his employer. When Allen first reported to Philadelphia's Little Rock farm club, he was the team's only African American. In retrospect the Phillies admitted their mistake in sending the 20-year old to strange, difficult surroundings. Unfortunately, the Little Rock experience might have caused permanent scarring.

Unable to patch their differences, the Phils and Allen parted company after 1969. But mutual satisfaction wasn't evident in St. Louis or Los Angeles either, where Allen spent one year each. However, his career suddenly rebounded after he joined the 1972 White Sox. Chicago manager Chuck Tanner was an old friend from western Pennsylvania not far from Allen's hometown. The two of them eventually co-owned racehorses. Allen caught fire early, continued hot, and led the American League in homers, runs batted in, and walks. His performance earned Allen the 1972 AL Most Valuable Player award.

Two years later, however, when he finished as league leader in home runs again, he walked out with a month left in the season.

Not welcomed back to Chicago, and after a trial with Atlanta, he returned to Philadelphia in 1975. He performed adequately, but was clearly winding down. Allen, at 35, finished his often contentious career in 54 games with the 1977 Athletics.

Discord had intruded on Dick Allen's personal life, too. But after his playing days he appeared more at ease within himself and with others. He owned several racehorses and sometimes served as a trainer. He attends card shows and old-timers' games, and he has shared a peace pipe with Frank Thomas, his former adversary. A full-time resident of California, Dick has become closely associated with his old ball club again. Its 1964 Rookie of the Year has been serving the Phillies in community relations as a fan development representative.

JEFF BAGWELL
1991   Houston Astros, National League

Personal Data: B. May 27, 1968, at Boston, MA.
Physical Attributes: 6′ 0″, playing weight 195 lbs. Bats right, throws right.
Rookie Year, 1991:   Primary position first base.
Career to Date, 14 years: Astros 1991–2004.

	BA	G	H	2B	3B	HR	RBI
1991	.294	156	163	26	4	15	82
Lifetime	.297	2,111	2,289	484	32	446	1,510

The Houston ball club has been in business for more than 40 years now. The Astros, who were first known as the Colt .45s, have not managed to capture a National League championship in those four-plus decades, but they have one Most Valuable Player to their credit. And a Rookie of the Year, too.

Both honors were achieved by the same man: Jeff Bagwell.

Based on the consistently productive numbers Bagwell has compiled, he will someday be a legitimate candidate for Cooperstown admission. In the meantime, as Jeff enters his late 30s, the Astros have every right to expect his offensive performance to continue to produce runs for them. As he has right from the start.

His impressive .294 average, 82 RBI, and double-figure home runs led to his Rookie of the Year salute in 1991. Just three years later his league-leading

Jeff Bagwell, Houston Astros, 1991
The only Astro in history to be named Rookie of the Year and later MVP. Jeff has averaged more than 100 runs batted in per season.
(Courtesy of Houston Astros)

116 runs batted in during only 110 games in the strike-shortened 1994 summer, a sparkling .368 batting average, and an NL-best 104 runs scored, clearly assured his MVP selection.

Since then, with the exception of 1995 when a broken hand sidelined him for one month, "Mr. Consistency Bagwell" drove home 111 or more runs six straight seasons. He totaled 135 RBI, a career milestone, in 1997. He missed the magic century mark by two when he accounted for 98 RBI in 2002, but returned to the 100 level again in '03.

When his 13th season, 2003, was finished, Bagwell's lifetime batting average was precisely .300. It was another reflection of his career's consistency. He had hit .273 in 1992 and turned in that marvelous .368 season of 1994. His other batting averages never dropped below .286 until 2003 (.278), nor did they exceed .320. All the others hovered near .300. Jeff's 14-season averages of 32 home runs and 108 RBI are other clear statistical indications of his year-by-year value to Houston.

Along the way, in addition to his other baseball accomplishments, Jeff, in 2000, joined the select quartet of Hank Aaron, Joe DiMaggio, Frank Robinson, and Ted Williams with 300 homers, 1,000 runs batted in, and 1,000 runs scored in their first 10 years. His 47 home runs that season set a still-standing franchise record. The next season he became the first Astro to accumulate a career mark of 3,000 total bases.

Bagwell is not yet ready to contemplate post-baseball activities. "I'm just thinking pretty much about the game and the next seasons," he says. "It's like my rookie season in a way. Even late that season, when guys on the team talked about me maybe winning the award, I still concentrated more on the game at hand. The main thing for a newcomer is to feel like you belong. Even after that first year it took me a while to realize I actually belonged in the big leagues."

Others had every confidence that Bagwell would, and did, fit in—as a ballplayer and a citizen. At the University of Hartford the Boston-born Bagwell hit .413 over three seasons. Twice he was ECAC Player of the Year, and he was inducted to the university's Hall of Fame in 1997. The Red Sox drafted him in the third round in 1989 (and later traded him to Houston for pitcher Larry Andersen). He was the Double-A Eastern League's MVP in 1990.

Jeff has been honored with the Middlesex, Connecticut, Chamber of Commerce Role Model of the Year Award, had his high school uniform number retired, and been chosen six times by Boston media as the New England Native Player of the Year.

Bagwell points with pride to a 2001 personal highlight, one that has no direct connection with a ball game. He and his wife Ericka, now full-time residents of Houston, became parents of Bryce Alicia that January. Two months later, as usual, he was at first base on opening day for the 11th successive year. Just another typical spring day for Houston fans to take Jeff Bagwell's presence for granted.

JOSE CANSECO
1986   Oakland Athletics, American League

Personal Data: B. July 2, 1964, at Havana, Cuba.
Physical Attributes: 6' 4 ", playing weight 240 lbs. Bats right, throws right.
Rookie Year, 1986:   Primary position outfield.
Total Career, 17 years: A's 1985–92; Rangers '92–94; Red Sox '95–96; A's '97; Blue Jays '98; Devil Rays '99–2000; Yankees '00; White Sox '01.

	BA	G	H	2B	3B	HR	RBI
1986	.240	157	144	29	1	33	117
Lifetime	.266	1,887	1,877	340	14	462	1,407

Jose Canseco started a celebratory tradition in Oakland. Honored in 1986 for his first-year achievements, he was the first of three successive Oakland players to be American League Rookies of the Year. Mark McGwire and Walt Weiss followed.

Jose was a significant contributor to the '86 Athletics. Coming off a 36-homer minor league season, he produced 33 home runs and 117 RBI—probably more than the A's had a right to expect.

Two years later, Jose Canseco added Most Valuable Player to his growing collection of trophies and accolades. In helping spark Oakland to the '88 World Series, Jose paced the AL with 42 homers and 124 runs batted in. He hit .307 that year. Only once more, primarily as a designated hitter for Boston in 1995, did he exceed .300.

Jose became baseball's first 40–40 man: 40 stolen bases, 42 home runs in 1988. Eventually he was one of just nine major leaguers with more than 400 homers and 200 steals. Interestingly, his base-path speed seldom translated into triples—only 14 lifetime. Canseco's power, though, was top-drawer. His career-high 44 homers in 1991 tied Cecil Fielder for the league lead. He ranks 26th, all-time, with 462 major league home runs. Jose is Oakland's third-best career home run hitter, and is second to McGwire in A's RBI.

Conversely, though, he's the all-time single-season strikeout leader at both Oakland and Toronto. And there's his infamous blooper—the fly ball bouncing from his head, over the fence, for a home run. He also pitched in relief in a blowout game, injured his elbow, and lost several months.

Despite nearly a dozen visits to the disabled list, Canseco continued to hit monstrous home runs as he moved to six other American League teams, and even back to Oakland for one year. He played independent league ball for a while. By then his personal life had usually made more headlines than baseball did. He was frequently cited for driving infractions. He once slammed a car into his first wife's automobile.

A widely publicized scrape involved Jose's arrest for assault and battery during a Miami nightclub brawl. He and twin brother Ozzie (a short-time big leaguer) were both charged. Jose was jailed briefly, then sentenced to house arrest. Subsequently he was arrested again after testing positive for steroids, a probation violation. Later he began a full-scale sale of his baseball trophies and jewelry, including World Series rings.

It is a reality of human nature that history will likely recall more of Jose's off-field escapades—and the bizarre on-field incidents—than his extraordinary baseball skills. When he and Mark McGwire exhibited their Bash Brothers abilities, it was power baseball at its very best.

ANDRE DAWSON
1977   Montreal Expos, National League

Personal Data: B. July 10, 1954, at Miami, FL.
Physical Attributes: 6′ 3 ″, playing weight 180 lbs. Bats right, throws right.
Rookie Year, 1977:   Primary position outfield. 21 stolen bases.
Total Career, 21 years: Expos 1976–86; Cubs '87–92; Red Sox '93–94; Marlins '95–96.

	BA	G	H	2B	3B	HR	RBI
1977	.282	139	148	26	9	19	65
Lifetime	.279	2,627	2,774	503	98	438	1,591

Of the nearly 10 dozen Rookies of the Year, Andre Dawson stands prominently among the most versatile of them. He hit for average, he hit with power, he excelled as a base runner, and he had one of the strongest outfield throwing arms of all time.

That combination of abilities was clearly evident to Rookie of the Year voters back in 1977, as well as to selectors who named him National League Most Valuable Player a decade later.

Andre was the first Montreal position player to win the Rookie honor. In 1987, by then with the Cubs, he became the first man in history to earn MVP laurels as a member of a last-place team. He chalked up career highs that season in leading the National League in home runs (49) and runs batted in (137).

Earlier, throughout his decade in Montreal, his offensive output was a model of consistency. He generally hit somewhere between .282 and .308 with two dozen or so home runs and 20 to 30 stolen bases. Defensively he and teammates Ellis Valentine and Warren Cromartie (and later Tim Raines) formed one of history's most powerful trios of outfield speed and throwing arms.

Following the 1986 season "The Hawk," as he was often nicknamed, decided to test the free-agent market. Wrigley Field was always his favorite ballpark to visit, and he signed on with the Cubs. It was a contentious period then. Owners were charged with colluding to limit free-agent salaries. Dawson, it was said, offered to sign a blank contract. The Cubs, however, would not agree to that.

Eventually Dawson signed for over $600,000. After he won the '87 MVP award, Chicago destroyed the original contract and wrote a new one that nearly tripled Andre's income.

During his six Chicago seasons the Hawk's overall average was .285 (a shade over his rookie year's). He averaged nearly 30 home runs a year.

When his marvelous career ended Dawson owned a trophy case full of mementos and citations. He had been named to eight NL All-Star teams, had won eight Gold Gloves, had been the only man in big league history to attain double digits in both homers and stolen bases for 12 straight seasons, and had tied the record of twice hitting two home runs in the same inning.

Andre Dawson, Montreal Expos, 1977
"The Hawk's" 19-year career featured 438 home runs. Noted for his excellent defensive ability, Dawson averaged nearly 10 outfield assists per season.
(Temple University Libraries, Urban Archives, Philadelphia, PA)

Just before turning 39, Andre moved to Boston, serving the Red Sox primarily as a designated hitter for two years. Then his final two seasons were played back in Miami, his hometown. He has long been a supporter of his native city, and felt that his presence might encourage fan support of the expansion Marlins. He retired just before Florida's 1997 World Championship campaign.

Although not in uniform anymore, Andre is still an active Marlin. Since 2000 he has covered numerous special assignments as assistant to the club's president. They include community activity, scouting, and occasional on-field instruction.

Andre, his wife, and two children live near Miami in Pinecrest, Florida. The lifelong ambassador of his home region was the proud recipient of a special salute a few years ago when the community of South Miami christened a street Andre Dawson Drive.

FRED LYNN
1975   Boston Red Sox, American League

Personal Data: B. February 3, 1952, at Chicago, IL.
Physical Attributes: 6′ 1 ″, playing weight 185 lbs. Bats left, throws right.
Rookie Year, 1975:   Primary position outfield. Led league in slugging average, doubles, runs scored. First man to win MVP award in rookie season.
Total Career, 17 years: Red Sox 1974–80; Angels '81–84; Orioles '85–88; Tigers '88–89; Padres '90.

	BA	G	H	2B	3B	HR	RBI
1975	.331	145	175	47	7	21	105
Lifetime	.283	1,969	1,960	388	43	306	1,111

Fred Lynn, Boston Red Sox, 1975
Holds the distinction as the first player to be crowned both Rookie of the Year and Most Valuable Player in the same season. Later hit history's only All-Star Game grand slam.
(Courtesy of Boston Red Sox)

Predicting who will be any season's Rookie of the Year is a tricky proposition. So the Boston Red Sox were cautious in their public prognosticating after watching Fred Lynn hit .419 and drive in 10 runs for them as a September call-up in 1974. He appeared to be something special, but only a lengthy trial the next spring would determine his legitimacy.

Legitimacy indeed! Not only did the young man seamlessly fit into a big league outfield. He sat American League opponents on their collective ears from April through September. With his exciting defensive play that often featured circus catches. With his .331 hitting and a league-leading .566 slugging average. With AL highs in doubles (47) and runs scored (105). And with 21 homers and 105 RBI.

Lynn's brilliant debut was a major factor in Boston's advancing to the World Series. And it was clear evidence to baseball's voting writers that Fred Lynn should be Rookie of the Year... *and* Most Valuable Player.

He was the sole owner of that dual distinction until Seattle's Ichiro Suzuki was similarly saluted 26 years later.

Even though recurring aches and pains would eventually cut into Fred's playing time, he was by no means a one-year wonder. During the five Red Sox seasons immediately following his rookie year Fred topped .300 three times. His best overall output was in 1979 when he posted career highs in batting (.333), slugging (.637), runs (116), home runs (39), and RBI (122).

Lynn and teammate Jim Rice almost "double-handedly" led Boston to 91 wins in '79, although Baltimore ran away with the American League East. Lynn and Rice had come to Boston together in late 1974, had both challenged for the Rookie of the Year award ultimately presented to Lynn, and together sparked the Red Sox offense for six years.

Rice continued as a dangerous Boston slugger throughout the 1980s. But Lynn would ply his trade 3,000 miles away for a while. Born in Chicago, Lynn had grown up in California and was eager to play for a West Coast team. In January 1981, following contentiousness over contract issuance dates, Boston traded him to the Angels for Joe Rudi, Jim Dorsey, and Frank Tanana. The transaction negated Lynn's expected application for free-agent status. But it did land him in California.

"I hated to see him go," says Don Zimmer, who was a Boston coach during the pennant-winning '75 season, and was later Lynn's Red Sox manager. "It seemed he could do no wrong in 1975. In the outfield he'd dive and dash and catch everything in sight. Fenway and Fred Lynn seemed to be a perfect fit for each other. I know he did some good things for the Angels, but I'm convinced his career would have been much more brilliant if he'd stayed at Fenway Park."

Fred's remaining 10 major league seasons did not match up favorably with his remarkable Boston accomplishments. With one or two exceptions he missed 40 to 60 games a year with injuries ranging from a broken rib, to torn knees, to various nagging ailments. His very first season in California was a strike year. He played in 76 games and hit only .219. He, Angels followers, and presumably his new employer were disappointed.

But Southern California fans would soon enjoy a season-long glimpse of the old Red Sox performer when Lynn hit .299 and drove in 86 runs for the AL West–winning 1982 Angels. And, in the League Championship Series against Milwaukee, he gave them a demonstration of the kind of dramatics he had so often delivered in a national spotlight.

Through no fault of Fred's, California lost the five-game series, in which Lynn delivered a .611 batting mark (11-for-18), two doubles, a home run, and five runs batted in. His overall eight-game LCS batting average, in 1975 and '82, was .517.

In other significant outings Fred was frequently at the forefront again. Representing the Angels in the All-Star contest's 50-year anniversary game at Chicago's Comiskey Park in 1983, Fred hit a grand-slam home run. No other player—before or since—has an All-Star grand slam to his credit.

First at Boston, then with the Angels, Lynn appeared in All-Star games in each of his first nine AL years. In 20 All-Star at bats he hit .300, clubbed four home runs, and totaled 10 RBI.

Aside from Boston, where he is still remembered for his excellent first six seasons, Lynn's career seems somehow diminished. Perhaps that's because he seldom played a full schedule. Or maybe because his first years were so remarkable that the others tend to suffer in comparison.

Whatever the reasons for falling a little short of baseball archives' top shelf, there is no argument that Fred Lynn was a most deserving recipient of Rookie of the Year honors. And the 1975 MVP award, to boot.

THURMAN MUNSON
1970   New York Yankees, American League

Personal Data: B. June 7, 1947, at Akron, OH. D. August 2, 1979.
Physical Attributes: 5′ 11″, playing weight 190 lbs. Bats right, throws right.
Rookie Year, 1970:   Primary position catcher.
Total Career, 11 years: Yankees 1969–79.

	BA	G	H	2B	3B	HR	RBI
1970	.302	132	137	25	4	6	53
Lifetime	.292	1,423	1,558	229	32	113	701

A model of consistency who seldom strayed far from his first year's .302 batting average, Thurman Munson is one of two Rookies of the Year whose careers were tragically ended by fatal injuries suffered in plane crashes. Ken Hubbs of the Chicago Cubs was the other.

Munson was far the better known of the two, for Hubbs had completed only two full seasons prior to his 1964 accident in Utah. Munson, however, played most of his career in New York Yankee prime-time visibility. Along the way he was one of a handful of Rookie award winners who became a Most Valuable Player. That was in 1976 when he, instead of later teammate Reggie Jackson, could have been dubbed Mr. October. Despite a World Series sweep by Cincinnati, Thurman paced the Yankees with a .529 Series batting average after going 10-for-23 a week earlier in the League Championship Series.

He wasn't finished yet with October brilliance. In 1977, then in '78, he hit .320 each time as the Yankees posted World Series wins over Los Angeles. Here's a summary of Munson's remarkable post-season accomplishments: in a total of 30 LCS and World Series games he merely had 46 hits in 129 at bats, a sparkling .357 average. Included among those nearly four dozen hits were nine doubles and three homers. He accounted for 22 RBI.

Thurman Munson, New York Yankees, 1970
An American League MVP, he hit .373 in 16 World Series games. The Yankees captain was victim of a 1979 fatal airplane crash.
(Temple University Libraries, Urban Archives, Philadelphia, PA)

The only time Thurman's numbers dipped significantly from his rookie year's was his sophomore summer when he finished at .251. But except for his .261 three years later he would register four more seasons of between .301 and .318, and chalk up two years when he hit between .280 and .297. Never a long-ball threat, Munson hit as many as 20 home runs just once, but during the midpoint of his prime (1975–77) he drove home 102, 105, then 100 runs. Mr. Consistency, indeed. He earned three Gold Gloves and was an American League All-Star team member seven times.

Mr. Leadership, too. Thurman was clearly the Yankees' team leader throughout the 1970s. He was accorded the distinction of being named New York's team captain, the first player so designated since the legendary Lou Gehrig. Gehrig's 4 was the first number retired by a big league baseball team. Munson's 15 is also among the permanently retired numbers on display in Yankee Stadium's Monument Park.

In the strange twists that fate sometime takes, both Gehrig and Munson died in their 30s. Thurman, having turned 32 only two months earlier, was hitting at his usual pace—.288 after 97 games. The American League scheduled August 2, 1979, as a day off for the Yankees, who had just concluded a series in Chicago. Munson decided to spend the day at his eastern Ohio home before rejoining the team later that night. He planned to use part of the day to work on some maneuvers he'd been learning as a fledgling pilot.

His single-engine plane went down in the early afternoon.

It would be another 17 years before the Yankees, for whom this Rookie of the Year and MVP had performed brilliantly, would win another World Series.

DON NEWCOMBE
1949   Brooklyn Dodgers, National League

Personal Data: B. June 14, 1926, at Madison, NJ.
Physical Attributes: 6' 4 ", playing weight 220 lbs.Throws right, bats left.
Rookie Year, 1949:   Primary position pitcher.
Total Career, 10 years: Dodgers 1949–51, '54–58; Reds '58–60; Indians '60.

	Record	ERA	G	GS	SO	IP
1949	17–8	3.17	38	31	149	244½
Lifetime	149–90	3.56	344	294	1,129	2,154⅔

How's this for a Rookie of the Year fulfilling his promise? Don Newcombe, the 1949 National League's top rookie, not only won *that* prestigious honor. Seven years later, as his career reached its pinnacle, he was awarded the Most Valuable Player and Cy Young awards.

It was the first, and only, time a player was accorded citations in all three of those major individual categories.

Old-timers sometimes fail to recall that Don Newcombe came forth from a new breed of African American stars. His rookie season was in the same era as other Rookies of the Year—Jackie Robinson, Sam Jethroe, Joe Black, and Jim Gilliam. But unlike that prominent quartet, whose best years might have

Don Newcombe, Brooklyn Dodgers, 1949
One of history's best hitting pitchers, he is the only player to have been Rookie of the Year, MVP, and Cy Young Award winner during his career.
(Courtesy of Los Angeles Dodgers)

originally surfaced back in the old Negro leagues, Newcombe was only 22 when he joined the Brooklyn Dodgers and 23 when he pitched them to the 1949 pennant.

Yes, Newk had apprenticed with the Negro leagues' Newark Eagles ...as a teenager. But not with the veteran stature attained by the aforementioned players. Newcombe's best days were ahead.

He didn't waste any time to show his capabilities. Don made his mound debut in May 1949 with a 3–0 shutout of Cincinnati. When the curtain dropped in late September, Newcombe had led the NL with five shutouts, had registered a 3.17 ERA, and, even though he missed the season's first month, finished with a 17–8 won-lost record. The only blemish was his final pitch of the season, in Game One of the World Series. New York's Tommy Henrich, leading off the ninth inning, hit it into Yankee Stadium's right-field stands to break a 0–0 deadlock.

Despite that particular loss (Don allowed only five hits), no sophomore jinx afflicted him. He went 19–11 in 1950, missing out on 20 victories when the pennant-winning Phillies defeated him in extra innings on the final day.

Newk captured the coveted 20 wins the following year. His 164 strikeouts led the league. Again, though, his last game of the season was eventful. For the third year in a row the opposition prevailed. Ninth inning. Final game of NL best-of-three playoff. Newcombe on the mound leading 4–2 over the home team New York Giants. A Brooklyn victory seemed likely. Suddenly Don appeared to tire. Two Giants reached base. Manager Chuck Dressen replaced Big Newk with Ralph Branca.

You know the rest. Bobby Thomson's three-run homer sent the Dodgers quietly back to Brooklyn.

Newcombe did not pitch again for nearly 30 months. Drafted into U.S. military service, Don missed two full seasons during what should have been his prime pitching years. When he returned in 1954 he looked rusty and turned in a modest 9–8 record. But then came two blockbuster summers.

Don went 20–5 to lead the 1955 Dodgers to another pennant...and to Brooklyn's first and only World Series crown. The following season was even better for Newk. He posted a 27–7 record, led the NL in winning percentage for the second successive season, won the Cy Young award, and was the league's Most Valuable Player.

Brooklyn, however, failed to repeat its world title performance, bowing to New York in seven games.

The next year was the Dodgers' last hurrah at storied Ebbets Field. Newcombe's record dropped to 11–12, and he and his teammates traveled to Los Angeles for the team's 1958 debut there. After 11 games the MVP and Cy Young winner of only two years earlier was traded to Cincinnati for slugger Steve Bilko and relief pitcher Johnny Klippstein.

Don at first seemed uncomfortable with a new team. But the following year, 1959, he was on target again. With a 13–8 record he posted a 3.16 ERA over 30 games. But 1959 would be Big Newk's last season in the spotlight.

He was dealt to Cleveland at midseason of 1960, won just six games in 36 appearances, and eventually packed his bags for Japan and a stint at first base for the Chunichi Dragons.

Maybe, if designated hitter spots had been open in the American League back then, Newcombe might have auditioned for one of them. National League followers knew him as one of the best hitting pitchers of all time.

Frequently he entered the lineup as a pinch hitter. In 878 major league at bats Newk was a .271 hitter. Rarely did someone pinch-hit for him. Don totaled 15 career homers, including seven in 1955 when he twice smacked two in a game. Not many pitchers have exceeded 100 RBI. Newcombe registered 108 over his career. In a surprise base-running move, he once stole home after hitting a triple against Pittsburgh.

Following his active career it was learned that Don was a victim of alcoholism. Eventually he worked hard to overcome addiction and was fully rehabilitated. He later visited baseball clubhouses to explain the dangers of illegal drug and alcohol abuse.

Today, more than 40 years after his playing days ended, Don Newcombe interestingly but forcefully tells his stories to various youth organizations in and around Los Angeles, where he is currently the Dodgers' director of community affairs.

Pete Rose, Cincinnati Reds, 1963
The game's all-time hits leader (4,256) was a three-time batting champ who 10 times recorded 200 or more base hits. He is major league baseball's most recent player-manager (Reds 1984–86).
(George Brace Collection)

PETE ROSE
1963   Cincinnati Reds, National League

Personal Data: B. April 14, 1941, at Cincinnati, OH.
Physical Attributes: 5′ 11″, playing weight 190 lbs. Bats both, throws right.
Rookie Year, 1963:   Primary position second base.
Total Career, 24 years: Reds 1963–78; Phillies '79–83; Expos '84; Reds '84–86.

	BA	G	H	2B	3B	HR	RBI
1963	.273	157	170	25	9	6	41
Lifetime	.303	3,562	4,256	746	135	160	1,314

Pete Rose is a man who has reached his middle 60s. Already. Never has the old cliché "time flies" seemed more apropos.

If you ever saw him play baseball it's hard to picture him as anything other than that energized, take-charge, impetuous youth who led Cincinnati's Big Red Machine into four World Series and drove himself to statistical heights that might not be matched for a long time.

Right from the first—splashing headlong into his 1963 Rookie of the Year season—you'd never characterize him as, say, shy. Brash, yes. No Caspar Milquetoast he. Rose quickly became known as "Charlie Hustle," a sobriquet for which he exhibited great pride. He customarily ran full-speed to first base after drawing a walk. He welcomed the opportunity to be in position to break up potential double plays. Remember his saving stab of a teammate's dropped pop fly in a World Series game? The infield brawl with New York's Bud Harrelson during the NL Championship series in 1973, Rose's MVP year? Or crashing into catcher Ray Fosse with an All-Star Game's winning run?

Rose's first-year numbers don't rank especially high among typical Rookie of the Year statistics. Nor did his second season's .269 average, with just moderate overall offensive production, foretell the magnificent career that would follow.

But, beginning in 1965, Charlie Hustle hit over .300 for nine straight seasons—three of them batting champion campaigns (including a career-high .348 in 1969). He surpassed .300 a total of 14 times during his 24 seasons as an active player en route to baseball's all-time base hit record total of 4,256. In 1978 he batted safely in 44 consecutive games, still a National League hitting-streak mark.

Rose stroked more than 200 hits in a season 10 times, paced the NL in doubles five times, and led in runs scored in four different years. Thought of as something of a banjo hitter—especially in his later seasons—Pete at one time was the National League's all-time home run hitter among switch-hitters. Overall he laced 160 regular-season home runs, hit five in postseason play, and once homered three times in a nationally televised game from Shea Stadium.

Nearly two decades have now passed since Rose last swung a bat officially, yet he still holds NL career records in games played, 3,562; at bats, 14,053; runs scored, 2,165; base hits, 4,256; singles, 3,215; and doubles, 746. He ranks fourth behind Hall of Famers Hank Aaron, Stan Musial, and Willie Mays in National League total bases. Pete is Cincinnati's team leader in seven career offensive categories.

After 16 productive years in Cincinnati, his hometown, free agent Pete Rose signed with the 1979 Philadelphia Phillies. His power had waned slightly, but he promptly hit .331 in his new uniform. His leadership qualities, as well as the examples he set with his aggressive play, are widely credited with molding a talented group of Phillies into a 1980 World Championship unit.

Pete played in one more World Series after that, his sixth, hitting .313 as Philadelphia lost to Baltimore in 1983. He went to Montreal briefly the following year before accepting a midseason invitation to return to Cincinnati as player-manager.

Over four full seasons and parts of two others with the Reds, Rose's creditable managing record is usually overlooked. That oversight is due, in large part, to his managership's abrupt conclusion. Cincinnati posted 412 victories, lost 373 games, and turned in a winning percentage of .525 under Rose's direction. He penciled himself onto the Reds lineup card 217 times through 1986. He is major league baseball's most recent player-manager.

Pete Rose's expulsion from baseball, by Commissioner A. Bartlett Giamatti in 1989, has been well documented and remains controversial. Throughout the '89 season several allegations concerning Rose's relationship with gamblers and his known visits to race tracks led to investigations of his betting on baseball games. Based on resultant findings, the Commissioner's Office and Rose negotiated a settlement for a lifetime ban from baseball. Provisions were made for a possible reinstatement, although, at this writing, the matter's status remains unchanged.

Soon after the banishment, Pete was found guilty of income tax evasion and was imprisoned for several months. Since then he has owned and operated restaurants, hosted a nationwide radio call-in program, appeared frequently at baseball memorabilia expositions, and regularly attended Induction Weekend at Cooperstown in an effort to attract public support for Hall of Fame consideration and for reinstatement to organized baseball.

Recent reports have suggested that Bud Selig, baseball's current commissioner, was giving close attention to Rose's request for reconsideration. However, following the 2004 publishing of a book in which Rose admits wagering on baseball while he managed the Reds, immediate reinstatement seemed doubtful.

Whatever the outcome, it is clear that Pete Rose's mighty records—from his Rookie of the Year award, to his Most Valuable Player season, to his six World Series appearances—will forever stand with distinction in baseball's archives. And for those of us who saw him play, his unbridled enthusiasm between the white lines will forever distinguish him as a model for the way the game should be played.

ICHIRO SUZUKI
2001   Seattle Mariners, American League

Personal Data: B. October 22, 1973, at Kasugai, Aichi prefecture, Japan.
Physical Attributes: 5′ 9″, playing weight 160 lbs. Bats left, throws right.
Rookie Year, 2001:   Primary position outfield. Rookie record for hits (242) and singles (192), 56 steals led league. Only second MVP in Rookie of Year season. Hit postseason division series record .600 (12-for-20).
Career to Date, 4 years: Mariners 2001–04.

	BA	G	H	2B	3B	HR	RBI
2001	.350	157	242	34	8	8	69
Lifetime	.339	634	924	114	29	37	242

When a ballplayer is known more widely by his first name than his last, you figure he must be quite a celebrity. This one, indeed, is. Shout out "EEE-cher-oh," and even occasional onlookers know you're referring to the 2001 American League Rookie of the Year. They might be hard-pressed to give you his surname, Suzuki, but they know him just the same.

Oh, you forgot he was Rookie of the Year! That's probably because you remember him as the AL's Most Valuable Player in '01. For only the second time in history, a Rookie of the Year was also the American League MVP. Boston's Fred Lynn, in 1975, was the other.

The summer of '01 was clearly a red-letter baseball season. Albert Pujols, whose exploits are chronicled in Chapter 7, was the National League's top rookie that year. If Suzuki and Pujols continue to build on their early brilliance, they could become only the third Rookie of the Year tandem eventually invited to Cooperstown. Both 1956 rookie award winners, Luis Aparicio and Frank Robinson, and then the 1967 duo of Rod Carew and Tom Seaver, were Hall of Fame inductees.

Some contend that Suzuki's rookie award ought to be accompanied by an asterisk. They feel

Ichiro Suzuki, Seattle Mariners, 2001
First Japanese position player to earn Rookie of the Year award. Only second player in history to win Most Valuable Player salute in rookie season.
(Courtesy of Seattle Mariners)

he should fall into some other category because he was a seasoned high-level professional before entering America's major leagues. Suzuki played nine years in Japan's top-grade circuits and was a three-time MVP there. That's a matter for another day, though, because his eligibility for Rookie of the Year consideration was in complete accordance with BBWAA selection criteria as outlined elsewhere.

Suzuki's first American League season was exceptionally brilliant, and well deserving of a Rookie of the Year award. If a Soph of the Year were ever cited, Ichiro would have captured that trophy, too.

Here is a sampling of the newcomer's rookie achievements:

More base hits (450) in first two seasons than any player in history . . . first man since Jackie Robinson to lead majors in batting and stolen bases in same season . . . 242 hits in 2001 were most since 1930 and had been exceeded only eight times then . . . second rookie ever to lead AL in batting . . . set rookie record for singles (192) . . . won Gold Gloves in 2001 and '02 . . . All-Star Game starter in rookie season...had hitting streaks of 23 and 21 games in 2001. His sophomore highlights include a .321 average, 31 steals, 208 hits, and a .388 on-base average.

With each passing season Ichiro closes in on several Mariners all-time records. His 56 stolen bases in 2001 were just four shy of the Seattle standard established by Harold Reynolds in 1987. One record that will be difficult to surpass is his own .600 batting average—12-for-20—in Seattle's 2001 Division Series victory over Cleveland.

As we see, professional experience notwithstanding, Suzuki came roaring out of the gate to generate immediate excitement. Two of the 2001 Mariners remembered Ichiro's rookie season with great admiration. Third baseman David Bell said,

> I know he was technically a rookie, but you'd never know it. He was already seasoned. The full package. Ichiro could do it all. Defensively, too, with a strong, accurate arm. He's a very intelligent young man, so no great adjustments were required. There was a little bit of a language barrier at first, but nothing significant. Kaz Sasaki, one of our pitchers, is also from Japan and was Rookie of the Year in 2000. His presence helped Ichiro. A translator was always around, too. And living in Seattle, with its large Asian population, had to add to his comfort level. Hey, he'd won seven or eight batting titles in Japan, so it didn't take a rocket scientist to figure he'd be Rookie of the Year. And deserved to be.

Seattle third base coach Dave Myers echoed some of Bell's observations.

> Sure, the culture change had to concern Ichiro at first, but the advantage he had was his years of high-level Japanese baseball experience. He's a real sharp kid, and picks things up quickly. He studied our game very closely, so he'd recognize any differences from the way baseball's played in Japan. And he fits into our clubhouse very well. Hasn't missed a beat from the beginning of 2001 right up to now.

Entering the 2004 season, Suzuki was just past his 30th birthday. His American League batting average had dipped slightly each year, but he still surpassed .300 annually, and he delivered more than 200 hits in each of his three big league seasons. Suddenly, as the '04 campaign unfolded, the 200-hit level seemed to be merely a stepping-stone for Ichiro. Not only did his batting average soar to a career-high .372, but Suzuki also established an all-time major league record of 262 base hits. His total surpassed the former standard of 257 hits by Hall of Famer George Sisler of the 1920 St. Louis Browns. After more than a dozen professional seasons now—nine in Japan and four in the United States—his base-path speed might soon ebb. But his sharp batting eye and his intensity level can be expected to keep Ichiro Suzuki's name in baseball headlines for years and, perhaps some day, on a hallowed wall at Cooperstown. If so, just "Ichiro" on a Hall of Fame plaque would be enough.

4
Dugout Directors

Rookies of the Year Who Became Managers

L ong after their special first seasons, when their playing days were finally finished, several Rookies of the Year continued with baseball in various capacities: Coaching, scouting, minor league piloting, broadcasting.

Eleven became big league managers.

Alvin Dark, 1948 Rookie of the Year from the Boston Braves, is one of only six men to have managed pennant winners in both major leagues—the 1962 San Francisco Giants and 1974 Oakland Athletics. Mike Hargrove skippered Cleveland to two American League titles, and Lou Piniella led Cincinnati to the 1990 World Championship. In his second term at Milwaukee, Harvey Kuenn managed the Brewers to their only pennant (1982).

Pete Rose and Frank Robinson are the only ones to have become player-managers, Rose the most recent. Bill Virdon, Frank Robinson, and Piniella—in addition to Dark—have managed four franchises. (Dark had the A's in both Kansas City and Oakland in addition to leading San Francisco, Cleveland, and San Diego.) Robinson and Piniella were still actively directing their teams' dugouts throughout the 2004 season.

And Ozzie Guillen, in 2004, took over the leadership of the White Sox with whom he won the 1985 AL Rookie of the Year award.

Except for Robinson and Rose, whose careers are summarized in preceding sections, the profiles of the other nine managers who had been Rookies of the Year follow.

Rookies of the Year Who Became Managers

Rookie, Year, Team	Team(s) Managed
Alvin Dark, 1948, Boston NL	San Francisco Giants 1961–64 Kansas City A's '66–67 Cleveland Indians '68–71 Oakland A's '74–75 San Diego Padres '77
Ozzie Guillen, 1985, Chicago AL	Chicago White Sox 2004–
Mike Hargrove, 1974, Texas AL	Cleveland Indians 1991–99 Baltimore Orioles 2000–03 Seattle Mariners '05–
Tommy Helms, 1966, Cincinnati NL	Cincinnati Reds (interim) 1988, '89
Frank Howard, 1960, Los Angeles NL	San Diego Padres 1981 New York Mets '83
Harvey Kuenn, 1953, Detroit AL	Milwaukee Brewers 1975, '82–83
Jim Lebebvre, 1965, Los Angeles NL	Seattle Mariners 1989–91 Chicago Cubs '92–93 Milwaukee Brewers '99
Lou Piniella, 1969, Kansas City AL	New York Yankees 1986–87, '88 Cincinnati Reds '90–92 Seattle Mariners '93–2002 Tampa Bay Devil Rays '03–
Frank Robinson, 1956, Cincinnati NL	Cleveland Indians 1975–77 San Francisco Giants '81–84 Baltimore Orioles '88–91 Montreal Expos 2002–
Pete Rose, 1963, Cincinnati NL	Cincinnati Reds 1984–89
Bill Virdon, 1955, St. Louis NL	Pittsburgh Pirates 1972–73 New York Yankees '74–75 Houston Astros '75–82 Montreal Expos '83–84

ALVIN DARK
1948   Boston Braves, Major League Rookie of the Year

Personal Data: B. January 7, 1922, at Comanche, OK.
Physical Attributes: 5′ 11″, playing weight 185 lbs. Bats right, throws right.
Rookie Year, 1948:   Primary position shortstop.
Total Career, 14 years: Braves 1946, '48–49; Giants '50–56; Cardinals '56–58; Cubs '58–59; Phillies '60; Braves '60.

	BA	G	H	2B	3B	HR	RBI
1948	.322	137	175	39	6	3	48
Lifetime	.289	1,828	2,089	358	72	126	757

When shortstop Alvin Dark outpolled Indians pitcher Gene Bearden and Phillies center fielder Richie Ashburn for 1948 Rookie of the Year honors, Cleveland and Philadelphia fans were outraged. They felt their local heroes deserved the award.

No question that Bearden and Ashburn performed exceptionally well in their inaugural seasons. But Dark did, too, in helping the Boston Braves to their first pennant in 34 years. The former LSU football star, who had a 13-at-bat trial in 1946 for Boston, quickly proved to be a catalyst for the veteran-laden '48 Braves.

Dark was already 26 when that championship season began. Immediately he exhibited leadership qualities that eventually led to a 13-year managing career. In the meantime, though, he was clearly an on-field leader who not only sparked Boston to its final National League pennant, but also captained the 1951 and '54 Giants to their last two pennants before they departed New York for San Francisco.

Alvin never equaled his .322 rookie-season batting average again. But he consistently hit in the .285–.300 range, was a formidable clutch hitter, was annually among league

Alvin Dark, Boston Braves, 1948
An on-field leader during his playing days, Dark later managed teams from each league into the World Series . . . one of only six men to do so.
(Boston Braves Historical Association)

leaders in doubles (his 41 led the NL in 1950), and even at age 37 sprinted for nine triples with the 1959 Cubs.

Dark's first managing assignment came with the 1961 San Francisco Giants. The following season he was a pennant-winning skipper for the first time. San Francisco lost an exciting seven-game World Series to the Yankees.

He is one of only six men to pilot flag winners in both major leagues. His 1974 Oakland A's finally gave him a World Series triumph by downing Los Angeles in five games. Dark's postseason managing record was 10–9.

Between his San Francisco and Oakland tenures, Alvin piloted the Kansas City Athletics and Cleveland Indians. He completed his dugout career with the 1977 Padres.

During his playing days Dark was occasionally reported to carry a racial bias. Some years later, Jackie Robinson, a baseball rival from a competitive standpoint, sternly told the New York press that the allegations against Dark simply were not true.

Robinson and Dark are the only two men to achieve Rookie of the Year plaudits for all of major league baseball. After 1948 the Baseball Writers' Association of America selected one top rookie from each league. Roy Sievers of the Browns and Brooklyn's Don Newcombe were the 1949 choices.

During the quarter century since he last managed a big league team, Alvin has been active as a motivational speaker. A few years ago he established the Alvin Dark Foundation, which benefits Christian missionaries.

He recently told the *Charlotte Observer* that, when not traveling, he plays 18 holes of golf twice a week, and might hit balls or play six holes the other days. Golfing today at his baseball playing weight, 185 pounds, Alvin doesn't go far to find a tee box. He and his wife Jackie live on a golf course in Easley, South Carolina.

OZZIE GUILLEN
1985   Chicago White Sox, American League

Personal Data: B. January 20, 1964, at Oculare del Tuy, Venezuela.
Physical Attributes: 5′ 11″, playing weight 164 lbs. Bats left, throws right.
Rookie Year, 1985:   Primary position shortstop.
Total Career, 16 years: White Sox 1985–97; Orioles '98; Braves '98–99; Devil Rays 2000.

	BA	G	H	2B	3B	HR	RBI
1985	.273	150	134	21	9	1	33
Lifetime	.264	1,993	1,764	275	69	28	619

If their newest manager can transfer his own upbeat enthusiasm to his charges, the 2005 Chicago White Sox will have taken further strides toward success.

Ozzie Guillen, Chicago White Sox, 1985
In 2004 this Venezuela native was the most recent Rookie of the Year to become big league manager when he returned to the Sox, his rookie team.
(Ron Vesely/Chicago White Sox)

Ozzie Guillen, the 11th Rookie of the Year to assume a big league managership, was a spark plug as a player and a coach. That contagious vigor is still there in his role of manager. During the 20 seasons since he was the American League's top 1985 rookie, Ozzie has carried a trademark smile and a spring in his step to the ballpark every day. To welcome him as Sox skipper in 2004, virtually all of his former managers contacted Ozzie with warm congratulations.

Guillen has returned to his major league roots where he continued a long tradition of excellence at shortstop. Among his predecessors were Hall of Famers Luke Appling and Luis Aparicio. Ozzie has been especially close to Aparicio over the years.

"He was the first Venezuelan to make the Hall of Fame," says Guillen proudly.

And he was my first winter league manager. Our families know each other well. When I was named Rookie of the Year it was extra special, because Luis had played the same position on the same team as I did. And he was a Rookie of the Year, too. People in our native Venezuela still talk about the Rookie award. I've always looked on it as something extra special. You have chances to lead the league or maybe be MVP anytime during a long career. But Rookie of the Year? Only once.

Ozzie is admittedly proud to be a major leaguer. He has a keen interest in baseball's history and traditions. The 1993 White Sox happened to be the opponent for the last game ever at Cleveland Stadium. During the postgame ceremonies eulogizing the old ballpark, a single member of the Chicago club stood silently and attentively in the Sox dugout—Ozzie Guillen, clearly eager to soak in those final historic moments.

With the exception of 1992, when he was injured most of the year, Guillen was a model of durability. He appeared in the Chicago lineup nearly every game for 12 seasons. Ozzie then served as an elder statesman at Baltimore, Atlanta, and finally Tampa Bay during his final four active seasons. He hit .400 for the Braves in the 1998 and 1999 NLCS.

In 2002, Florida manager Jeff Torborg hired his old White Sox shortstop as the Marlins' third base coach—a post he held through the 2003 World Championship season.

During his Florida tenure Ozzie discussed leaders' responsibilities:

> Coaching's harder than playing. You have 25 guys to worry about; not just yourself. I try to learn all the time. I've learned a lot from every manager I played for. I think the best advice I can offer is this: Go out there and concentrate on your job today. Yesterday . . . last year . . . have nothing to do with today. Just do your best today!

As a manager Ozzie Guillen has players, coaches, a front office, and media to be concerned with. From all accounts, and not surprisingly, the White Sox skipper covers all those bases with a firm, understanding touch of professional class.

MIKE HARGROVE
1974   Texas Rangers, American League

Personal Data: B. October 26, 1949, at Perryton, TX.
Physical Attributes: 6' 0 ", playing weight 195 lbs. Bats left, throws left.
Rookie Year, 1974:   Primary position first base.
Total Career, 12 years: Rangers 1974–78; Padres '79; Indians '79–85.

	BA	G	H	2B	3B	HR	RBI
1974	.323	131	134	18	6	4	66
Lifetime	.290	1,666	1,614	266	28	80	686

Unlike most Rookies of the Year, who compile impressive résumés at high minor league levels, Mike Hargrove jumped from two good Class A seasons directly to the majors . . . and to first-year honors.

The Texas Rangers invited him, as a nonroster player, to 1974 spring training. He's been connected with professional baseball ever since.

"Grover," as he's commonly nicknamed, broke from the '74 gate
quickly and finished with solid
Rookie of the Year credentials—134
hits in 131 games and a .323 average.

He hit .303 the next year, added
some power, and smilingly touched
on a common superstition. "After I
won Rookie of the Year, many people warned me about the sophomore
jinx. How come you don't hear them
talking to the other second-year players about it?"

Mike played five seasons in Texas,
hitting over .300 three times. A brief
tour with the Padres (52 games in
1979) was followed by six and a half
years in Cleveland until his 12-year
career concluded with a lifetime .290
batting average.

Mike Hargrove, Texas Rangers, 1974
Nicknamed "Human Rain Delay" for frequently stepping
from the batter's box, Mike later managed Cleveland to
two American League pennants.
(George Brace Collection)

Given the sobriquet "Human
Rain Delay" for his deliberate pauses
at the plate between pitches, Hargrove's batting eye was considered
one of baseball's best. Twice he led the American League in drawing walks.
He struck out, on average, only once in more than 11 at bats, an excellent ratio
in modern baseball.

Upon retirement as an active player, Mike became a field manager. Younger
fans know him best in that role. He recently recalled:

> Dan O'Brien and Hal Keller, two Rangers officials, once asked if I'd thought
> about managing eventually. Well, yes and no. But not seriously back then. Then I
> thought . . . when you're on the bench, like everybody else you second-guess your
> manager. Study his theories. Try to see why some work and some don't. So yes,
> when the Indians gave me shot at minor league managing, I figured why not.

Three years as a farm system skipper followed. Then Grover joined the
Indians as a coach for a year and a half before succeeding John McNamara as
manager in 1991. He took the rebuilt Indians to the postseason five straight
years (1995–99) before his four-year managing tenure in Baltimore, starting in
2000. His Indians twice advanced to the World Series, losing out to Atlanta and
Florida. Hargrove has since embarked on a third managerial stint, this one with
Seattle.

While reviewing his Rookie of the Year award, Hargrove noted that he never piloted a player's Rookie of the Year season:

I thought Kenny Lofton had a good shot in 1992 at Cleveland. [Lofton was edged out by Pat Listach.] Eventually I did have the pleasure of managing a couple of the award winners later in their careers—Marty Cordova and Cal Ripken in Baltimore. And when I was playing, my Cleveland teammate Joe Charboneau was the 1980 winner. Joe was a great guy and quite a character. But all those stories about removing bottle caps with his eye socket, and so forth, were exaggerations.

Baltimore terminated Mike's manager contract after 2003, and he quickly rejoined Cleveland as senior baseball adviser. Throughout '04, before joining the 2005 Mariners, he worked with the Indians' minor league staff and with the team's major league coaches.

"Mike Hargrove . . . will always be a Cleveland Indian," said general manager Mark Shapiro. Perhaps that's so in Mike's mind, too.

"As a kid, I grew up a Cleveland fan," he's said. And during his four seasons with Baltimore, Mike and his wife Sharon maintained a permanent residence at the Cleveland-area home where their five children were raised.

Evidently the Rangers' only Rookie of the Year is revered and well remembered back in his old boyhood neighborhoods, too. The baseball complex at Perryton, Texas, High School, from which he was graduated, was recently named Mike Hargrove Field.

TOMMY HELMS
1966   Cincinnati Reds, National League

Personal Data: B. May 5, 1941, at Charlotte, NC.
Physical Attributes: 5′ 10 ″, playing weight 165 lbs. Bats right, throws right.
Rookie Year, 1966:   Primary position third base.
Total Career, 14 years: Reds 1964–71; Astros '72–75; Pirates '76–77; Red Sox '77.

	BA	G	H	2B	3B	HR	RBI
1966	.284	138	154	23	1	9	49
Lifetime	.269	1,435	1,342	223	21	34	477

Tommy Helms is among the more overshadowed of major league baseball's 116 Rookies of the Year. Yet his career reflects solid consistency, high-ranking longevity, and a defensive capability rarely equaled by his award-winning counterparts.

Officially a rookie in 1966, although having seen brief National League service in the preceding two seasons, Helms posted a .284 batting average as the Reds struggled to a seventh-place finish. It was the following year when Cincinnati began rising to its legendary Big Red Machine status. And Helms, for five straight seasons, was an infield mainstay—mostly at second base.

The keystoner's defensive performance was among the league's best for a decade. All the while, he generally hit in the .270 to .290 range, and he wound up with a sparkling .980 career fielding percentage.

Two years after his .983 fielding average in 150 games helped the Reds to their 1970 pennant, Helms was involved in a blockbuster trade. He and teammates Lee May and Jimmy Stewart were dealt to Houston for five players. Among them was Joe Morgan, who solidified his Hall of Fame credentials soon after during the Big Red Machine's heyday.

Helms, meanwhile, was a productive contributor with the Astros for three seasons before concluding his 14-year active career with brief stops in Pittsburgh and Boston.

But his baseball life was far from over. A long-time major league coach, he assisted manager Pete Rose at Cincinnati in the late 1980s. Helms then twice managed the Reds as a fill-in for Rose in 1988 and again, for 37 games, when Rose was forced to retire a year later. Cincinnati posted a combined record of 28–36 under Helms' field management.

Tommy has continued to follow professional baseball over the years from Evansville, Indiana, where he spent time in the automobile dealership business. One of his fondest special baseball memories is from 1970. Helms was never considered to be a power hitter, but he's forever in the Reds' archives as their first player to hit a home run at Cincinnati's newly opened Riverfront Stadium.

FRANK HOWARD
1960   Los Angeles Dodgers, National League

Personal Data: B. August 8, 1936, at Columbus, OH.
Physical Attributes: 6' 7 ", playing weight 255 lbs. Bats right, throws right.
Rookie Year, 1960:   Primary position first base.
Total Career, 16 years: Dodgers 1958–64; Senators/Rangers '65–72; Tigers '72–73.

	BA	G	H	2B	3B	HR	RBI
1960	.268	117	120	15	2	23	77
Lifetime	.273	1,902	1,774	245	35	382	1,119

He was known as Hondo. And also the Capital Punisher. The latter nickname referred to his long-ball power when he starred for the second-edition Washington Senators. It could also have applied to his hometown, Ohio capital Columbus, where he was an All-American basketball player at Ohio State University.

But baseball is where Frank Howard gained national prominence and where he chose to concentrate his career. The 1960 National League Rookie of the Year enjoyed a 16-year tenure as a player and nearly three decades more as big league manager and coach.

After poling 123 home runs in five-plus seasons for the Los Angeles Dodgers, with whom he excelled in the 1963 World Championship season, Howard was traded to Washington for pitcher Claude Osteen. In seven seasons with the Senators he cranked out another 237 homers. Many of them were legitimate tape-measure blasts. Twice he led the American League in home runs and was the RBI leader with 126 in 1970.

One of Frank's long-remembered feats of strength was a six-game stretch in 1968 when he smacked 10 home runs in 20 at bats. For the second of three times he ranked within the top 10 in MVP voting. He was an American League All-Star four times.

When the Washington franchise moved to Texas in 1972, Howard played in 95 games with the Rangers before Detroit purchased his contract. By then, nearing age 37, he was winding down. After the '93 season Frank decided to give Japanese baseball a try.

His first game in Japan was his last. Striking out, in his very first at bat, he injured his back. Frank Howard never played another game.

He had, however, developed a reputation as a knowledgeable baseball man who was popular among players and fans. Soon after returning from Japan he instructed minor leaguers for a while. He donned a major league uniform again in 1977 as a Brewers' coach. Four years later he was named manager at San Diego and, in 1983, was elevated from the Mets coaching staff to pilot New York's final 116 games that year.

Howard returned to coaching the following season and, through the remainder of the 20th century, was assigned coaching duties with the Mariners, the Yankees, the Mets again, and the expansion Devil Rays.

Today, residing again in the Washington, DC, area, Frank Howard reflects with pride on his Rookie of the Year selection, on the long home runs that typified his career, and on the satisfaction that he was widely considered the best player in the expansion Senators' 11-year history.

HARVEY KUENN
1953   Detroit Tigers, American League

Personal Data: B. December 4, 1930, at West Allis, WI. D. February 28, 1988.
Physical Attributes: 6' 2 ", playing weight 187 lbs. Bats right throws right.
Rookie Year, 1953:   Primary position shortstop. Led league with 209 hits and 679 at bats.
Total Career, 15 years: Tigers 1952–59; Indians '60; Giants '61–65; Cubs '65–66; Phillies '66.

	BA	G	H	2B	3B	HR	RBI
1953	.308	155	209	33	7	2	48
Lifetime	.303	1,833	2,092	356	56	87	671

He led the league in hits (198) for the fourth time, in doubles (42), and in batting, a career high .353. And for all that, Detroit's Harvey Kuenn earned a one-way trip out of town. Across the lake to Cleveland.

In one of baseball's best known, oft-repeated true stories—the "swap of the century" on the eve of opening day 1960—batting champion Kuenn and 1959 home run leader Rocky Colavito traded places.

Fans in both cities were irate. Teammates were befuddled. Neither player added strength to his new club. Presto, both teams dropped two positions in the standings from 1959. Reasons for the failed transaction probably involved general manager egos, particular that of Cleveland's Frank Lane. Yet, while the Indians and Tigers both suffered, the traded players continued to be productive for many years.

Colavito's role was that of slugger. Kuenn was a singles hitter, a hit-and-run specialist, a table setter, an aggressive hustler. From the moment he arrived at Detroit in late 1952 from a sterling collegiate career at the University of Wisconsin, Harvey Kuenn's big league success was virtually preordained.

Harvey Kuenn, Detroit Tigers, 1953
Managed Brewers to their only AL flag in 1982. Was a consistent hitter with a lifetime .303 batting average over 15 American and National League seasons.
(Temple University Libraries, Urban Archives, Philadelphia, PA)

By the following autumn, with his first full season completed, Kuenn had led the American League with a career-high 209 hits. He was clearly Rookie of the Year. No sophomore jinx would detour this fellow. His 201 hits led the AL again. In seven of his eight Tiger seasons he exceeded .300. After the infamous trade he would twice hit over .300 again and would match or surpass .290 two other times.

His first Cleveland campaign was his last Cleveland season. Despite Harvey's .308 batting average, the Indians wanted more power (which they had before "the trade"!), so Kuenn went to San Francisco for Willie Kirkland. He stayed in the Bay area five seasons, hit well there, and was part of the Giants' 1962 World Series squad. But injuries and illness began to slow him down. And after short stints with the Cubs and Phillies, Harvey's career was over. He was a consistent hitter to the end—his .296 average that last year enabled him to finish with a lifetime .303 average.

Kuenn returned to Wisconsin. When the Brewers moved into Milwaukee, Harvey coached for a while despite growing diabetes problems and cardiac concerns. He served as interim manager for the final 1975 game. Returning to the director's seat six weeks into the 1982 season, he led the team from fifth place to the World Series before St. Louis won out in seven games. Milwaukee's heavy hitters became widely known that summer as "Harvey's Wallbangers."

Harvey retired after the '83 season. He spent his latter years assisting with a family restaurant-lounge operation and as a Brewers adviser. But diabetes would take its toll, and his heart finally gave out in Peoria, Arizona, where Harvey planned to follow 1988 spring training.

He was only 57. Harvey Kuenn deserves to be remembered for his Rookie of the Year award and his excellent 15-year career. Not for a goofy trade.

JIM LEFEBVRE
1965   Los Angeles Dodgers, National League

Personal Data: B. January 7, 1942, at Inglewood, CA.
Physical Attributes: 6' 0 ", playing weight 180 lbs. Bats both, throws right.
Rookie Year, 1965:   Primary position second base.
Total Career, 8 years: Dodgers 1965–72.

	BA	G	H	2B	3B	HR	RBI
1965	.250	157	136	21	4	12	69
Lifetime	.251	922	756	126	18	74	404

When a first-year player leads his team in home runs and is solid enough to play in 156 games, he's likely to be considered for Rookie of the Year nomination. And that's just what transpired for Dodger second baseman Jim Lefebvre in 1965.

That home run figure was only 12, a comparatively low leadership total. Those dozen roundtrippers happened to be the fewest to lead a pennant winner since 1947 when another rookie, Jackie Robinson (matching teammate Pee Wee Reese), also stroked 12 to pace the Brooklyn Dodgers.

Lefebvre, pronounced La-FEE-ver, showed some added power when he hit 24 homers his sophomore season. He also had career highs in batting average (.274) and RBI (74) that year, and he hit his team's only home run when Baltimore pitching limited Los Angeles to only two runs over the 1966 four-game World Series sweep. During his first World Series, in 1965, Jim hit .400.

He is frequently remembered as a key member of Los Angeles's all-switch-hitting infield of the middle to late '60s. It featured two Rookies of the Year—Lefebvre and third baseman Jim Gilliam, the 1953 rookie award winner. Wes Parker played first; Maury Wills was the shortstop.

Although Lefebvre's career was a relatively short one—eight major league seasons plus four more in Japan—he continued in baseball as a coach, a big league manager, and a sought-after hitting guru.

When he was still an active player, he made several acting appearances in television bit roles.

Returning from Japan, Jim coached at Los Angeles, San Francisco, and Oakland. As player, coach, and manager, he was known for his intensity and strong personality. After Tom Lasorda removed Jim from the Dodger coaching staff, the two engaged in a brief public altercation at a television studio.

Jim's first managership was from 1989 through '91 at Seattle. He elevated the Mariners to their first winning season (1991), but was dismissed at year's end after some disputes with the front office surfaced over his lineup choices. He was hired immediately thereafter by the Cubs, and ran their dugout for two seasons. Lefebvre was a Brewers batting coach when manager Phil Garner was fired in late 1999. Jim replaced him, as interim skipper, for the schedule's remainder.

A full-time resident of Scottsdale, Arizona, Jim Lefebvre is still widely recognized for his ability to coach hitters. Every off-season major leaguers hire him to analyze their batting techniques and remove the glitches.

LOU PINIELLA
1969   Kansas City Royals, American League

Personal Data: B. August 28, 1943, at Tampa, FL.
Physical Attributes: 6' 0 ", playing weight 182 lbs. Bats right, throws right.
Rookie Year, 1969:   Primary position outfield.
Total Career, 18 years: Orioles 1964; Indians '68; Royals '69–73; Yankees '74–84.

	BA	G	H	2B	3B	HR	RBI
1969	.282	135	139	21	0	11	68
Lifetime	.291	1,747	1,705	305	41	102	766

Lou Piniella played his first major league game two teams and five years before he was officially, and appropriately, named American League Rookie of the Year.

At age 21 he recorded one at bat for the 1964 Orioles. Lou went to the plate five times for the '68 Indians, not nearly enough appearances to impair his rookie status. But, in 1969, when he delivered the team's first hit and scored the first run in history for the expansion Kansas City Royals, he was off and running toward Rookie of the Year honors. And a productive 18-season big league career.

More than three decades later, and perhaps best known by young fans as a successful 18-year field manager, Piniella reminisced about his early baseball days:

> I struggled in the minors for the better part of six years before everything came together in '69. Finally, the hard work paid off. And gave me a sense of pride and accomplishment. Joe Gordon, the old second baseman, was the Royals manager. He let the players play, and I'm forever grateful for the chance he gave me. With a good first season behind me—and by then I was 26—no sophomore jinx affected me at all, and I was fortunate enough to come right back with an even better year.

Lou hit .301 in 1970, homered 11 times, and drove in a career-high 88 runs.

"Baseball of the 1960s was more a sport than the commercial enterprise it is now," Piniella says.

> There weren't many endorsements or appearances for Rookies of the Year back then. Now, rookies are more accepted by the veterans than before. Of course, with more teams now, more opportunities exist for rookies. Even though my numbers were OK in '69, I thought that Chicago's Carlos May would be the top rookie. But he was injured in a firearms accident in early August. Fortunately, he recovered and had a good career.

Piniella also continued to excel. His 33 doubles led the AL in 1972 when he made the All-Star team. Unlike many rookies whose performances decline, Lou exceeded his .282 first-year average 10 times. Twice in Kansas City and five times in 11 seasons at New York, Piniella hit .301 or better.

His active career ended at age 39, but he continued in baseball's forefront. He managed the Yankees briefly in 1986, '87, and '88, was the New York GM and broadcaster for a while, then took over the Cincinnati managership in 1990. That year his Reds swept favored Oakland in the World Series.

In 1993, Piniella signed on as Seattle manager. He led the Mariners to their most successful decade, taking them to the postseason four times. Seattle's 116 victories in 2001 represent an all-time American League record. After 10 years in the Great Northwest, Lou returned to his native Tampa, Florida, area to pilot the Devil Rays.

In what many consider the majors' toughest division, Piniella in 2004 had the Rays playing their most competitive brand of baseball in the expansion club's seven-year existence.

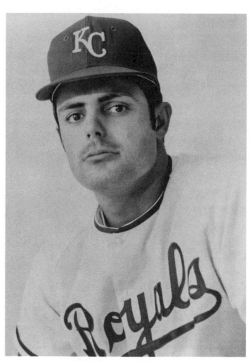

Lou Piniella, Kansas City Royals, 1969
Lou's rookie season was also the expansion Royals' first year. He and Alvin Dark are the only Rookies of the Year to eventually manage World Champions.
(Photo courtesy of Kansas City Royals)

BILL VIRDON
1955   St. Louis Cardinals, National League

Personal Data: B. June 9, 1931, at Hazel Park, MI.
Physical Attributes: 6′ 0 ″, playing weight 175 lbs. Bats left, throws right.
Rookie Year, 1955:   Primary position outfield.
Total Career, 12 years: Cardinals 1955–56; Pirates '56–65, '68.

	BA	G	H	2B	3B	HR	RBI
1955	.281	144	150	18	6	17	68
Lifetime	.267	1,583	1,596	237	81	91	502

The St. Louis Cardinals are one of baseball's most successful, most competitive, and fan-friendliest franchises. Sure, there's been a glitch here and there, but by and large the Cardinals contend far more often than not.

But sometimes you wondered if they had something against Rookies of the Year. Their own.

Wally Moon, for example. In 1954 he was the Cardinals first rookie honoree. A few years later he was a Dodger, traded away for Gino Cimoli.

St. Louis boasted two successive Rookies of the Year. Bill Virdon was the 1955 winner. Two years later he, too, was gone. "Trader" Frank Lane, who later orchestrated the infamous 1960 Kuenn for Colavito American League transaction, was the Cardinals' general manager in 1956. Lane dealt the popular Virdon to Pittsburgh for the soon-forgotten Dick Littlefield and Bobby Del Greco.

For several seasons after that deal, the Cardinals were usually just mediocre. You'll never know whether Moon and Virdon might have made a difference.

We do know, however, that Bill Virdon earned great respect as a defensive standout (Gold Glove–winning center fielder) and timely hitter for 10 years with Pittsburgh. He was a major contributor to the Pirates' first league title in 33 years and their first World Series win since 1925. It was Virdon's sharp grounder that struck a pebble and hit Yankee shortstop Tony Kubek in the throat to keep a late-inning rally alive. Eventually Bill Mazeroski smacked his 1960 Series–winning home run.

Bill Virdon, St. Louis Cardinals, 1955
Traded early in career, he helped spark Pittsburgh to its first title in 33 years. Later won 995 games as manager of the Pirates, Yankees, Astros, and Expos.
(Temple University Libraries, Urban Archives, Philadelphia, PA)

One man whom Virdon outpolled for rookie honors was his eventual team-mate, Hall of Famer Roberto Clemente. Virdon recalled:

I thought Roberto might win it, but I was glad to be in a position for that kind of recognition. People asked if there'd be pressure to have a good sophomore year. Pressure's only what you make of it, and I just tried to do a good job every game. Competition, you know, has a lot to do with that. Sure, by your second year pitchers know you better, but by then I was familiar with most of them, too. And it happened that my best year at bat was my sophomore season.

Pirates manager Danny Murtaugh and Virdon had great respect for each other. When Bill's playing days ended, Murtaugh hired him as a coach. Virdon eventually succeeded Murtaugh as Pittsburgh manager and, in his first year, led the team to the 1972 NL East title. But at midseason the next year, with the team at roughly .500, ownership rehired Murtaugh to replace Virdon.

Virdon was a manager again in 1974, this time with the Yankees. But when new owner George Steinbrenner learned that Billy Martin was available to manage, Virdon went; Martin came. His next managing stint was his most successful. Eight years at Houston . . . and the Astros' first division championship (1980).

Bill bowed out of managing in 1984 after two seasons at Montreal. Overall he posted a winning log as manager, 995–921.

He stayed connected with baseball after that, and finally retired from the field after assisting Pirates manager Lloyd McLendon as a full-time coach and adviser through the 2002 season.

A relaxed Bill Virdon then headed to his home near Springfield, Missouri, where his growing family includes seven grandchildren and four great-grandchildren.

Rookies of the Year by Franchise (1947–2004)

ANAHEIM/CALIFORNIA ANGELS
Tim Salmon, 1993

BALTIMORE ORIOLES
Ron Hansen, 1960

Curt Blefary, 1965

Al Bumbry, 1973

Eddie Murray, 1977

Cal Ripken Jr., 1982

Gregg Olson, 1989

(St. Louis Browns)
Roy Sievers, 1949

BOSTON RED SOX
Walt Dropo, 1950

Don Schwall, 1961

Carlton Fisk, 1972

Fred Lynn, 1975

Nomar Garciaparra, 1997

CHICAGO WHITE SOX
Luis Aparicio, 1956

Gary Peters, 1963

Tommie Agee, 1966

Ron Kittle, 1983

Ozzie Guillen, 1985

CLEVELAND INDIANS
Herb Score, 1955

Chris Chambliss, 1971

Joe Charboneau, 1980

Sandy Alomar Jr., 1990

DETROIT TIGERS
Harvey Kuenn, 1953

Mark Fidrych, 1976

Lou Whitaker, 1978

KANSAS CITY ROYALS
Lou Piniella, 1969

Bob Hamelin, 1994

Carlos Beltran, 1999

Angel Berroa, 2003

MILWAUKEE BREWERS
Pat Listach, 1992

(Seattle Pilots)
none

MINNESOTA TWINS
Tony Oliva, 1964

Rod Carew, 1967

John Castino, 1979 (co-winner)

Chuck Knoblauch, 1991

Marty Cordova, 1995

(Washington Senators)
Albie Pearson, 1958

Bob Allison, 1959

NEW YORK YANKEES
Gil McDougald, 1951

Bob Grim, 1954

Tony Kubek, 1957

Tom Tresh, 1962

Stan Bahnsen, 1968

Thurman Munson, 1970

Dave Righetti, 1981

Derek Jeter, 1996

Rookies of the Year by Franchise (1947–2004) (continued)

American League (continued)

OAKLAND ATHLETICS
Jose Canseco, 1986
Mark McGwire, 1987
Walt Weiss, 1988
Ben Grieve, 1998
Bobby Crosby, 2004

(Kansas City Athletics)
none

(Philadelphia Athletics)
Harry Byrd, 1952

SEATTLE MARINERS
Alvin Davis, 1984
Kazuhiro Sasaki, 2000
Ichiro Suzuki, 2001

TAMPA BAY DEVIL RAYS
none

TEXAS RANGERS
Mike Hargrove, 1974

(expansion Washington Senators)
none

TORONTO BLUE JAYS
Alfredo Griffin, 1979 (co-winner)
Eric Hinske, 2002

National League

ARIZONA DIAMONDBACKS
none

ATLANTA BRAVES
Earl Williams, 1971
Bob Horner, 1978
David Justice, 1990
Rafael Furcal, 2000

(Milwaukee Braves)
none

(Boston Braves)
Alvin Dark, 1948
Sam Jethroe, 1950

CHICAGO CUBS
Billy Williams, 1961
Ken Hubbs, 1962
Jerome Walton, 1989
Kerry Wood, 1998

CINCINNATI REDS
Frank Robinson, 1956
Pete Rose, 1963
Tommy Helms, 1966
Johnny Bench, 1968
Pat Zachry, 1976 (co-winner)
Chris Sabo, 1988
Scott Williamson, 1999

COLORADO ROCKIES
Jason Jennings, 2002

FLORIDA MARLINS
Dontrelle Willis, 2003

HOUSTON ASTROS
Jeff Bagwell, 1991

Rookies of the Year by Franchise (1947–2004) (continued)

National League (continued)

LOS ANGELES DODGERS
Frank Howard, 1960
Jim Lefebvre, 1965
Ted Sizemore, 1969
Rick Sutcliffe, 1979
Steve Howe, 1980
Fernando Valenzuela, 1981
Steve Sax, 1982
Eric Karros, 1992
Mike Piazza, 1993
Raul Mondesi, 1994
Hideo Nomo, 1995
Todd Hollandsworth, 1996

(Brooklyn Dodgers)
Jackie Robinson, 1947
Don Newcombe, 1949
Joe Black, 1952
Jim Gilliam, 1953

MILWAUKEE BREWERS
Note: see American League
Brewers joined National
League in 1998

MONTREAL EXPOS
Carl Morton, 1970
Andre Dawson, 1977

NEW YORK METS
Tom Seaver, 1967
Jon Matlack, 1972
Darryl Strawberry, 1983
Dwight Gooden, 1984

PHILADELPHIA PHILLIES
Jack Sanford, 1957
Dick Allen, 1964
Scott Rolen, 1997

PITTSBURGH PIRATES
Jason Bay, 2004

ST. LOUIS CARDINALS
Wally Moon, 1954
Bill Virdon, 1955
Bake McBride, 1974
Vince Coleman, 1985
Todd Worrell, 1986
Albert Pujols, 2001

SAN DIEGO PADRES
Butch Metzger, 1976 (co-winner)
Benito Santiago, 1987

SAN FRANCISCO GIANTS
Orlando Cepeda, 1958
Willie McCovey, 1959
Gary Matthews, 1973
John Montefusco, 1975

(New York Giants)
Willie Mays, 1951

The Short Timers

Rookies of the Year with Short Careers

I t's obvious that any young player who is named Rookie of the Year exhibits great potential. Most of the award winners, indeed, continue to fulfill a promise that results in lengthy big league tenures.

Of the 91 Rookies of the Year whose playing days ended before 2004, the average career was roughly 12 years. That's longer than baseball's overall average, as you might expect of the exceptionally talented.

A few exceeded 15 seasons in the majors. And fewer than a half dozen played for more than 20 years.

Twelve Rookies of the Year registered what we call short-time careers. Some suffered injuries that curtailed their advancement. Others—Sam Jethroe and Joe Black come to mind—were former Negro leaguers who had passed typical prime-time age when organized baseball finally permitted them to participate. Some simply ran out of gas before normal time was up. Joe Charboneau and Bob Hamelin would be included in that group. And one player, Ken Hubbs, died in a tragic accident after just two full major league seasons.

All the players whose careers are outlined in this chapter played seven seasons or fewer. Despite their relatively early departures from the "show," they sparkled during their Rookie of the Year season.

SAM JETHROE
1950   Boston Braves, National League

Personal Data: B. January 20, 1922, at East St. Louis, IL. D. June 16, 2001.
Physical Attributes: 6′ 1″, playing weight 178 lbs. Bats both, throws right.
Rookie Year, 1950:   Primary position outfield. 35 stolen bases led NL.
Total Career, 4 years: Braves 1950–52; Pirates '54.

	BA	G	H	2B	3B	HR	RBI
1950	.273	141	159	28	8	18	58
Lifetime	.261	442	460	80	25	49	181

Back when base stealing was a rare offensive strategy, Sam Jethroe delighted fans with his swiftness and daring.

However, he had already passed his 28th birthday—some say years earlier—when his 1950 rookie season began. Three years later the major league tenure of "Jethroe the Jet" was effectively over. Only two other Rookies of the Year, Joe Charboneau and Ken Hubbs, had shorter careers.

By 1950 many of the position players who had led Boston to the NL pennant two years earlier were in the twilight of their careers. To add speed to its aging lineup, Boston purchased Jethroe from the Brooklyn organization.

Sam Jethroe, Boston Braves, 1950
Sam "The Jet" played only three full seasons. He was noted for his base stealing, as well as for being the city of Boston's first African American major leaguer.
(Boston Braves Historical Association)

That transaction reflected a significant change taking place in baseball. Jethroe was Boston's first black baseball player. The Red Sox didn't play their first African American, Pumpsie Green, for nearly another decade.

Jethroe, like pathfinder Jackie Robinson, had been a Negro league standout in his mid-20s. But when the color ban was lifted, many Negro league stars were past their primes. Hall of Famer Monte Irvin was already 30 when he joined the 1949 New York Giants. Satchel Paige claimed to be 42 upon signing with Cleveland in 1948. Jethroe, at a reported 28, was baseball's eldest Rookie of the Year for 50 years until Seattle's Kazuhiro Sasaki (age 32) won the 2000 award.

At Boston it was base stealing and his ability to cover most of Braves Field's outfield that kept center fielder Sam Jethroe's name in 1950 headlines. He stole 35 bases. Runner-up Pee Wee Reese had 17. Sam batted .273 with 18 home runs and 28 doubles. His 1951 figures were almost duplicates; .280, 29 doubles, 18 homers, and another 35 steals.

Jethroe's career started to decline in 1952. Home runs were less frequent, steals dropped to 28, and for the third straight year he led National League outfielders in errors. The Braves bought Sam eyeglasses, but his outfield play remained unstable. Age, several seasons with the Negro league's Cleveland Buckeyes, and three National League campaigns with few days off had taken their toll.

Sam never again played for Boston. He suited up with Pittsburgh for just two games . . . and one hitless at bat . . . in 1954. Less than four years after being saluted Rookie of the Year, Sam Jethroe's major league career was finished. However, he continued in uniform for another five Triple-A years with Toledo and Toronto.

Back in his adopted home city of Erie, Pennsylvania, Sam occasionally played in the semipro Glenwood League. His focus, though, was on business. A respected local entrepreneur, he operated restaurants and lounges over the following two dozen years.

After retirement Sam worked zealously to acquire pension benefits and health insurance assistance for retired Negro leaguers.

Survived by Elsie, his wife of 58 years, "Sam the Jet" died in June 2001. At age 79. Or 80. Maybe 84, as his family says. "He told baseball people he was born in 1922. But we never located a birth certificate," said his granddaughter, Carla. "But my mom said he was 84 when he passed, so subtract that from 2001 and he was born in 1917!"

Regardless of what his age might have been, Sam's memory of long-ago games, at bats, and baseball friendships remained clear. Even though a racial barrier delayed his entering organized baseball, Sam Jethroe proudly cherished his Rookie of the Year recognition and his place in history as Boston's first black major leaguer.

JOE BLACK
1952   Brooklyn Dodgers, National League

Personal Data: B. February 8, 1924, at Plainfield, NJ. D. May 16, 2002.
Physical Attributes: 6′ 2″, playing weight 220 lbs. Throws right, bats right.
Rookie Year, 1952:   Primary position pitcher.
Total Career, 6 years: Dodgers 1952–55; Reds '55–56; Senators '57.

	Record	ERA	G	GS	SO	IP
1952	15–4	2.15	56	2	85	142⅓
Lifetime	30–12	3.91	172	16	222	414

Joe Black, the popular 1952 National League Rookie of the Year, was a starting pitcher in the World Series that year. He started three Series games, including a complete-game six-hit 4–2 Brooklyn victory in the opener against the Yankees.

Ironically, he'd been a starter only twice during the Dodgers' regular season.

His Rookie of the Year honors were based primarily on his outstanding relief pitching. Relieving 54 times, the big right-hander clearly earned the rookie trophy for his 15–4 record and sparkling 2.15 ERA. His strikeout/walk ratio was better than 2 to 1.

Joe Black, like many of his contemporaries, such as Jackie Robinson, Sam Jethroe, Monte Irvin, and Satchel Paige, had excelled in the old Negro leagues in his younger days. Joe was 28 when he first appeared for the Dodgers, just a few weeks shy of Robinson's and Jethroe's ages when those two earlier Rookies of the Year made major league debuts.

Black's first year was clearly his best. He had winning records in three of his remaining five seasons, but his earned run average ballooned when his vaunted fastball and curve lost some of their potency. Early in his fourth season he was dealt to Cincinnati where, frequently in a starting role, he was 5 and 2 in 1955. He then relieved in 32 games for the 1956 Reds before concluding his relatively short big league career over 13 innings with Washington in 1957.

After his playing career Joe was an executive with Greyhound in Phoenix, was on the board of directors of the Baseball Assistance Team, and later worked for the expansion Arizona Diamondbacks in community relations. His cheery demeanor made him a welcome visitor to major league clubhouses, in pressrooms, and at civic functions relating to young student-athletes. Technically, he was Doctor Black. Joe received an honorary doctorate degree from Morgan State University, from which he was graduated in 1950.

Black was a long-time resident of the Phoenix area. He passed away there, at age 78, in May 2002. As a fitting tribute to Joe and his close interest in baseball's Arizona Fall League, the league's Most Valuable Player is now awarded the prestigious Joe Black Trophy. It's another symbol of a lasting legacy to 1952's amiable NL Rookie of the Year who had the distinction of being the first African American pitcher to win a World Series game.

HARRY BYRD
1952   Philadelphia Athletics, American League

Personal Data: B. February 3, 1925, at Darlington, SC. D. May 14, 1985.
Physical Attributes: 6′ 1″, playing weight 188 lbs. Throws right, bats both.
Rookie Year, 1952:   Primary position pitcher.
Total Career, 7 years: A's 1950, '52–53; Yankees '54; Orioles '55; White Sox '55–56; Tigers '57.

	Record	ERA	G	GS	SO	IP
1952	15–15	3.31	37	28	116	228⅓
Lifetime	46–54	4.35	187	108	381	827⅔

The Philadelphia Athletics, one of the American League's eight charter teams, spent much of their 54-year Pennsylvania lifetime in or near first place . . . or else fighting to escape the basement. The A's won nine pennants during manager Connie Mack's 50-year reign. But they also finished last, or next to last, 22 times before transferring to Kansas City in 1955.

A "last hurrah" in Philadelphia was recorded in 1952 when the ball club, by then managed by Jimmie Dykes, posted a winning record (79–75) to finish a respectable fourth, just two games below third place. More than a half dozen individuals turned in standout performances. One of them was right-hander Harry Byrd, whose 15 wins and a solid 3.31 ERA lifted him to Rookie of the Year honors.

Based on Byrd's achievements, as well as the productive accomplishments of several teammates, Philadelphia management foresaw a return to glory days. First baseman Ferris Fain led the league with a .327 batting average. He was also tops in doubles and third in base hits. Southpaw Bobby Shantz (24–7; .774

Harry Byrd, Philadelphia Athletics, 1952
Prior to the franchise's move to Kansas City, then on to Oakland, right-handed pitcher Harry Byrd was the Philadelphia A's only Rookie of the Year.
(Philadelphia Athletics Historical Society)

winning percentage) was the '52 MVP. Fain, Eddie Joost, and Elmer Valo ranked third through fifth in walks. Slugger Gus Zernial hit 29 homers and drove home 100 runs to place fourth in the AL in both categories. Yes, the future looked bright.

Alas, it wasn't. Trades removed some of the regulars, and others suffered injuries, while some of the remaining A's never again matched their '52 performances. Rookie of the Year Byrd was one of those.

He led the league in his sophomore season. But in a negative category. Twenty losses. Harry logged only 11 victories. His ERA ballooned from his rookie year's 3.31 to 5.51 in 1953.

Byrd was shipped off to the Yankees in an 11-player transaction. New York benefited, and so did Byrd—briefly. He was 9–7 with a respectable 2.99 ERA in 1954. But three more trades soon followed, including a 17-man blockbuster between the Yanks and Orioles. By then Byrd's best days were well behind him, and his relatively short career ended in 1957.

Harry Byrd was only 60 at the time of his 1985 death in his native Darlington, South Carolina. Over the decades he took great pride in having been the Philadelphia Athletics' only Rookie of the Year.

DON SCHWALL
1961   Boston Red Sox, American League

Personal Data: B. March 2, 1936, at Wilkes-Barre, PA.
Physical Attributes: 6' 6", playing weight 200 lbs. Throws right, bats right.
Rookie Year, 1961:   Primary position pitcher. 10 complete games.
Total Career, 7 years: Red Sox 1961–62; Pirates '63–66; Braves '66–67.

	Record	ERA	G	GS	SO	IP
1961	15–7	3.22	25	25	91	178⅔
Lifetime	49–48	3.72	172	103	408	743

Maybe it's Fenway Park's intimidating left-field wall. Or, simply the way the chips have fallen over the past half century and more.

Fact is, of the five Red Sox Rookies of the Year, just one was a pitcher. Big right-hander Don Schwall, in 1961. He was on the major league stage for only seven years. But his first one was a dandy, and well deserving of the rookie honors.

A former basketball player at the University of Oklahoma, Schwall pitched so well in his first months in Boston that he was selected to the All-Star team. The second 1961 game (the third of four summers when two All-Star Games were booked) was played at Fenway Park, and Schwall, already a local favorite, pitched three innings in the 1–1 tie. Rain, and not a commissioner's edict, ended the contest.

"Just getting to the big leagues was a lifetime dream come true for me," said Don recently. "But I guess striking out Stan Musial in the All-Star Game was that first year's highlight. Later the Rookie of the Year selection really capped the season. I hadn't given the award much thought, because I wasn't even on the big league roster when the season began."

Schwall's career took a downturn, but not a full nosedive, after that. He had a 9–15 log in 1962, then was traded to Pittsburgh for slugger Dick Stuart. For the next four seasons he pitched at roughly a .500 pace and was assigned both spot starting and bullpen work. He went to the Braves in mid-1966, pitched in just one game for Atlanta in 1967, and called it a career. A new career, though, immediately beckoned.

Don went into the investment business before 1967 was over. In his late 60s he was still active and comfortable, having served as a vice president at both E. F. Hutton and Paine Webber over the years.

Johnny Pesky, a Red Sox coach during Schwall's Boston years, remembers Don's excellent rookie season and shares disappointment that the pitcher's career ended quickly. "But," smiles Pesky, "he's a good man, and it's gratifying to see how well he's done as a businessman."

The Rookie of the Year award remains at the forefront of Don Schwall's baseball memories.

"There's no question that it's helped my business career. Forty some years later, and still it brings me publicity periodically. I get to go to baseball card functions from time to time, and the Rookie of the Year honor is always mentioned."

Don and his family continue to reside in Pittsburgh, where he's still active in the investment business.

KEN HUBBS
1962   Chicago Cubs, National League

Personal Data: B. December 23, 1941, at Riverside, CA. D. February 15, 1964.
Physical Attributes: 6′ 2″, playing weight 175 lbs. Bats right, throws right.
Rookie Year, 1962:   Primary position second base.
Total Career, 3 years: Cubs 1961–63.

	BA	G	H	2B	3B	HR	RBI
1962	.260	160	172	24	9	5	49
Lifetime	.247	324	310	44	13	14	98

From that time back in the early 20th century when Johnny Evers was poetically immortalized with shortstop Joe Tinker and first baseman Frank Chance, the Chicago Cubs have been blessed with several outstanding second basemen. Perennial headliners Rogers Hornsby, Billy Herman, and Ryne Sandberg are among others who come to mind.

Forty-some years ago it appeared that Ken Hubbs would join that prominent list of celebrated pivot men. Fate, however, suddenly intervened.

The popular 1962 National League Rookie of the Year was tragically killed when a private plane he was piloting crashed in Utah during a February snowstorm. Less than two weeks later Hubbs was to have reported for the Cubs' 1964 spring training.

Ken was still 10 months shy of his 23rd birthday.

During Hubbs' brilliant rookie year, Chicago officials had delighted in Ken's promise, which seemingly accelerated week after week into a record-setting performance.

By season's end he had established a big league standard with 78 consecutive errorless games. His successful handling of 418 chances over that stretch was also a record.

In addition to his Rookie of the Year salute, the agile second baseman was honored as the first rookie to win baseball's Gold Glove. And at the plate Hubbs' 661 at bats was a National League record at the time. During eight of those consecutive at bats the youngster was perfect. Against Philadelphia, in late May, he stroked eight singles in eight trips to the plate in leading Chicago to a doubleheader sweep.

Ken's premature final season was something of a letdown immediately following his rookie success. His batting average dipped to .235. But he cut down on his league-leading strikeouts of the previous year, and he continued to deliver defensive brilliance. Chicago management was convinced that Hubbs would consistently progress into a long-time fixture in its infield.

Instead, his sadly abbreviated career of 324 games was the shortest of any National League position player ever honored as Rookie of the Year.

MARK FIDRYCH
1976   Detroit Tigers, American League

Personal Data: B. August 14, 1954, at Worcester, MA.
Physical Attributes: 6' 3", playing weight 175 lbs. Throws right, bats right.
Rookie Year, 1976:   Primary position pitcher. League-leading 2.34 ERA and 24 complete games. Started All-Star Game.
Total Career, 5 years: Tigers 1976–80.

	Record	ERA	G	GS	SO	IP
1976	19–9	2.34	31	29	97	250⅓
Lifetime	29–19	3.10	58	56	170	412

Some people called him a flake. His antics and gangly appearance reminded others of television's "Big Bird." Ergo, he was soon known as Mark the Bird. In truth Mark Fidrych was a legitimate phenomenon.

He advanced to the major leagues a few weeks after the 1976 season had begun and pitched a two-hitter in his first start. Less than three months later, at age 21, he was the American League's starting pitcher in the All-Star Game at Philadelphia. Three months after that, Fidrych was hailed as the AL Rookie of the Year.

The honor was genuinely earned. Virtually unknown except in his native Massachusetts locales and within the Detroit Tigers organization, Mark Fidrych suddenly became baseball's biggest drawing card of 1976. His brilliant pitching, combined with on-field showmanship, attracted full houses throughout the American League.

He talked to himself on the mound. He insisted that balls be removed "because they had hits in them." He'd sometimes delay games by smoothing out cleat marks from the pitching mound's surface.

An entertainer, yes. But foremost, Mark Fidrych delivered a potent fastball and wicked slider that propelled him to a 19–9 rookie-season record. The tall right-hander led the AL with a 2.34 earned run average and with 24 complete games.

Fidrych's future seemed exceedingly bright. Unfortunately for him, and for the Tigers' box office, Mark's big league future consisted of only four more years and a disappointing 10–10 record.

His sophomore season began decently enough. But soon knee and shoulder problems developed. Fidrych appeared in only 11 games, winning six of them with a good 2.89 ERA. The ailments persisted, though. Mark attempted to regain his old form, but took the mound for only three games in 1978, four in '79, and nine in 1980. Over those three seasons he completed but three of his 16 starts.

Boston signed the Bird to a minor league contract, but his comeback efforts were fruitless. In a 1982 Triple-A game he faced Dave Righetti, another Rookie of the Year, at Pawtucket. More than 9,000 fans attended. Fidrych, though, was clearly ineffective. In early 1983, at age 29, he retired from professional baseball.

Sadly, and too late, it was determined that Mark had a torn rotator cuff that caused his arm problems years earlier. The malady had not been diagnosed properly until 1985.

Mark Fidrych seamlessly returned to a quieter life. He retired to New England and turned to farming. In recent years the former flamboyant "Bird," the popular 1976 Rookie of the Year, has resided near Northboro, Massachusetts. Never having lost his enthusiasm for baseball, he still turns up for an occasional old-timers' game or a baseball exhibit.

BUTCH METZGER
1976   San Diego Padres, National League Cowinner

Personal Data: B. May 23, 1952, at Lafayette, IN.
Physical Attributes: 6′ 1″, playing weight 185 lbs. Throws right, bats right.
Rookie Year, 1976:   Primary position pitcher. 16 saves.
Total Career, 5 years: Giants 1974; Padres '75–77; Cardinals '77; Mets '78.

	Record	ERA	G	GS	SO	IP
1976	11–4	2.92	77	0	89	123⅓
Career	18–9	3.74	191	1	175	293⅔

Clarence Edward (Butch) Metzger holds two baseball records. On the positive side, one of the records is most victories without a loss at the start of a career, 12. The other mark is of a dubious nature. Butch's total career consisted of fewer innings played than any other of history's 116 Rookies of the Year. Two hundred ninety-three and two-thirds innings.

The husky right-hander started only one big league game. But for a two-year period he was one of baseball's most highly regarded relief pitchers. Unfortunately, severe arm problems forced a hasty finish to his career.

Originally signed by the Giants, Metzger made his major league debut with them by turning in a respectable 1–0 record in 10 games toward the tag end of the 1974 season. But the team negotiated a trade during the winter, and Butch,

Butch Metzger, San Diego Padres, 1976
Relief pitcher began his big league tenure with a record 12 straight victories at the start of a career. Shared '76 NL rookie honors with Pat Zachry.
(Courtesy of San Diego Padres)

along with shortstop Tito Fuentes, went to San Diego in exchange for Derrel Thomas. Metzger spent most of 1975 in San Diego's minor league system.

Then came Butch's watershed season. An 11–4 record, 16 saves, and an ERA under three clearly represented the finest year of his short career. Victories in each of his first 10 decisions in 1976, combined with 1–0 records at San Francisco two years earlier and then 1–0 again for the '75 Padres, enabled Butch to match Hooks Wiltse's all-time mark of 12 wins in a row at the start of a career. Wiltse, like Metzger, broke in with the Giants. In Wiltse's case they were the New York Giants back in 1904.

Sharing honors was nothing new for Metzger. He and Cincinnati's Pat Zachry received equal billing for 1976 Rookie of the Year. That's the only time in history that National League cowinners were elected.

Metzger's tenure in the spotlight was short-lived, primarily because of a persistently sore arm. Butch was traded to St. Louis in early 1977. He was able to pitch 115 innings for the Cardinals, but was sold to the Mets prior to 1978. By then his arm was no longer effective, and New York dealt Butch to Philadelphia at midseason.

He never took the mound for the Phillies, nor for any major league team again. Now a resident of Sacramento, California, the promising 1976 co–Rookie of the Year was out of baseball at age 26.

JOHN CASTINO
1979   Minnesota Twins, American League cowinner

Personal Data: B. October 23, 1954, at Evanston, IL.
Physical Attributes: 5′ 11″, playing weight 175 lbs. Bats right, throws right.
Rookie Year, 1979:   Primary position third base.
Total Career, 6 years: Twins 1979–84.

	BA	G	H	2B	3B	HR	RBI
1979	.285	148	112	13	8	5	52
Lifetime	.278	666	646	86	34	41	249

If ever a Rookie of the Year seemed oblivious to the nasty "sophomore jinx," John Castino appears to be that man. His second year, in fact, turned out to be his overall best in a short career ended by a serious back problem after only six seasons.

Year two featured John's only .300 season. He averaged .302 and posted career highs in home runs (13) and runs batted in (64). Those figures represented an impressive follow-up to his 1979 Rookie of the Year campaign's respectable .285 average, five homers, and 52 RBI.

John's rookie-season figures bore close resemblance to the performance recorded by Toronto's Alfredo Griffin. When writers' ballots were officially tabulated, Castino and Griffin had tied for Rookie of the Year honors. It was the only year cowinners were named in the American League. Here's how the two infielders compared:

> Castino, 3B—.285, 13 doubles, 8 triples, 5 home runs, .962 fielding average.
> Griffin, SS—.287, 22 doubles, 10 triples, 2 home runs, .956 fielding average.

Castino reflects on that season's rookie competition: "I wasn't surprised that Alfredo and I tied in the voting. Frankly, it was a fairly weak class of rookies in '79. As the season progressed I figured I had a chance. I look on the rookie award as a very nice honor. It continues to bring recognition to me."

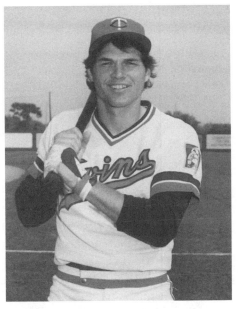

John Castino, Minnesota Twins, 1979
Back injuries limited John to his six-year career. He and Toronto's Alfredo Griffin were the American League's only co Rookies of the Year.
(Courtesy of Minnesota Twins)

As we've seen, it was surely no impediment to his second season's performance. In his third year, 1981, Castino's nine triples led the league. A year later John, primarily a third baseman to that point, was switched to second when young Gary Gaetti took over the hot corner post for the Twins. Only two years after that, and with just eight 1984 games to his credit, John Castino's big league days were over.

He had been victimized frequently by back pains. Finally a fused disc brought his baseball career to a certain finish.

Fortunately John was soon physically fit for somewhat more sedentary activities. He exited the disabled list, and for nearly two decades he has been senior vice president of Wealth Enhancement Group, a financial services organization.

From his home in Edina, Minnesota, near the Twin Cities, John reflects on his Rookie of the Year season when he lined up at third base for 143 games and at shortstop for five others. He points to one particular moment:

"It was a home game against the Yankees. I'll never forget the standing ovation I received for defensive plays that day."

JOE CHARBONEAU
1980   Cleveland Indians, American League

Personal Data: B. June 17, 1955, at Belvedere, IL.
Physical Attributes: 6' 2", playing weight 205 lbs. Bats right, throws right.
Rookie Year, 1980:   Primary position outfield/designated hitter.
Total Career, 3 years: Indians 1980–82.

	BA	G	H	2B	3B	HR	RBI
1980	.289	131	131	17	2	23	87
Lifetime	.266	201	172	26	4	29	114

One comparative measure of quantity is its greatest number. Conversely, there's its lowest number or least amount. How many jelly beans in the jar? Which golfer had the fewest strokes? Et cetera. Thus it is with Rookies of the Year. Statistical achievements. The youngest. Eldest. Most hits. Lowest ERA. Et cetera, et cetera.

The greatest number of seasons logged by any Rookie of the Year was 24. Pete Rose and Carlton Fisk did that. As for fewest career games played by a Rookie of the Year, Joe Charboneau appeared in only 201.

Super Joe, they called him. A sobriquet bestowed after his very first home game with the 1980 Cleveland Indians. He went 3-for-3 that day. And even though he would rarely turn in similar performances, his .289 that year, combined with 23 home runs and 87 RBI, earned him Rookie of the Year honors and helped Cleveland post its best record during a generally dismal 10-year stretch.

But Joe Charboneau's career effectively ended the same year it began. After 1980 he played in merely 70 more big league games. He hit just six more homers, and batted only .211. Why?

The combination of a painful back injury and the subsequent inability to hit consistently doomed him. Regardless, as he told the *Akron Beacon Journal,* "I'm thankful for the time I had. I wish I wouldn't have been hurt so early in my career, but I have no regrets. I enjoyed every minute of it."

Teammates and writers enjoyed his off-field antics, which, according to his friend and former teammate Mike Hargrove, were often exaggerated. Whether or not Super Joe opened beer bottles with his eye socket or shaved off tattoos with razors, Hargrove says Joe was a charismatic young man who was a well-liked teammate. And a productive one in that 1980 Rookie of the Year season.

Charboneau was only 27 when his big league dream died. Joe later appeared in the film *The Natural,* then drifted in and out of various other jobs for several years before returning to baseball. Not the major leagues, but to instructional and mentoring assignments.

The father of two boys, Charboneau still lives in the Cleveland area. He's a regular at Indians fantasy camps and frequently conducts baseball clinics for young players. Additionally, Joe has served as the hitting coach with the former Canton-Akron AA club and for two teams in the independent Frontier League. He's regarded as a talented instructor. As one minor leaguer says, "How could you not learn from someone with his experience?"

Now five decades old, Joe Charboneau is a successful baseball teacher and morale booster. Yet despite that, the 1980 American League Rookie of the Year will forever be characterized as a "one-year wonder."

PAT LISTACH
1992   Milwaukee Brewers, American League

Personal Data: B. September 12, 1967, at Natchitoches, LA.
Physical Attributes: 5′ 9″, playing weight 170 lbs. Bats both, throws right.
Rookie Year, 1992:   Primary position shortstop. 54 stolen bases.
Total Career, 6 years: Brewers 1992–96; Astros '97.

	BA	G	H	2B	3B	HR	RBI
1992	.290	149	168	19	6	1	47
Lifetime	.251	503	444	63	13	5	143

Shortstop Pat Listach, arguably one of baseball's most forgotten freshmen, holds the distinction of being the only Milwaukee Brewer christened Rookie of the Year.

And he had to fight off Kenny Lofton's formidable challenge to earn the award.

More than a decade later many fans are surprised that Lofton was only the bridesmaid. Kenny, after all, continues to make baseball headlines while Listach long ago disappeared from big league view. But for one particular special summer Listach narrowly outpolled Lofton for Rookie of the Year honors. Because, by the numbers, voters figured Pat for the slightest of edges.

For example, after virtually the same total of games played and at bats, Listach nipped Lofton with 168 hits to 164 ... 19 doubles to 15 ... 47 RBI to 42 ... a .290 batting average to .285. But Kenny edged Pat, too: 96 runs

Pat Listach, Milwaukee Brewers, 1992
This former shortstop is still active in baseball as a minor league coach. To date he is the Brewers' only Rookie of the Year.
(Larry Stoudt)

scored to 93 . . . 8 triples to 6 . . . 5 homers to 1 . . . 66 stolen bases to 54. Obviously, both had solid years. In fact, with Lofton's setting the pace, they ranked one-two in AL steals.

Unfortunately Listach was unable to sustain his first year's performance. Except for .296 in an injury-riddled 1994, his batting average never exceeded .244 again. Pat averaged only 12 steals per year over his remaining five seasons. By late 1996 he was out of the American League en route to Houston, where his .182 average in 52 games expedited his big league departure. He had just turned 30.

Before joining the 1997 Astros, Listach had been traded, with pitcher Graeme Lloyd, to the Yankees. But New York complained that Milwaukee, then still in the American League, delivered physically damaged goods in Lloyd. The transaction was revised. Listach returned to Milwaukee for Ricky Bones. Soon thereafter Pat went to Houston, his final big league stop.

The former Arizona State star tried to recapture his 1992 form via minor league service in the Cleveland and Philadelphia organizations. When that attempt failed, he vowed to remain a baseball lifer in some capacity.

Perhaps managing is in the offing. Since 2001, Listach has been hitting coach for the Cubs' Iowa AAA club, which he interim-managed to a 27–28 record in 2002 after Iowa skipper Bruce Kimm was promoted to the Chicago managership. He has also coached in the Arizona Fall League.

In the off-seasons Pat, his wife Lisa, and their four children live in Houston, Texas. Despite high hopes for additional baseball leadership roles in his future, Listach still occasionally looks back. Especially to that exciting 1992 Rookie of the Year season.

BOB HAMELIN
1994   Kansas City Royals, American League

Personal Data: B. November 29, 1967, at Elizabeth, NJ.
Physical Attributes: 6′ 0″, playing weight 235 lbs. Bats left, throws left.
Rookie Year, 1994:   Primary position first base.
Total Career, 6 years: Royals 1993–96; Tigers '97; Brewers '98.

	BA	G	H	2B	3B	HR	RBI
1994	.282	101	88	25	1	24	65
Lifetime	.246	497	313	70	3	67	209

Typical of Rookie of the Year award winners, Bob Hamelin displayed great potential for a lengthy baseball career.

Unfortunately for Bob and the Kansas City Royals, his promising 1994 season was essentially a last hurrah. Four years and two more franchises later he had played his final major league game.

Coulda, shoulda, woulda, if. The lament of golf's duffers or many a baseball manager who stayed with his starter one hanging slider too long. Bob Hamelin wonders how things might have turned out differently.

Platooned for much of his official rookie season, Hamelin hit with decent consistency (.282) and with good power (24 home runs) in just under 400 plate appearances. He had a productive slugging percentage of .599, a figure that ranked a solid fifth in the American League.

His overall performance impressed BBWAA voters who selected him 1994 Rookie of the Year over a Cleveland outfielder named Manny Ramirez. Hamelin's individual statistics that year would be, by far, his career's best.

Mysteriously he never got untracked in 1995. Some onlookers recalled that Hamelin was out of shape when he reported to spring training. Bob Boone, his Royals manager, remembers that more than two weeks were required for Hamelin to be ready for spring games.

> After the season began, Bob was simply overmatched. He couldn't seem to adjust to American League pitchers he'd faced for the first time the year before. I had to send him out for a while [to AAA Omaha in mid-June]. When he returned, his game was still at loose ends. It developed that one of his problems involved some vision issues. He began to wear glasses in the batter's box. Still, no improvement. And, of course, his confidence was disappearing.

Hamelin, even with corrective lenses, was unable to adjust satisfactorily. After 1996, when his home run output was reduced to nine, the Royals declined to renew his contract. At Detroit the following season he showed spurts of reclaiming his earlier form when he finished at .270 with 18 homers. Then Milwaukee gave him an opportunity in 1998. But with a .219 average in 146 at bats—often as a pinch hitter or defensive replacement—Bob Hamelin's major league tenure was ended.

The next year, attempting a comeback in the Tigers system, he was hitting .226 with five home runs and just 20 RBI for Toledo when he removed himself from the lineup in the early innings of a mid-June game. He was 31 years old.

Bob Hamelin, the promising Rookie of the Year just five years earlier, never played professional baseball again.

KAZUHIRO SASAKI
2000   Seattle Mariners, American League

Personal Data: B. February 22, 1968, at Sendai City, Japan.
Physical Attributes: 6′ 4″, playing weight 212 lbs. Throws right, bats right.
Rookie Year, 2000:   Primary position pitcher. 37 saves.
Total Career, 4 years: Mariners 2000–03.

	Record	ERA	G	GS	SO	IP
2000	2–5	3.16	63	0	78	62⅔
Lifetime	7–16	3.14	228	0	242	223⅓

Until arm ailments sidelined him for two months and limited his appearances to 35 games and only 33⅓ innings in 2003, Kazuhiro Sasaki held a special distinction among the 29 pitchers who have won Rookie of the Year accolades. When his brief four-year tenure concluded, the lanky right-hander owned a career earned run average (3.14) that was lower than his rookie year's ERA.

Every other rookie-award-winning hurler's career total has exceeded his first year's ERA mark.

The Tokyo-area native owns at least two other rookie distinctions. At age 32 he was the eldest Rookie of the Year. That's four years older than Jackie Robinson was in 1947, and older than the reported age 28 of Sam Jethroe in 1950. The other distinction: Kaz, as he is popularly nicknamed, is the first Japanese-born player to be an American League Rookie of the Year. His fellow countryman

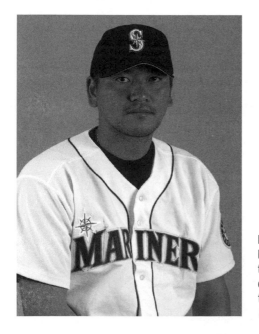

Kazuhiro Sasaki, Seattle Mariners, 2000
Kaz, officially the eldest Rookie of the Year (32), is the only pitcher among Rookies of the Year to conclude a career with an ERA lower than his freshman season's.
(Courtesy of Seattle Mariners)

Hideo Nomo preceded him by five years when he was chosen as the National League's top rookie in 1995.

Kazuhiro continued to make his winter home in Japan during his American League career. More recently he announced that he would be there permanently, too. Kaz, a free agent, departed Seattle for a 2004 Japanese baseball contract. He, his wife Kaori, and their daughter Reina and son Shogo are residents of Yokohama.

Sasaki, who arrived in Seattle in 2000 with 10 years of professional Japanese baseball under his belt, became the Mariners' all-time saves leader (119) after only three seasons. Quickly established as the team's closer, Kaz never started any of the 228 Seattle games in which he appeared.

When asked to comment about winning the Rookie of the Year award, Sasaki clearly expressed delight and appreciation. Through his interpreter, Allen Turner, he also remarked that he'd expected Oakland's Terrence Long to be the 2000 recipient.

Baseball mementos Kaz took with him back to Japan—in addition to the Rookie of the Year trophy—are two All-Star team selections, the Mariners Pitcher of the Year award in his rookie season, and the coveted *Seattle Post-Intelligencer's* Sports Star of the Year salute in 2000.

Available Only Once

Other Rookies of the Year

From Roy Sievers in 1949 when the St. Louis Browns were still in business, to the 21st century's free agents with bulging wallets, "Rookie of the Year" remains one of baseball's most coveted awards. And it's available only once.

ROY SIEVERS
1949   St. Louis Browns, American League

Personal Data: B. November 18, 1926, at St. Louis, MO.
Physical Attributes: 6′ 1″, playing weight 195 lbs. Bats right, throws right.
Rookie Year, 1949:   Primary position outfield.
Total Career, 17 years: Browns 1949–53; Senators '54–59; White Sox '60–61; Phillies '62–64; Senators '64–65.

	BA	G	H	2B	3B	HR	RBI
1949	.306	140	144	28	1	16	91
Lifetime	.267	1,887	1,703	292	42	318	1,147

The old St. Louis Browns, who started life as the 1901 Milwaukee Brewers and now operate as the Baltimore Orioles, seldom had much to brag about. During their 52 years in Missouri, they won one American League pennant and usually finished deep in the second division.

In 1949, St. Louis typified its hapless play. Second baseman Gerry Priddy and third baseman Bob Dillinger led the AL in errors at their positions. Only one pitcher, Ned Garver (12–17), posted an earned run average under four (3.98). Four hurlers had ERAs of 5.06 or higher. Dillinger, whose .324 average was the league's third best, was one of only two Browns to surpass .300.

The other was the team's most consistent bright spot: Rookie of the Year Roy Sievers.

Roy slammed 16 home runs en route to a 91-RBI total and a career-best .306 average. Outpolling Detroit's Johnny Groth and Chicago's Gus Zernial for the rookie award, he became the Baseball Writers' Association of America's first official American League Rookie of the Year. In the award's first two years—1947 and '48—the BBWAA had selected just one player from major league baseball's entire 16-team field. Jackie Robinson and Alvin Dark were both National Leaguers.

Sievers reflects on the award:

Its real impact lives on, because it's something I'll always be remembered for. In retrospect, my fondest memories revolve around playing with so many of baseball's all-time greats. It was a real thrill to put on a big league uniform and play with and against so many Hall of Famers and other All-Stars for 17 years.

Roy Sievers, St. Louis Browns, 1949
First American Leaguer, and only Brown, to win Rookie of the Year award. In midcareer he established long-ball records for the original Washington Senators.
(Allied Photocolor)

After five seasons in St. Louis—the Browns' final years there before shifting to Baltimore—Roy was traded in 1954 to Washington, where he turned in prime-time performances. He totaled 81 homers and 222 RBI over 1957 and '58 for the Senators, leading the league in both categories in '57. Later, with the White Sox, he recorded virtually identical 1960 and '61 seasons by hitting .295 both years with 28 and 27 home runs, respectively, and 93 and 92 RBI. He concluded his productive career with two and a half seasons at Philadelphia and finally 45 games with the expansion Washington club.

"I coached for a year at Cincinnati after that. Hoped to have 20 years in big league uniforms," he muses. "However, it didn't work out. I managed in the minors for a while, though. Some of my players—including Duffy Dyer and George Hendrick—got to the majors."

With baseball behind him, Roy was employed for 18 years by a trucking firm in St. Louis, his hometown. He's now retired, "Playing golf, fishing, and enjoying the fruits of life."

Perhaps he sometimes relaxes with an old movie. If it happens to be *Damn Yankees*, he'll see Roy Sievers again . . . old number 2 in wide-angle newsreel clips in the persona of the film's mythical Joe Hardy . . . once more slugging home runs for the Washington Senators.

WALT DROPO
1950   Boston Red Sox, American League

Personal Data: B. January 30, 1923, at Moosup, CT.
Physical Attributes: 6′ 5″, playing weight 220 lbs. Bats right, throws right.
Rookie Year, 1950:   Primary position first base. Tied for league RBI lead with 144.
Total Career, 13 years: Red Sox 1949–52; Tigers '52–54; White Sox '55–58; Reds '58–59; Orioles '59–61.

	BA	G	H	2B	3B	HR	RBI
1950	.322	136	180	28	8	34	144
Lifetime	.270	1,288	1,113	168	22	152	704

It's hard to imagine that anyone could make a more thunderous entrance than Walt Dropo did over the course of his 1950 Rookie of the Year season.

Often known as Moose, for his formidable physique (6′ 5″, 220 pounds in his rookie year)—and because he hailed from the town of Moosup, Connecticut— the 27-year-old slugger clouted 34 home runs and hit .322 in his first full big league season. He also tied for the AL lead in runs batted in with teammate Vern Stephens, the Red Sox shortstop. More than a half century later his 34-homer total still ranks as a Boston rookie record.

Dropo made his only All-Star team that first season. He went 1-for-3, with a triple, in the American League's extra-inning loss at Comiskey Park.

Walt Dropo, Boston Red Sox, 1950
Dropo's 34 homers remain a Red Sox rookie record. And his hitting safely in 12 straight at bats for Detroit in 1952 is another record still on the books.
(Courtesy of Boston Red Sox)

Walt Dropo had been something of a New England legend years earlier for his tape-measure home runs while representing the University of Connecticut. The Red Sox eventually auditioned him for 11 relatively unspectacular games in 1949. There was little indication, then, that Moose would be an All-Star starter just nine months later.

Nineteen-fifty, however, would be Dropo's signature season. Injuries limited him to 99 games and only 11 homers in 1951. He hit .239. Halfway through the next year he was a key figure in a nine-man trade with Detroit. The transaction included such luminaries as George Kell, Johnny Pesky, and pitcher Dizzy Trout. Walt finished the season with 29 home runs. But he would not reach the 20-homer level again. And, after that marvelous 1950 debut, Dropo never reached 100 RBI in any season.

Once, during his two and a half years in Detroit, Dropo reentered the national spotlight. In July 1952 he hit safely in 12 consecutive at bats, a record that's still on the books.

After Walt's Detroit stint he was transferred regularly. Chicago's White Sox for three years. Cincinnati for 89 games over parts of two seasons. Finally Baltimore, where his career ended in 1961.

He didn't idle for long. Walt and two of his brothers developed a successful importing business, trading primarily with China. Later he operated an insurance enterprise in the Boston area, where he still resides.

In reviewing his baseball days, Dropo told writer Edward Kiersh, "Yes, I broke in with a bang, only to tail off to where I should have been. Very average. Truthfully, I never thought I was going to be a Ted Williams. I must admit, though, that [after the big Rookie of the Year season] I was disappointed about not living up to expectations."

GIL MCDOUGALD
1951   New York Yankees, American League

Personal Data: B. May 19, 1928, at San Francisco, CA.
Physical Attributes: 6' 0", playing weight 175 lbs. Bats right, throws right.
Rookie Year, 1951:   Primary position third base.
Total Career, 10 years: Yankees 1951–60.

	BA	G	H	2B	3B	HR	RBI
1951	.306	131	123	23	4	14	63
Lifetime	.276	1,336	1,291	187	51	112	576

HERB SCORE
1955   Cleveland Indians, American League

Personal Data: B. June 7, 1933, at Rosedale, NY.
Physical Attributes: 6' 2", playing weight 185 lbs. Throws left, bats left.
Rookie Year, 1955:   Primary position pitcher. Led league with 245 strikeouts.
Total Career, 8 years: Indians 1955–59; White Sox '60–62.

	Record	ERA	G	GS	SO	IP
1955	16–10	2.85	33	32	245	227⅓
Lifetime	55–46	3.36	150	127	837	858⅓

Upon hearing of Ralph Branca, you expect Bobby Thomson's name to follow immediately. Like the other shoe dropping. Branca and Thomson. As in bread and butter or scotch and soda.

So, also, are two American League Rookies of the Year forever linked: Herb Score and Gil McDougald. Both achieved notable successes during their relatively short careers. But history obscures their accomplishments by focusing on one shocking instant.

The line drive.

It hastened Score's premature major league departure. And it overshadowed McDougald's numerous contributions that helped spark the New York Yankees to eight pennants in the 10 years he played for them.

The evening of May 7, 1957, was chilly, as it usually was at midspring in Cleveland Stadium. Casey Stengel's visiting Yankees had set sights on another

Herb Score, Cleveland Indians, 1955
His rookie record of 245 strikeouts stood for 29 years. At age 24 he was struck by a batted ball. The resultant injury hastened Score's 1962 retirement.
(Courtesy of the Herb and Nancy Score family collection)

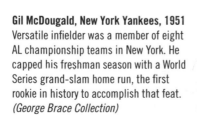

Gil McDougald, New York Yankees, 1951
Versatile infielder was a member of eight AL championship teams in New York. He capped his freshman season with a World Series grand-slam home run, the first rookie in history to accomplish that feat.
(George Brace Collection)

pennant, their seventh of the 1950s. The Indians were New York's most formidable challengers during that decade, having posted runner-up finishes in five of skipper Al Lopez's six Cleveland years and having won the 1954 flag with a then American League record 111 wins.

Cleveland's Herb Score, Rookie of the Year two years earlier, was new manager Kerby Farrell's starting pitcher that night. The southpaw, with a 2–1 early-season record, was the staff's ace. He'd face a Yankee roster that included sluggers Mickey Mantle, Yogi Berra, Bill Skowron, and Hank Bauer. And shortstop Gil McDougald.

Early innings. Tight game. Then the line drive.

McDougald's bat met a fastball that rocketed directly back at Score. It smashed into his right eye socket. Little matter that McDougald had singled. Or that Cleveland eventually won the game. The focus was not on the box score. Instead, could Score see? More important, would he survive? Never losing consciousness, he lay on the field for several minutes attended by medics. Soon an ambulance raced him to the hospital.

Herb Score recovered. In time his eyesight returned. A broken nose and lacerations soon healed. But, at age 24, his best pitching was now behind him.

Score had been pegged a likely Hall of Famer during his 1955 Rookie of the Year season. He combined a 16–10 record with a 2.85 earned run average. He baffled opponents with 245 strikeouts, a rookie record that stood until Dwight Gooden broke it 29 years later.

Herb's ascension to baseball's penthouse seemed a sure thing. Especially when his second year was even better . . . a 20–9 log, a 2.53 ERA, and a league-leading 263 strikeouts.

But then came his fifth game of 1957. The line drive. A promising career suddenly turned upside down.

Herb climbed "back on the horse" 49 weeks later for the first time since the accident. He was limited to three innings. He pitched sparingly for the remainder of 1958, then displayed spurts of his early form with nine wins and 147 strikeouts in 1959. The Philadelphia Sports Writers Association honored Score with its prestigious Most Courageous Athlete Award.

Clearly, though, his rookie-year effectiveness was dramatically reduced. Herb was traded to the White Sox. He won six games and lost 12 for Chicago over two seasons. Then, after four relief appearances and a 0–0 record in 1962, he retired. At age 29.

By 1960, at Chicago, Score was no longer in the regular starting rotation. Coincidentally, 1960 was Gil McDougald's final season. He was 32.

Today, with hazy hindsight, some fans seem astonished that McDougald— and not his freshman teammate Mickey Mantle—was 1951 Rookie of the Year. But why not? Gil had the better year. Baseball insiders weren't surprised. Mantle, after all, was only 19 then, with limited minor league experience. McDougald was coming off a 1950 Texas League MVP season. Over the years the Yankees have had eight Rookies of the Year to their credit. McDougald was the first.

Mantle, of course, soon advanced rapidly toward superstar status. McDougald meanwhile was building a decade of the reliable versatility that Stengel admired. Gil participated in no fewer than 119 games during any of his 10 seasons, and he played all infield positions except first base. Twice he was New York's primary shortstop. In four other seasons he was the principal second baseman. He lined up at third for four years.

Gil's rookie season featured a .306 batting average with career highs of 14 homers and 14 steals. Then came McDougald's first World Series, a national showcase. His seven RBI led the Yankees to a six-game Series triumph over the New York Giants. In Game Five he became the first rookie to hit a World Series grand-slam home run.

Despite switching from infield position to position, McDougald's offense was a model of consistency. His yearly home runs ranged from 11 to 14 over his first eight seasons. He led the AL with nine triples in 1957. The previous year he registered a career-high .311 batting average.

In the seven-game 1958 World Series win over Milwaukee, Gil stroked two homers, averaged .321, and scored five runs. An American League All-Star five times, Gil's single drove home a run to help win the 1958 game at Baltimore.

Following the 1960 season, the American League added the Los Angeles Angels and the second edition Washington Senators. McDougald was selected by Washington in the expansion draft. Still young and relatively healthy, he decided to retire.

He revisits the Yankee clubhouse for old-timers' games and special tributes from time to time. In 1966, Gil began a 10-season tenure as head baseball coach at New York's Fordham University—not far from Yankee Stadium.

More than 500 miles away, and soon after his retirement as an active player, Herb Score also returned to his old ballpark. In 1964, Herb was hired to broadcast Indians games. He stayed behind radio and television microphones for 34 years, retiring in 1998.

Sadly both of these Rookies of the Year have been victimized with physical problems in recent years. Gil McDougald is hearing impaired. Although he has a cochlear implant that helps in face-to-face conversations, it's difficult for him to engage in telephone interviews. So his wife Lucille spoke for him in a recent talk with baseballsavvy.com.

"Gil says it was all about the team then, those 10 years with the Yankees, when the game was very competitive and the guys were like a family." Speaking from their Wall, New Jersey, home, she said, "As much as Gil enjoyed baseball, he would have pursued basketball if not for the fact he wasn't tall enough or quick enough."

In Ohio, Herb Score's medical chart keeps growing longer. Just a week or so after retiring from announcing, he was seriously injured when his car and a tractor-trailer collided near Canton. Ironically, he was heading to Florida following his induction to the Akron-area Broadcasters Hall of Fame the previous evening. Herb sustained severe hip, head, and pelvic injuries.

"He never completely rebounded," said his wife, Nancy. "Herb has suffered a stroke in the meantime, and has broken some bones in falls." He was hospitalized near the Score's Lakewood, Ohio, home for several months in late 2003 and early '04.

"I can't begin to tell you how much courage Herb has shown during his recent adversity," says Nancy Score. "His bravery and optimism are truly inspiring."

Soon a half century will have passed since two strapping young athletes and their major league teammates cheerfully suited up for a game of baseball one spring evening in Cleveland.

Now, even though Herb Score and Gil McDougald achieved headlined excellence at the highest level of their professional calling, they're mainly remembered for one brief frightening tragedy.

That terrifying line drive.

JIM (JUNIOR) GILLIAM
1953   Brooklyn Dodgers, National League

Personal Data: B. October 17, 1928, at Nashville, TN. D. October 8, 1978.
Physical Attributes: 5' 10 1/2", playing weight 175 lbs. Bats both, throws right.
Rookie Year, 1953:   Primary position second base. Led league with 17 triples.
Total Career, 14 years: Dodgers 1953–66.

	BA	G	H	2B	3B	HR	RBI
1953	.278	151	168	31	17	6	63
Lifetime	.265	1,956	1,889	304	71	65	558

No player is related to the Dodgers' geographical transition era more than Jim Gilliam.

He was a already a Brooklyn veteran when the franchise moved to California in 1958. Then he delivered nine more productive seasons for the Los Angeles Dodgers.

Earlier nicknamed Junior, as the youngest member of the old Negro league's Baltimore Elite Giants, Gilliam was an immediate record setter in 1953 when he won the National League Rookie of the Year honors. He paced the NL in triples with 17 and collected 100 walks, a personal high.

Those bases on balls reflected his extremely sharp batting eye. Invariably his walks outdistanced strikeouts by three or four to one; in over more than 7,000 career at bats Gilliam fanned only 416 times, a figure ranking among baseball's all-time best.

Junior's entrance to the Brooklyn lineup was noteworthy beyond his statistical accomplishments. It required the Dodgers to move icon Jackie Robinson from his accustomed second base post to third . . . and eventually the outfield. Gilliam played 149 games at second in 1953, and capped his rookie season by hitting .296 with two home runs in a six-game World Series loss to New York.

Before his career was over, Gilliam also played numerous games at third and in the outfield—mostly after Robinson's retirement. Regardless of his defensive assignments, Gilliam was clearly an inspirational leader who helped send the Dodgers to seven World Series during their 1950s and '60s heydays. He registered more than 100 runs scored in each of his first four seasons, and three times ranked second to another Rookie of the Year, Willie Mays, in stolen bases. Once in Brooklyn and another time at Los Angeles, Jim Gilliam was selected for the National League All-Star team.

In 1965 he returned from a brief retirement to play third base in baseball's first all-switch-hitting infield (Wes Parker—first, Jim Lefebvre—second, Maury Wills—shortstop).

Gilliam's final active season, 1966, was the only year in which he played fewer than 100 games. Two of his 88 games were at first base, the only times he ever played that position.

When the '67 season began, Junior was still in a Dodgers uniform. He'd signed on as a coach, a post he held until his unexpected death from a brain hemorrhage just before the team's 1978 World Series appearance. He was less than two weeks shy of his 50th birthday. Jim's uniform number 19 has since been permanently retired by the ball club.

Dusty Baker, a Dodger outfielder during part of Gilliam's coaching career, said this of his friend: "Jim Gilliam was a good man. He taught me a lot. I always thought he would have been a great manager."

BOB GRIM
1954   New York Yankees, American League

Personal Data: B. March 8, 1930, at New York, NY. D. October 23, 1996.
Physical Attributes: 6' 1", playing weight 175 lbs. Throws right, bats right.
Rookie Year, 1954:   Primary position pitcher.
Total Career, 8 years: Yankees 1954–58; A's '58–59; Indians '60; Reds '60; Cardinals '60; A's '62.

	Record	ERA	G	GS	SO	IP
1954	20–6	3.26	37	20	108	199
Lifetime	61–41	3.61	268	60	443	759²/₃

Of the 29 pitchers who've been Rookies of the Year since 1947, Bob Grim is the answer to a dandy barroom trivia question.

"Who, among pitchers who won the award, was the only 20-game winner in his rookie season?"

Tom Seaver is a Rookie of the Year who wound up in the Hall of Fame. Don Newcombe was once an MVP. Several Rookies of the Year became perennial All-Star pitchers or frequently led their league in key statistical categories.

But Bob Grim, of the 1954 Yankees, is the only one who won 20 games in his Rookie of the Year season.

His feat, and sadly his name, are long forgotten by casual fans. So, too, is his team's ironic accomplishment that year. Under manager Casey Stengel, the New Yorkers won 103 games in 1954. It was the only year during Stengel's successful 12-year Yankees managership that his team posted 100 or more wins. Despite that victory total, and Bob Grim's brilliant debut, New York finished second to Cleveland's record-setting (at the time) 111 wins.

Stengel used Grim as a spot starter (20 games) and relieved with him 17 times. With eight complete games, a league-leading eight wins in relief, and a solid 3.26 ERA, Grim was a legitimate Rookie of the Year. Totaling 199 innings that season, he's the only pitcher to win 20 games with fewer than 200 innings pitched.

Bob Grim, New York Yankees, 1954
Of all pitchers to win the coveted freshman award, he's the only one to have posted 20 wins (20–6) in his Rookie of the Year season.
(Temple University Libraries, Urban Archives, Philadelphia, PA)

Bob never approached that victory total again. However, he posted 12 wins, all in relief, led the American League with 19 saves, and made his lone All-Star appearance in 1957. It was his last full season with the Yankees.

Arm miseries, surfacing during a game in Detroit, had encroached on Grim's durability as early as his sophomore season. In 1958, and spot starting, he was traded to Kansas City. Pitching respectably, but without the fastball and whipping slider of his early years, he appeared in 66 games with the Athletics over nearly two seasons.

Grim's career, clearly on a slide by then, wound down with 44 games—all in relief—for three teams in 1960. Then, after a season off, his ledger closed with 12 games and a 0–0 record for Kansas City again in 1962.

His name seldom appeared on sports pages after his retirement, except for an occasional "sports highlights of yesteryear" note. Yet, for the remainder of his life, Bob took pride in his unique distinction as the only Rookie of the Year pitcher with 20 wins in his first big league season.

Bob Grim was 66 when he passed away in October 1996 at Shawnee, Kansas.

WALLY MOON
1954   St. Louis Cardinals, National League

Personal Data: B. April 3, 1930, at Bay, AR.
Physical Attributes: 6' 0", playing weight 169 lbs. Bats left, throws right.
Rookie Year, 1954:   Primary position outfield.
Total Career, 12 years: Cardinals 1954–58; Dodgers '59–65.

	BA	G	H	2B	3B	HR	RBI
1954	.304	151	193	29	9	12	76
Lifetime	.289	1,457	1,399	212	60	142	661

Wally Moon was selected as the National League's 1954 Rookie of the Year because he deserved to be. A half century later, casual observers might be wondering why neither one of two other freshmen—Hank Aaron and Ernie Banks—got the honor instead. Simple. Wally Moon had a better 1954 than they did.

Nobody disputes that Aaron and Banks performed brilliantly over long careers that propelled them to well-deserved admission to the Hall of Fame. But in their first years together, Wally Moon, the Cardinals' very first Rookie of the Year, outplayed them.

Moon's .304 presaged his batting consistency. He followed up with .295, .298, and .295 averages over the next three seasons, although he never reached his rookie season's hit total (193) and runs scored (106) again. But after a .238 "downer" in only 108 games during the 1958 season, Wally was traded to Los Angeles, with Phil Paine, for outfielder Gino Cimoli.

The Dodgers, just a year removed from Brooklyn, played their home games at Los Angeles's Memorial Coliseum then. That's where Wally became widely known for his "Moon shots." They were the home runs the left-handed-hitting outfielder golfed over a 42-foot-high screen situated just 250 feet down the left-field line. Moon was generally credited with revitalizing Dodger spirit, as the team climbed from seventh place in 1958 to the '59 World Series championship. "Consistent" Wally was back to .302, and led the NL in triples with 11. The following year, 1960, he won a Gold Glove.

Ironically, Moon was a more productive home run hitter during his five St. Louis seasons than in his seven Dodger years. He hit 78 dingers for the Cardinals, 64 as a Dodger. In fact his first big league at bat for St. Louis was a home run.

Wally hit more than .300 twice and .299 another time during his first three seasons in Los Angeles. But injuries slowed him down in 1962, and his playing time became more and more limited. After two hitless pinch-hitting efforts in the Dodgers' 1965 World Series triumph over Minnesota, Moon's playing career was ended. Later he appeared at old-timers' games from time to time for several years.

Now the man who outshone some notable Hall of Famers back in 1954 is a resident of Bryan, Texas.

Tony Kubek
1957   New York Yankees, American League

Personal Data: B. October 12, 1936, at Milwaukee, WI.
Physical Attributes: 6' 3", playing weight 190 lbs. Bats left, throws right.
Rookie Year, 1957:   Primary position outfield/infield. Versatile defender with 50 games in outfield, 80 at short, third, and second.
Total Career, 9 years: Yankees 1957–65.

	BA	G	H	2B	3B	HR	RBI
1957	.297	127	128	21	3	3	39
Lifetime	.266	1,092	1,109	178	30	57	373

Tony Kubek stands apart from most other Rookies of the Year—in several ways. First, the 1957 American League's rookie award winner is probably better known to most fans under 50 as a prominent baseball announcer. What's more, he won the rookie accolade despite having no set defensive position. And he was still a shade under 21 when his rookie year ended. Later, he suffered one of the most headlined World Series injuries of all time.

Although Tony's minor league credentials were satisfactory, he wasn't counted on for a major role when the New York Yankees opened 1957 spring training. But his versatility soon caught manager Casey Stengel's attention. He made the big league roster and was expected to be a valuable fill-in. Valuable indeed. Teammates' injuries enabled Kubek to enter 127 games that first season. Stengel welcomed Kubek's flexibility and enthusiasm, and played the newcomer at all three outfield and three infield positions at one time or other.

Tony's first-year .297 helped his team reach the World Series. New York faced the Braves, who had been transplanted to Milwaukee only four years earlier. Kubek was thrilled, because Milwaukee was his hometown. When the Series moved there from New York for Game Three, Tony Kubek, then one week shy of his 21st birthday, showed his family and old neighborhood friends why he had earned a spot in the national limelight. The youngster hit two homers that day and drove home four runs in a 12–3 victory.

Kubek eventually played in 37 World Series games. The next time he made notable Series headlines was in the 1960 Yanks-versus-Pirates thriller. Late in the seventh game a ground ball hit a scuff mark or pebble in the Forbes Field base path just as Tony, at shortstop, was about to field it. Instead the ball smacked into his throat, forcing him from the lineup and into a hospital. The quirky bounce kept a home team rally alive. Pittsburgh tied the game, then eventually won it on Bill Mazeroski's legendary ninth-inning home run.

From then on the versatile Kubek was primarily a shortstop. But his career was interrupted by military service in 1962 (he missed 109 games that year) and surprisingly concluded in 1965. Tony was only 29 then, but called it quits after learning from Mayo Clinic medical experts that nagging back pains likely resulted from a broken neck sustained, and undiagnosed, years earlier.

He returned to New York to announce his retirement. Kubek had often been kidded about his shyness, so he was as astonished as his old teammates when NBC offered him a job as analyst for its "Game of the Week." It was the start of a 30-year television tenure that earned him growing admiration from the broadcasting community and from millions of fans who would know him better for his microphone work than his successful nine-year big league baseball career. Tony also handled Toronto Blue Jays broadcasts for many years.

Now in his late 60s, Rookie of the Year and award-winning broadcaster Tony Kubek lives with his family in Appleton, Wisconsin . . . not far from his 1957 World Series exploits at the age of 20.

JACK SANFORD
1957   Philadelphia Phillies, National League

Personal Data: B. May 18, 1929, at Wellesley Hills, MA. D. March 7, 2000.
Physical Attributes: 6' 0", playing weight 190 lbs. Throws right, bats right.
Rookie Year, 1957:   Primary position pitcher. Led league with 188 strikeouts.
Total Career, 12 years: Phillies 1956–58; Giants '59–65; Angels '65–67; A's '67.

	Record	ERA	G	GS	SO	IP
1957	19–8	3.08	33	33	188	236²⁄₃
Lifetime	137–101	3.69	388	293	1,182	2,049¹⁄₃

At 27, Jack Sanford was considered an elder among Rookies of the Year. But, as you might surmise, he entered the big leagues with more baseball, and life, experiences than younger first-year players usually bring with them.

Sanford had joined the Phillies for three late-season games in 1956 following seven successful minor league seasons and two years in the U.S. military. When the '57 schedule opened, he was already penciled into Philadelphia's starting rotation. By midseason he had become the ace of a staff that still included legendary "Whiz Kids" Robin Roberts and Curt Simmons.

Finishing with a 19–8 record, Sanford led the league in strikeouts. Only three National League rookie pitchers, to that point, had ever exceeded Sanford's 188 K's—Hall of Famers Grover Alexander, Christy Mathewson, and Dizzy Dean. One more victory would have enabled Sanford to join teammate Roberts as the Phils' lone 20-game winners since Alexander's dazzling achievements back in the 19-teens.

A 20-win season, however, was not to be until five years later. By then Jack was employed by the Giants, to whom he was traded for the battery of Ruben Gomez and Valmy Thomas. Neither distinguished himself in Philadelphia, but in 1962 Sanford had his best ever season by posting a 24–7 log to pace San Francisco into a seven-game World Series. He completed 13 of his 38 starts, then followed with a league-leading 42 starting assignments in 1963. After that, though, his effectiveness as a starter decreased quickly. A shoulder injury was largely responsible for a 5–7 record in 1964, and a trade to the California Angels soon followed. From 1965 until his career ended with the Kansas City Athletics in 1967, Sanford was essentially a relief pitcher. His best year as a fireman was 1966—a 13–7 record and a 3.83 ERA. Twelve wins came in relief, a league-leading relievers' standard that season.

Finished as a player, Sanford stayed active in athletics by working as a golf pro briefly, then scouting for the Orioles. His 12-year major league mark of 137 wins against 101 losses is considered a laudable performance from a man who

Jack Sanford, Philadelphia Phillies, 1957
Nineteen-game winner and league strikeout leader during rookie season. Then, in 1962, registered 24 victories for pennant-winning San Francisco Giants. *(The Rich Westcott Collection)*

was 27 years old when he became Rookie of the Year. Jack Sanford was just over two months shy of his 71st birthday when he passed away at Beckley, West Virginia, in March 2000.

ALBIE PEARSON
1958   Washington Senators, American League

Personal Data: B. September 12, 1934, at Alhambra, CA.
Physical Attributes: 5′ 5″, playing weight 140 lbs. Bats left, throws left.
Rookie Year, 1958:   Primary position outfield.
Total Career, 9 years: Senators 1958–59; Orioles '59–60; Angels '61–66.

	BA	G	H	2B	3B	HR	RBI
1958	.275	146	146	25	5	3	33
Lifetime	.270	988	831	130	24	28	214

One of the American League's specially honored rookies might also have been the league's Tiniest Man of the '60s. Whether or not that were so...and some historians would suggest Freddie Patek as a contender for that title...Albie Pearson was a giant among the AL's newcomers in 1958 when he became the first Washington Senator chosen Rookie of the Year.

A left-handed-hitting outfielder, Pearson had apprenticed in the Red Sox farm system before a trade sent him to Washington. Despite an excellent fresh-man performance that produced sound credentials, he was dispatched to rival Baltimore less than two months into the next season. The trade was a genuine curiosity—from both sides' viewpoints—for the Senators obtained Lenny Green, who was also a left-handed-batting outfielder with about the same speed, batting average potential, and power as Pearson's.

In Baltimore, Albie was unable to approach his rookie season numbers. So when the American League expanded to ten teams in 1961, he was made available to the new franchises and was selected by the Angels, then known as the Los Angeles Angels.

Pearson hit his stride in California, returning to his Rookie of the Year form...and then some. During five full seasons there he hit .288 once and .304 another time, and he led the league with 115 runs in 1962. The following season Albie was the AL's starting center fielder in the All-Star Game at Cleve-land, where he delivered a pair of hits in four at bats. His double was the game's only extra-base hit.

That '63 campaign, however, was Pearson's last productive season. Recurring back spasms disabled him frequently during the next two years. And after just two 1966 games, and three hitless at bats, he retired from active play.

He didn't avoid other activities, though. Since putting aside his baseball uni-form, Albie Pearson has engaged in several vocations and avocations, including disc jockeying and radio evangelism. He also served as a golf professional for a while. These days Albie sends greetings from his home in Danville, California.

BOB ALLISON
1959   Washington Senators, American League

Personal Data: B. July 11, 1934, at Raytown, MO. D. April 9, 1995.
Physical Attributes: 6′ 3″, playing weight 205 lbs. Bats right, throws right.
Rookie Year, 1959:   Primary position outfield. Nine triples led league.
Total Career, 13 years: Senators/Twins 1958–70.

	BA	G	H	2B	3B	HR	RBI
1959	.261	150	149	18	9	30	85
Lifetime	.255	1,541	1,281	216	53	256	796

That old chestnut about Washington—"First in war, first in peace, last in the American League!"—was always good for a giggle. But, in reality, the line was apocryphal.

True, the old Senators (first known as the Washington Nationals) were seldom serious pennant contenders. Yet, during their 60 seasons in the nation's capital, they finished in the cellar only 10 times, ended 20 seasons in the first division, won three pennants, and captured one World Series. The ball club left Washington after the 1960 season to become the Minnesota Twins, and took along Bob Allison, the American League's 1959 Rookie of the Year.

Had Allison and promising youngsters such as Harmon Killebrew and Earl Battey not been transferred to the Midwest, Washington might soon have housed another pennant contender. Instead, Minnesota reached the World Series only four years later. And Bob Allison was a major contributor to the Twins' rapid improvement.

He continued to produce the kind of long-ball power that led to his Rookie of the Year selection. After stroking 45 home runs during two full seasons at Washington, Allison stayed on course in Minnesota by hitting between 22 and 35 homers in eight different seasons. Along the way he led the league in runs scored with 99 in 1963.

Bob and his roommate, Killebrew, formed an explosive one-two punch that thrilled Twins fans. Allison, in a 1963 game, homered in three consecutive at bats. He and Killebrew became the 20th century's first teammates to hit grand slams in the same inning. Ironically, one of those four-RBI shots was relinquished by Cleveland right-hander Jim Perry, who had been Rookie of the Year runner-up to Allison in 1959.

Although Allison had very little batting-box success in postseason action, he is still remembered four decades later for his diving, backhand catch to save a World Series game for the '65 Twins against Los Angeles. It was a typical example of his hustling style of play.

Turning 35, Allison began to experience medical problems that would hasten his career's end after 13 seasons. A victim of ataxia, which affects voluntary muscular movement, his health deteriorated slowly but steadily. William Robert Allison was only 60 when he succumbed at Rio Verde, Arizona.

In 1959 he was the second and last Washington Senator to be chosen Rookie of the Year. Old-time Senators fans still believe Allison would have helped spark their team to glory if only it had stayed put in Washington a little while longer.

RON HANSEN
1960   Baltimore Orioles, American League

Personal Data: B. April 5, 1938, at Oxford, NE.
Physical Attributes: 6' 3", playing weight 190 lbs. Bats right, throws right.
Rookie Year, 1960:   Primary position shortstop.
Total Career, 15 years: Orioles 1958–62; White Sox '63–67; Senators '68; White Sox '68–69; Yankees '70–71; Royals '72.

	BA	G	H	2B	3B	HR	RBI
1960	.255	153	135	22	5	22	86
Lifetime	.234	1,384	1,007	156	17	106	501

At 6′ 3″, Ron Hansen was taller than most shortstops. But his height was just one of many distinctions to which this 1960 American League Rookie of the Year can lay claim.

The list starts before his first full big league season did. When the Orioles gave the youngster trial runs late in 1958 and 1959, he recorded exactly zero hits in 23 at bats. Not much of an audition.

Undeterred, Baltimore put him in its 1960 lineup. All the rookie did was post career-high marks in home runs (22) and runs batted in (86), and play shortstop the entire nine-inning All-Star Game at Yankee Stadium. With two singles, Hansen was the only American League All-Star with multiple hits. At season's end he was named on 22 of the 24 Rookie of the Year ballots. Oriole teammates Jim Gentile and Chuck Estrada also received votes.

Hansen never led the league in any offensive category. His rookie year, in fact, was his finest overall. Yet he was a clubhouse leader and, except for lengthy absences with back injuries and six months away with the U.S. Marines in 1962, Ron totaled 15 big league seasons with five different teams.

Distinctive performances would surface again from time to time. With Washington, versus Cleveland in 1968, he chalked up the majors' first unassisted triple play in 41 years. Earlier that year he'd been dealt to the Senators, by Chicago, for Tim Cullen. Less than a week after his historic triple play, he was traded back to the White Sox. For . . . Tim Cullen.

It's the only time in history that two men were traded for each other *twice* in the *same* season.

Hansen's defense was steadily solid. He led the league's shortstops in double plays three times. He was a four-time assists leader. And in 1965, during his first tour with Chicago, he set two records for chances accepted: 18 in the first game, then 10 in the nightcap, for a new doubleheader standard of 28 total chances.

Ron was only 31 when back problems surfaced. After he was traded to the Yankees following the 1969 season, his playing time was severely limited. He appeared in only 120 New York games over two seasons, and retired in 1972 after just 30 at bats for Kansas City.

Hansen has done spring training coaching and minor league managing in the meantime. This first Oriole to be honored with a Rookie of the Year award still resides in Maryland, not far from Baltimore.

TOM TRESH
1962   New York Yankees, American League

Personal Data: B. September 20, 1937, at Detroit, MI.
Physical Attributes: 6' 1", playing weight 180 lbs. Bats both, throws right.
Rookie Year, 1962:   Primary position shortstop.
Total Career, 9 years: Yankees 1961–69; Tigers '69.

	BA	G	H	2B	3B	HR	RBI
1962	.286	157	178	26	5	20	93
Lifetime	.245	1,192	1,041	179	34	153	530

One fellow's detour can be another's opportunity. Such was the case for two New York Yankee Rookies of the Year.

The 1957 rookie award winner, Tony Kubek, missed 109 games in 1962 to fulfill a military assignment. His departure opened the way for young Tom Tresh to make his own name among a long line of distinguished Yankee shortstops. He promptly turned in the best season-long performance of his career. The son of veteran catcher Mike Tresh, Tom was a vital ingredient in New York's drive toward a World Series triumph over San Francisco.

Tresh never missed a beat. He carried his regular-season effectiveness into the Series, where he hit .321 with one home run, drove in four runs, and scored five.

"I remember those early years well," he mused.

I played on the Richmond farm team in 1961. In September, when rosters can expand, the Yankees called me up for a few games [nine games; eight at bats]. What a thrill to enter the Yankee Stadium locker room. Another thrill soon followed. The uniform they assigned me was number 15, "Old Reliable" Tommy Henrich's old number. And I'm also proud to have been associated with the man who wore number 15 after me. Thurman Munson, another Rookie of the Year.

Tom's official first season, 1962, featured career highs in four major categories—.286 batting average, 93 RBI, 94 runs, 157 games played. He never had another year like that one. Uncle Sam returned Kubek in 1963, so Tresh was moved to the outfield. He held that post into 1969 when he was traded to Detroit, his native city. Hitting just .224 in 94 games with the '69 Tigers, Tom called it a career. He was only 32.

I knew my playing days were numbered after a 1967 incident in the second spring training game. I fielded a grounder on wet grass and in my haste to nail a runner I turned awkwardly. The runner was out, but so was my knee. Five knee operations followed. After surgery in the spring of 1970 I knew my playing days were over.

Tresh, though, would stay officially connected with young athletes for three more decades. He was part of Central Michigan University's administration for two tenures over 27 years. Tom was director of career placement for several years. And he was a part-time baseball coach—no surprise there—for 14 seasons.

Now fully retired, Tom Tresh occasionally participates in baseball fantasy camps, and he looks forward to annual old-timers' weekends at Yankee Stadium. He and his wife are full-time residents of Venice, Florida. Several of their grandchildren live nearby.

"As you can imagine," grins Tom, "retirement isn't particularly quiet."

GARY PETERS
1963   Chicago White Sox, American League

Personal Data: B. April 21, 1937, at Grove City, PA.
Physical Attributes: 6′ 2″, playing weight 200 lbs. Throws left, bats left.
Rookie Year, 1963:   Primary position pitcher. League-leading 2.33 ERA.
Total Career, 14 years: White Sox 1959–69; Red Sox '70–72.

	Record	ERA	G	GS	SO	IP
1963	19–8	2.33	41	30	189	243
Lifetime	124–103	3.25	359	286	1,420	2,081

Gary Peters had tasted baseball's proverbial "cups of coffee" during four brief call-ups with the Chicago White Sox before exploding in 1963 with a spectacular Rookie of the Year summer. It typified Gary's durability and capability,

Gary Peters, Chicago White Sox, 1963
A 20-game winner in his sophomore season, Gary twice led the American League in earned run average. He posted a 1.98 ERA in 1966.
(Courtesy of Chicago White Sox)

which were key elements in his producing double-digit victory totals in eight of his 10 full major league seasons.

Seven times he exceeded 200 innings pitched, including a career high 273²⁄3 in 1964 when his 20 wins led the American League and helped vault the Sox to just one game short of pennant winner New York. Then, in 1967, Chicago, Minnesota, Detroit, and Boston all entered the last weekend with a chance to take the title. But the underdog Kansas City Athletics derailed Chicago, for whom Gary had posted a league-leading 1.98 ERA in 204 2/3 innings. The Red Sox prevailed, culminating their "Impossible Dream" season.

In 1970, Peters was traded to Boston, where he registered a 33-and-25 record over three seasons before retiring from baseball after the '72 campaign. "I was ineffective that last year because of arm and back injuries," he remembers. "But overall I really enjoyed my baseball years. Three special highlights still stand out. The pair of one-hitters I pitched, and a grand-slam home run I hit against the Yankees in 1968." It contributed to his 19 career homers and .221 batting average compiled back before designated hitters were discovered.

Another special achievement was Gary's sterling All-Star Game appearance in 1967. He turned in three perfect innings with four strikeouts along the way.

Peters received several offers to stay in baseball, but he wanted to discontinue heavy travel and get away from big cities. He worked in construction administration and management for 28 years before retiring in 2000. In recalling his rookie season recently, from his Sarasota, Florida, home, Peters said he became aware of a Rookie of the Year possibility in August. But he figured that his teammate Pete Ward also had an excellent chance to win.

"Strangely, the award didn't have much of an effect on me until after I had retired," says Gary. "But since then it's generated a lot of fan mail, card show appearances, and other opportunities that bring back many pleasant memories."

TONY OLIVA
1964   Minnesota Twins, American League

Personal Data: B. July 20, 1940, at Pinar del Rio, Cuba.
Physical Attributes: 6′ 1″, playing weight 175 lbs. Bats left, throws right.
Rookie Year, 1964:   Primary position outfield. .323 batting average, 217 hits, 43 doubles, and 109 runs led league.
Total Career, 15 years: Twins 1962–76.

	BA	G	H	2B	3B	HR	RBI
1964	.323	161	217	43	9	32	94
Lifetime	.304	1,676	1,917	329	48	220	947

Tony Oliva has not yet been invited to Cooperstown for Hall of Fame induction ceremonies. He should have been. And someday might be.

His sparkling 1964 Rookie of the Year achievements were merely savory appetizers for the accomplishments that followed. Tony's skillful batsmanship, alone, is enough to merit Hall of Fame votes. Here's a sampling of his accomplishments.

Rookie season: led American League in batting (.323), hits (217 to establish AL rookie standard at the time), runs (109), doubles (43). Led major leagues with club-record total bases (374), extra-base hits (84), multihit games (71). Hit career-high 32 home runs.

Second year: league leader in batting average (.321) and hits (185).

Succeeding years: three-time leader in hits and doubles, and, in 1971, paced AL in slugging average and a career-best .337 batting average.

When the Twins suffered a 1965 World Series loss to Los Angeles, Oliva struggled, hitting only .192. But in 1969 and '70, in helping his team to the American League Championship Series against Baltimore both years, Tony chipped in with a .440 batting average that included two home runs.

Only the voters (and nonvoters?) themselves can explain Oliva's absence from Cooperstown. Perhaps his prime days were overlooked because teammate Harmon Killebrew was hitting numerous headlined home runs. Or because fellow Twin and Rookie of the Year Rod Carew surpassed Tony's solid batting averages. Yes, his team appeared on national telecasts less than some "big market" clubs did. Still, that's no excuse for Cooperstown omission. After all, Killebrew and Carew played in Minnesota, too. Perhaps Tony himself was unwittingly the culprit. Because, after his marvelous early seasons, his consistent .290ish annual production might have seemed like off years by comparison.

Tony, whose given name is Pedro (he used his brother's passport to enter the United States for baseball), was simply among the most dangerous hitters of his day. Until sustaining a serious 1971 knee injury, he was a Gold Glove winner as early as his sophomore year. Knee surgery, the first of seven such operations, limited Tony to 10 games in 1972 (when he hit a typical .321). From then on, for his final four years, he was the Twins' primary designated hitter.

The Minnesota Twins continue to offer him their highest respect. They've retired his number 6. And since his retirement he's held various posts within the team's administration. Currently he's a member of Minnesota's broadcast unit and has served part-time as a minor league hitting instructor.

The old Washington Senators became the Twins back in 1961. After these four-plus decades Tony Oliva still ranks among Minnesota's top five in 11 different batting categories. In fact, as a member of some prominent power-hitting Twins' editions, his 220 homers are third best in Minnesota history.

CURT BLEFARY
1965   Baltimore Orioles, American League

Personal Data: B. July 5, 1943, at Brooklyn, NY. D. January 28, 2001.
Physical Attributes: 6' 2", playing weight 195 lbs. Bats left, throws right.
Rookie Year, 1965:   Primary position outfield.
Total Career, 8 years: Orioles 1965–68; Astros '69; Yankees '70–71; A's '71–72; Padres '72.

	BA	G	H	2B	3B	HR	RBI
1965	.260	144	120	23	4	22	70
Lifetime	.237	974	699	194	20	112	382

When 21-year-old Curt Blefary entered the big league arena in 1965, his debut season's performance was heralded as an omen that the Baltimore Orioles were on track toward annual contention for the American League pennant.

Curt was one of the remaining ingredients needed for a title, which came the following year. Frank Robinson would join Blefary, Boog Powell, Brooks Robinson, Paul Blair, Luis Aparicio, and a group of fine young pitchers to lead Baltimore to its 1966 World Championship.

Blefary's Rookie of the Year season, 1965, turned out to be the best of the eight years in which he played for five clubs in both leagues. The left-handed-hitting outfielder hit a solid .260 that initial season and stroked 22 home runs for the O's. He never equaled that .260 again, although his power numbers over the next two years remained high. In the '66 flag-winning season he hit 23 homers, and he followed with 22 and a career-high 81 RBI in 1967.

But after falling off to an even .200 the next year, he had worn out his Baltimore welcome. The Orioles traded him and a minor league prospect to Houston for four players including pitcher Mike Cuellar, who would star during the Orioles three straight pennants in 1969, '70, and '71.

Upon arriving in Houston, Blefary switched defensive positions and immediately led the National League in assists (103) by first basemen. He also improved his batting average to .253. Basically, however, his days as a major league regular were ending.

Able to recapture neither his hitting consistency nor his power performance, Curt spent his last three big league seasons with the Yankees, Oakland, and finally 82 games at San Diego in 1972. He finished his career with a creditable 112 home runs . . . most of them during his four Baltimore seasons.

At age 57, in early 2001, Curt Blefary passed away at his Pompano Beach, Florida, home after suffering from pancreatic cancer and related ailments. Both his life and his baseball career ended prematurely.

TOMMIE AGEE
1966   Chicago White Sox, American League

Personal Data: B. August 9, 1942, at Magnolia, AL. D. January 22, 2001.
Physical Attributes: 5′ 11″, playing weight 195 lbs. Bats right, throws right.
Rookie Year, 1966:   Primary position outfield.
Total Career, 12 years: Indians 1962–64; White Sox '65–67; Mets '68–72; Astros '73; Cardinals '73.

	BA	G	H	2B	3B	HR	RBI
1966	.273	160	172	27	8	22	86
Lifetime	.255	1,129	999	170	27	130	433

Now and then a player is primarily remembered for one game or perhaps one series. Or even a single play. Mickey Owen in the 1941 World Series? Fred Merkle? Maybe Bucky Dent?

How about Tommie Agee? Casual fans might be hard-pressed to recall that he was the 1966 American League Rookie of the Year. But they're quick to tell you of his amazing center-field catches and a key home run in the New York Mets' 1969 World Series triumph over Baltimore.

He immediately followed that Series by hitting .286 and .285 in 1970 and '71, and driving home over 70 runs each year. By then his solid Rookie of the Year season had been long overlooked.

When Agee won that award he'd already auditioned briefly with Cleveland in each of three seasons starting in 1962. And, after a headlined trade with Tommy John to Chicago for Rocky Colavito and Camilo Carreon, the White Sox gave him a 10-game trial in late 1965.

Then he blossomed. Only 24, he registered the best overall performance of his 12-season major league career. Agee pounded out 22 home runs in 1966 and posted career highs in RBI (86) and stolen bases (44). He delivered solid defense, too, committing only seven outfield errors in 150 games played.

The dreaded sophomore jinx, however, zeroed in on Agee. He dropped off significantly in virtually all offensive categories the next year. And with Al Weis— also a '69 World Series standout—Chicago traded Tommie to the Mets for four players, including pitcher Jack Fisher and veteran outfielder Tommy Davis.

He started slowly in New York, but rebounded with three productive seasons—'69 through '71. However, Agee faded in 1972 and finished his career the following year with Houston and St. Louis. He hit just .222 in a combined 109 games for the Astros and Cardinals.

Tommie Agee continued to follow baseball after that, but various physical ailments surfaced. The man who won the American League's 1966 rookie honors, but who is most often remembered for one spectacular World Series, lived his latter years in the New York area. He died there, of an apparent sudden heart attack, at age 58.

STAN BAHNSEN
1968 New York Yankees, American League

Personal Data: B. December 15, 1944, at Council Bluffs, IA.
Physical Attributes: 6' 2", playing weight 185 lbs. Throws right, bats right.
Rookie Year, 1968:   Primary position pitcher.
Total Career, 16 years: Yankees 1966, '68–71; White Sox '72–75; A's '75–77; Expos '77–81; Angels '82;
Phillies '82.

	Record	ERA	G	GS	SO	IP
1968	17–12	2.05	37	34	162	267⅓
Lifetime	146–149	3.61	574	327	1,359	2,528

As we see elsewhere in this book, only 29 pitchers, among the 116 honorees, have won the BBWAA's Rookie of the Year award. When you remember the promise they all displayed as freshmen, it might seem surprising that just 11 of those 29 ever posted one or more 20-victory seasons.

Stan Bahnsen, the American League's top rookie in 1968, is one of them.

Bob Grim, another Yankee, is the only one of the 11 whose 20 wins came in his rookie season.

It is a fact that Stan Bahnsen never led his league in any significant statistical category—except the dubious "most losses" listing (21, against 18 wins for the 1973 White Sox). He never earned postseason notoriety either, having pitched a mere one and a third innings for his fourth team, Montreal, in that convoluted 1981 split season's Divisional Playoff Series.

But when you focus on his overall 16-season accomplishments, the positives stand out. Breaking in, then hurling five seasons with the New York Yankees, Stan registered a 54–41 record. Remember—and this goes back a while now—the Yankees were a mediocre to downright poor team back then. The Steinbrenner regime would not debut until a year or two after Bahnsen was dealt to the White Sox. In his four full New York seasons Stan's ERA never exceeded 3.83. In fact, in his '68 Rookie of the Year season, his earned run average was a brilliant 2.05.

Wouldn't 2.05 be a league-leading figure, you ask? Well, '68 was the so-called Year of the Pitcher. Bob Gibson, Denny McLain, and a few dozen others mowed down batsmen with regularity. Carl Yastrzemski's .301 led the AL. As strong as Bahnsen's performance was, it failed to be a league best.

His lone 20-win season (21–16) came in 1972, his first year in Chicago. His ERA rose a bit for the next few years—after baseball lowered the height of the pitchers mound. Still, the big right-hander annually started between 28 and 40 games through 1974.

Soon, however, his stamina disappeared. By then, essentially a reliever, he was sent to Oakland, Montreal, California, and finally Philadelphia where he pitched in eight games, all in relief, registering an 0–0 log to complete 1982 . . . and his major league tenure.

Stan's career, 146 wins combined with a 3.61 ERA, is best remembered for his Rookie of the Year output and his notable New York seasons that immediately followed.

In recent years Stan Bahnsen has been a resident of Pompano Beach, Florida.

TED SIZEMORE
1969   Los Angeles Dodgers, National League

Personal Data: B. April 15, 1945, at Gadsden, AL.
Physical Attributes: 5′ 10″, playing weight 165 lbs. Bats right, throws right.
Rookie Year, 1969:   Primary position second base.
Total Career, 12 years: Dodgers 1969–70; Cardinals '71–75; Dodgers '76; Phillies '77–78; Cubs '79; Red Sox '79–80.

	BA	G	H	2B	3B	HR	RBI
1969	.271	159	160	20	5	4	46
Lifetime	.262	1,411	1,311	188	21	23	430

The Dodgers, both the Brooklyn and Los Angeles varieties, have turned out more than a fair share of stellar second basemen. Four of them—Jim Gilliam, Jim Lefebvre, Ted Sizemore, Steve Sax—performed so well right out of the chute that they won Rookie of the Year honors. Another, Davey Lopes, had an excellent career although he missed out on the major rookie honor. Jackie Robinson, the BBWAA's very first Rookie of the Year who's best remembered as a second baseman, debuted at first base for Brooklyn throughout 1947.

Ted Sizemore, the 1969 National League top rookie, is perhaps the least recalled member of that celebrated group of Dodger second basemen. Yet he played important roles for three contending teams over a respected 12-year big league career.

His fine first Los Angeles season was followed with his highest single-year batting average, .306. Whereupon the Cardinals, impressed with Ted's bat control and patience, traded for him by sending slugger Dick Allen to Los Angeles. By hitting directly behind Lou Brock in the St. Louis batting order, Sizemore enhanced and protected his popular teammate's base-stealing efforts. The two of them were mainstays throughout Ted's five St. Louis seasons.

Sizemore returned to Los Angeles for one year at midcareer, then went to Philadelphia, where he registered his most productive single season.

By then he was accustomed to playing the role of bridesmaid. Philadelphia's 1977 edition, with Sizemore at second, is considered by many analysts as the franchise's all-time best squad. On a team that featured sluggers Mike Schmidt and Greg Luzinski, with Larry Bowa, Bob Boone, Steve Carlton, Tug McGraw, Garry Maddox, and others also contributing significantly, steady Ted Sizemore was, again, largely overlooked. Insiders, however, understood his great value. His production included a .281 batting average, 47 RBI, and a league-leading participation in 104 double plays. Ted's .986 fielding average—he committed only 11 errors in 152 games—was a career best.

The Chicago Cubs also were aware of Sizemore's talents. They traded Manny Trillo for him after 1978. At age 33, though, his skills began to fade. Late in 1979, Ted was sent to Boston where he hit .261 in 26 games. After nine outings the following year his Red Sox days, and his career, ended.

In evaluating Sizemore's 12-year career, his protection of St. Louis base thief Lou Brock stands out. So does Ted's defensive versatility. Participating in a total of 1,411 regular-season games, including four behind the plate, he played every position except pitcher and first base.

CARL MORTON
1970   Montreal Expos, National League

Personal Data: B. January 18, 1944, at Kansas City, MO. D. April 12, 1983.
Physical Attributes: 6′ 0″, playing weight 200 lbs. Throws right, bats right.
Rookie Year, 1970:   Primary position pitcher.
Total Career, 8 years: Expos 1969–72; Braves '73–76.

	Record	ERA	G	GS	SO	IP
1970	18–11	3.60	43	37	154	284⅔
Lifetime	87–92	3.73	255	242	650	1,649⅓

The expansion Montreal Expos had entered the National League just one year earlier. But already, when their 1970 season ended, the second-year franchise boasted of the league's Rookie of the Year.

Even though his team was still beset with severe growing pains, right-hander Carl Morton proved to be one of the new franchise's early bright spots. And this success came only two years after he had been converted from playing the outfield to pitching. Ironically, representing a last-place team that year, Morton outpolled Bernie Carbo of the league champion Reds for the top rookie laurel.

Morton had spent most of the late 1960s as an outfielder in the Braves' organization. But he was selected from the Atlanta system, by the Expos, during the 1968 expansion draft. He started pitching regularly throughout the summer of '69, and was called up to Montreal for the season's final month. He started eight games, was 0–3, and registered an unspectacular 4.66 ERA. But as soon as his official rookie season began the next spring, Carl turned things around dramatically.

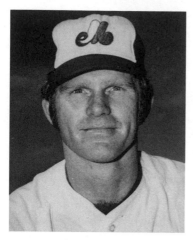

Carl Morton, Montreal Expos, 1970
This right-handed pitcher, who died at age 39, was the first Rookie of the Year from a Canadian team. He registered 18 victories in 1970.
(Temple University Libraries, Urban Archives, Philadelphia, PA)

Then 26, he quickly became the Montreal staff ace. He was clearly Rookie of the Year on merit. Morton turned in an 18–11 record with a 3.60 ERA in 285 innings. He completed 10 of the 43 games he started. But things reversed suddenly the next year, and he won only 10 games while losing 18. After just a 7–13 log in '73 he was traded back to Atlanta.

Carl averaged 15 victories there for three seasons. However, when he won only four of the 24 games he started in 1976, he, four others, and cash were dealt to Texas for outfielder Jeff Burroughs.

Burroughs would play nine more big league seasons. Morton, whose eight-season totals included a creditable 87–92 record and a 3.73 earned run average, would never appear in the majors again. Texas shipped him to the minors. Soon he retired from baseball. Just six years later, while jogging in Tulsa, Oklahoma, Morton was stricken with a fatal heart attack. He was only 39.

As an eerie coincidence Thurman Munson, of the American League, died in a tragic airplane accident at the age of 32.

Munson and Carl Morton were both Rookies of the Year in 1970.

Chris Chambliss
1971   Cleveland Indians, American League

Personal Data: B. December 26, 1948, at Dayton, OH.
Physical Attributes: 6′ 1″, playing weight 195 lbs. Bats left, throws right.
Rookie Year, 1971:   Primary position first base.
Total Career, 17 years: Indians 1971–74; Yankees '74–79; Braves '80–86; Yankees '88.

	BA	G	H	2B	3B	HR	RBI
1971	.275	111	114	20	4	9	48
Lifetime	.279	2,173	2,109	392	42	185	972

Baseball insiders knew of Chris Chambliss's potential. After all, Cleveland made him the nation's number one selection in the 1970 free-agent draft. However, few would have predicted then that Chambliss would be American League Rookie of the Year just 22 months later.

Chris gave them a preview in 1970 when he won the Triple-A batting crown (.342 at Wichita). He was still at Wichita in '71. But for only 11 games. The Indians promoted him in late April, and he proceeded to hit .275 in 111 games en route to Rookie of the Year honors.

"Best thing about that award," Chris recalls, "is the instant recognition that comes with it. Of course the trade to New York [three years later], and being a Yankee for six years, magnified the exposure."

One headlined home run—his dramatic 1976 shot in the ninth inning to win the deciding ALCS game for New York over Kansas City—still seems to overshadow Chambliss's numerous other achievements during a craftsmanlike 17-season career.

Exclusively a first baseman, except for 24 designated hitter assignments, Chris was a Gold Glove winner. He hit over .280 eight times, with a full-season high of .304 for New York in 1975. At Atlanta, where he played after leaving New York in 1980, Chris's 37 doubles in '80 tied Hank Aaron's Atlanta record at the time. Then, in 1986, he led the National League with 20 pinch hits.

Not until his sixth big league season, however, did he reach double-digit home runs.

"I'd always studied hitting techniques and style," he says. "Finally, after six years, I learned about hitting zones and started to focus on that aspect of batting."

He mastered hitting disciplines so well that, after retiring as an active player, he's spent 15 years teaching them. He was hitting coach with Joe Torre's Cardinals and Yankees from 1993 through 2000, held the same post with the '02 Mets, then was a Mets minor league batting instructor throughout 2003.

Chris also has minor league managing achievements to his credit. In five years his charges posted 372 wins. They won a championship at London, Ontario, where he was the 1990 Eastern League manager of the year. He earned similar honors the next summer in the Southern League.

Chambliss is clearly sincere saying, "I'm truly happy serving as a batting instructor." Still, you get a feeling that he'd welcome an opportunity to give major league skippering a try. In the meantime, in his middle 50s, Chambliss donned a big league uniform again in 2004 as the Cincinnati Reds batting coach, a position he maintained in 2005.

EARL WILLIAMS
1971   Atlanta Braves, National League

Personal Data: B. July 14, 1948, at Newark, NJ.
Physical Attributes: 6′ 3″, playing weight 215 lbs. Bats right, throws right.
Rookie Year, 1971:   Primary position catcher.
Total Career, 8 years: Braves 1970–72; Orioles '73–74; Braves '75–76; Expos '76; A's '77.

	BA	G	H	2B	3B	HR	RBI
1971	.260	145	129	14	1	33	87
Lifetime	.247	889	756	115	6	138	457

The Braves boasted of two Rookies of the Year (Alvin Dark and Sam Jethroe) during the award's first four years. Both players represented the team when it was still housed in Boston. Ironically, over the club's subsequent successful decade in Milwaukee, none of its first-year players—including Henry Aaron—was ever the freshman honoree.

Not until the Braves had transferred to Atlanta did the franchise produce another Rookie of the Year. Earl Williams, a hard-hitting catcher, captured the 1971 National League award. His long-ball production, 87 RBI including a career-high 33 home runs, enabled him to outballot Philadelphia's Willie Montanez.

Williams suffered no sophomore jinx in 1972, as he matched his runs-batted-in production of the preceding season, came within two batting average points of his opening year's .260, and checked in with 28 homers. But he would rarely perform consistently well after that, and by the end of the 1977 season at Oakland, Williams' big league career was finished. He was 29.

During 1972, that second solid year with the Braves, Williams often voiced displeasure with his position as catcher. So Atlanta frequently stationed him at either first base or third. When that season ended, the Braves had an opportunity to trade Earl to the American League. It turned out to be one of baseball's most lopsided transactions. In return for Williams and minor leaguer Taylor Duncan, who would play in scarcely more than 100 major league games later in the decade, Atlanta claimed four Baltimore Orioles. Included were three solid starters: pitcher Pat Dobson, catcher Johnny Oates, and Davey Johnson who smacked 43 home runs in '73, a single-season record for second basemen.

Earl Williams' productivity, meanwhile, was starting a steady decline. He totaled only 36 home runs in two seasons at Baltimore. By 1975 he'd been returned to Atlanta, this time primarily as a first baseman. He hit .240 that year. As he moved on to Montreal, then Oakland, his average continued to decline. In that last year with the Athletics, though, Earl again got his wish to play somewhere other than behind the plate. He was often a first baseman or designated hitter, and appeared in only 26 games as a catcher.

Away from baseball for more than a quarter century, Williams has resided in central New Jersey, not far from his Newark birthplace.

JON MATLACK
1972   New York Mets, National League

Personal Data: B. January 19, 1950, at West Chester, PA.
Physical Attributes: 6′ 3″, playing weight 205 lbs. Throws left, bats left.
Rookie Year, 1972:   Primary position pitcher.
Total Career, 13 years: Mets 1971–77; Rangers '78–83.

	Record	ERA	G	GS	SO	IP
1972	15–10	2.32	34	32	169	244
Lifetime	125–126	3.18	361	318	1,516	2,363

As you would expect, starting pitchers who've won National League Rookie of the Year laurels registered extremely impressive figures in their debut seasons. Thus, their well-earned places in the spotlight.

Included in that distinguished group are such notable names as Seaver, Gooden, Newcombe, Valenzuela, Wood. But the starter who recorded the best rookie season earned run average . . . 2.32 . . . was New York Mets southpaw Jon Matlack. Among the 215 base hits he allowed in '72 was Hall of Famer Roberto Clemente's 3,000th—and very last—hit.

Seaver was the deservedly acknowledged ace of the Mets staff that 1972 season, as he was throughout his teammate Matlack's first five years in New York. Nevertheless, Matlack was a key member of an excellent pitching squad. He went to the starting post with regularity—nearly three dozen times a summer—and posted 13 or more wins in each of his first five full seasons.

Matlack was selected to three All-Star teams during that period, and shared 1975 All-Star MVP honors with Bill Madlock. Jon also led the National League in shutouts twice: 1974 (7) and 1976 (6).

For a frightening day or so, in 1973, Mets fans everywhere concerned themselves more with Jon's survival than with his pitching statistics. In early May, the same month 16 years after another Rookie of the Year, Herb Score, had been felled by a batted ball, a line drive struck Jon above his left eye. An anguished Marty Perez was the Atlanta batter who smacked a laser shot toward the mound. Matlack was rushed to a hospital. Happily he displayed amazing recuperative powers.

"I spent three days in the hospital," he told Kevin Czerwinski for MLB.com. "But eight days later I was pitching again. Yes, I was nervous that first game back, but I realized I wasn't going to flinch when the ball came in my direction." Before 1973 ended, Matlack had tossed a complete game shutout in the League Championship Series and won a World Series game against Oakland.

In late 1977 the Mets decided to reduce payroll and start rebuilding. As part of a four-team deal, Jon was traded to Texas. He spent six years with the Rangers, winning 43 games and losing 45. Twice his victory total reached double figures. He was a reliever and spot starter in his final two seasons.

Since his retirement as a player, Matlack has been a coach and instructor in the Tigers' organization.

Even though his solid career doesn't quite merit a Cooperstown plaque, Jon Matlack and his wife, Dee, can almost see the Hall of Fame's shadows and feel its aura. Their permanent home, in Norwich, New York, is not far from the hallowed site.

AL BUMBRY
1973   Baltimore Orioles, American League

Personal Data: B. April 21, 1947, at Fredericksburg, VA.
Physical Attributes: 5′ 8″, playing weight 170 lbs. Bats left, throws right.
Rookie Year, 1973:   Primary position outfield. Tied for league lead in triples with Rod Carew (11). 23 stolen bases. .500 slugging average.
Total Career, 14 years: Orioles 1972–84; Padres '85.

	BA	G	H	2B	3B	HR	RBI
1973	.337	110	120	15	11	7	34
Lifetime	.281	1,496	1,422	220	52	54	402

Even baseball's most ardent followers would likely concede that the name Al Bumbry might not flow automatically through their lips when quickly naming the most productive Baltimore Orioles of the past half century. But that might be an embarrassing oversight.

Over 12 full seasons, Al Bumbry, the American League's 1973 Rookie of the Year, was among the elite Orioles in terms of steadiness and durability.

For starters, he played in more than 100 of Baltimore's games 10 times. Seldom was he seriously injured. Since the franchise moved to Maryland in 1954 after its half-century run as the St. Louis Browns, Bumbry's career accomplishments in numerous offensive categories rank him among Baltimore's top 10:

Games played—9th, 1,428 . . . at bats—9th, 4,958 . . . runs—6th, 772 . . . hits—8th, 1,403 . . . doubles—8th, 217 . . . total bases—8th, 1,883 . . . batting average—10th, .283

If those numbers are not convincing enough, here's more confirmation that Al Bumbry was a special Baltimore Oriole for a long time:

His 252 career stolen bases set a team record back in 1984. (Since then Brady Anderson's 307 Oriole steals exceeded those of Bumbry, who still holds second place.)

Then there's the matter of triples. He legged out 11 in his 1973 Rookie of the Year season. In one September game alone, against Milwaukee, he sprinted for three triples to tie a major league record that's likely to remain permanently unbroken.

The Orioles of Al Bumbry's time were strong contenders year in and year out. He appeared in 11 World Series games with them—1979 and 1983—and was an important member of four Baltimore division winners. Al made the American League All-Star team in 1980, a season in which he hit .318 with nine triples. That year he became the first of the modern Orioles to get 200 hits. He totaled 205. For the third time Al surpassed .300.

Following his playing career, which ended with 68 games at San Diego in 1985, Bumbry returned to the Baltimore area, where he followed the Orioles closely and, in 1995, served as one of their coaches. He and his family now live in nearby Lutherville, Maryland.

Too often overshadowed in history by such Oriole teammates as Jim Palmer, Brooks Robinson, Eddie Murray, manager Earl Weaver, Reggie Jackson, and his close friend Cal Ripken, Jr., Al Bumbry proudly looks back on a satisfying big league career. And with typical modest pride, he also reflects on some serious pre-baseball days when he earned a Bronze Star for his U.S. military heroism in Vietnam.

GARY MATTHEWS
1973   San Francisco Giants, National League

Personal Data: B. July 5, 1950, at San Fernando, CA.
Physical Attributes: 6′ 2″, playing weight 185 lbs. Bats right, throws right.
Rookie Year, 1973:   Primary position outfield.
Total Career, 16 years: Giants 1972–76; Braves '77–80; Phillies '81–83; Cubs '84–87; Mariners '87.

	BA	G	H	2B	3B	HR	RBI
1973	.300	148	162	22	10	12	58
Lifetime	.281	2,033	2,011	319	51	234	978

Gary Matthews, a popular and thoughtful baseball "lifer," believes the foundation for success is to play with consistency that begets the character necessary for longevity.

This 1973 National League Rookie of the Year personified just that kind of a successful career pattern. Gary's first full season, for San Francisco at age 22, produced a .300 batting average and double-digit doubles (22), home runs (12), and stolen bases (17).

How does that relate to Gary's 13 full-season averages? You could almost pre-print them on opening day. A 13-year batting average of .284, 23 doubles a year, 18 home runs, and 14 successful steals.

A long career's average does not necessarily denote consistency. But on the Matthews' log it does. He rarely differed much from year to year. Gary hit .300 thrice—.300, .304, .301. He stroked between 12 and 20 homers in 10 of his 13 full seasons. He hit between 20 and 30 doubles nine times.

That, indeed, is consistency. And those 13 full and three partial seasons clearly translate into longevity. They also factored into his teams' successes, especially at his final two NL stops. Nicknamed Sarge, Matthews helped the 1981 Phillies to a split-season division title. Two years later he sparked Philadelphia to the 1983 World Series. En route, with three homers, eight RBI, and a .429 average against Los Angeles, he was the NLCS Most Valuable Player. The very next year Gary's .291 batting and 82 RBI helped lead the Cubs to a division crown and their first postseason appearance in 39 years.

Matthews' playing career ended in 1987. After several years in private industry, he returned to the Cubs in 1995 as minor league hitting coordinator. Gary then went to Toronto as hitting coach and broadcaster before coaching at Milwaukee in 2002. In 2003 he signed on as Dusty Baker's hitting coach in Chicago, where Gary and his wife Sandra reside.

Comparing broadcasting and baseball, Gary said, "There's pressure in both. But more so on the field. There a manager's the man with the real pressure."

Gary confesses that he'd likely consider a managerial opportunity, should one be presented. But instead of dwelling on it he devotes full concentration to his coaching duties, and clearly enjoys working for manager Baker.

He was asked to describe any differences now compared to his Rookie of the Year summer of 1973.

"Media coverage," he quickly answered. "So much more today. There's so much focus on 'celebrity' now. So when I work with young players today, I stress that consistency and longevity breed winning. It's always been more important than personal stats."

Bet that Gary preaches that philosophy to his five children, one of whom is Gary, Jr., a veteran major league outfielder. Another boy, Delvon, was a Brewers farmhand in the early 2000s.

BAKE MCBRIDE
1974   St. Louis Cardinals, National League

Personal Data: B. February 3, 1949, at Fulton, MO.
Physical Attributes: 6′ 2″, playing weight 190 lbs. Bats left, throws right.
Rookie Year, 1974:   Primary position outfield.
Total Career, 11 years: Cardinals 1973–77; Phillies '77–81; Indians '82–83.

	BA	G	H	2B	3B	HR	RBI
1974	.309	150	173	19	5	6	56
Lifetime	.299	1,071	1,153	167	55	63	430

For a while the Cardinals had a habit of sending away promising young outfielders shortly after they'd won Rookie of the Year honors. Bill Virdon and Wally Moon, from the 1950s, are good examples.

Bake McBride, two decades later, was another one.

It's not that these fellows were one-year wonders, either. McBride, for instance, had turned in excellent figures during his three full St. Louis seasons. He followed his rookie year's .309 with .300, then .335 performances. But after 43 games in 1977 he was traded to Philadelphia for three oft-forgotten players of modest talent.

The Phillies were delighted to have Arnold McBride on their side. He contributed immediately, hitting .339 for them in 85 games. Many close observers consider the 1977 team the strongest Phillies combine of all time. McBride, usually overshadowed in history by such teammates as Steve Carlton, Mike Schmidt, Larry Bowa, Pete Rose, Greg Luzinski, Tug McGraw, Garry Maddox, and Bob Boone, was a popular catalyst as Philadelphia was a postseason entrant in four of his five years there. Bake hit .304 with a home run and five RBI in 1980 as the Phillies won their only World Series title.

During that '80 regular season, alternating from the leadoff slot to third and sometimes cleanup in the batting order, McBride posted a career high 87 RBI and hit .300 again—this time .309.

Knee troubles, though, had surfaced before Bake reached age 30. After the satisfying 1980 season, he never played regularly again. He was limited to 58 outings in the strike-shortened '81 campaign. When he did play, his knees ached.

Cleveland signed him for the 1982 and '83 seasons. His batting eye was as sharp as ever, but he was unable to muster much power even though he averaged .311 in 97 games in two years with the Indians. He was only 34 when he called it quits.

Seven times, over his 11 partial or full big league seasons, McBride hit .300 or better. He finished his career just one percentage short of the coveted .300.

Before his legs failed him, Bake was considered an excellent defender. In 1978 he led NL outfielders in fielding and in one outing that year tied a major league record with 10 chances in a game.

Despite being often overshadowed by glamorous Phillies teammates, Bake was fondly remembered and loudly cheered by Philadelphia fans when he returned in late 2003 for Veterans Stadium's closing ceremonies. Despite the balky knees that took him out to right field for ceremonial goodbyes, Bake McBride, with a wide grin, seemed right at home again.

JOHN MONTEFUSCO
1975   San Francisco Giants, National League

Personal Data: B. May 25, 1950, at Long Branch, NJ.
Physical Attributes: 6′ 1″, playing weight 180 lbs. Throws right, bats right.
Rookie Year, 1975:   Primary position pitcher.
Total Career, 13 years: Giants 1974–80; Braves '81; Padres '82–83; Yankees '83–86.

	Record	ERA	G	GS	SO	IP
1975	15–9	2.88	35	34	215	243⅔
Lifetime	90–83	3.54	298	244	1,081	1,651⅔

Had the 1975 National League Rookie of the Year been born a decade or so later, he might have become a character actor on television's "The Sopranos," a show set in New Jersey, for John Montefusco, a Long Branch native, was a legitimate self-proclaimed character.

Like baseball's flamboyant Dizzy Dean, Montefusco lived up to his boasts. But for just a short time.

Dean wasn't the only notable pitcher whom Montefusco resembled. As we see elsewhere in this book, the career ERAs of virtually all pitchers who won Rookie of the Year honors are invariably higher than their first year's. Montefusco was no exception. After his second full season, he never again (except for four outings at age 36) matched his rookie year's 2.88 ERA.

Nicknamed the Count of Montefusco, John's flair was similar to Detroit's Mark (the Bird) Fidrych, who was Rookie of the Year just one year after Montefusco's official debut. The Count's career would exceed the Bird's by several years.

Apologists for left-handers, citing Dean, Montefusco, and Fidrych, emphasize that some of baseball's "flakes" aren't necessarily southpaws.

Montefusco's 1975 statistics were legitimate Rookie of the Year numbers. A 15–9 log. A 2.88 ERA. A 215-strikeout total, second best in the league. Although he never again fanned that many, his career strikeout/walk ratio was better than two-to-one . . . 1,081–513.

The Count's second season nearly mirrored his first. He won 16 games and lowered his ERA slightly to 2.84. In the season finale he spun a no-hitter. It was one of his six shutouts, a league-leading figure. After the no-hitter, and despite making 169 more career starts, he never registered another shutout.

Soon arm ailments reduced Montefusco's effectiveness. He won only 25 Giants games over the next four years. Atlanta signed him for a season, then traded him to San Diego. Late in the 1983 campaign he was dealt to the Yankees. His pitching suddenly revived. Perhaps his return to the New Jersey/New York area gave him a lift. The Mouth That Roared, another nickname from his early seasons, went 5–0 for the Yankees. His combined San Diego–New York log was 14–4. Was his career, indeed, back on track?

It seemed so. After 11 starts he had a 5–3 record with the 1984 Yankees. But severe arm trouble developed. His big league days were effectively over. He started seven games over the next two years, won none and lost none, and retired at age 36.

Yes, his pitching effectiveness had disappeared. But not his zest for pranks, for fellowship with old neighborhood cronies and teammates alike, and for recounting those early career successes that included hitting a home run in his first big league at bat. And who knows? The Count still lives in New Jersey. Maybe he'll yet audition for "The Sopranos."

PAT ZACHRY
1976   Cincinnati Reds, National League Cowinner

Personal Data: B. April 24, 1952, at Richmond, TX.
Physical Attributes: 6′ 5″, playing weight 180 lbs. Throws right, bats right.
Rookie Year, 1976:   Primary position pitcher.
Total Career, 10 years: Reds 1976–77; Mets '77–82; Dodgers '83–84; Phillies '85.

	Record	ERA	G	GS	SO	IP
1976	14–7	2.74	38	28	143	204
Lifetime	69–67	3.52	293	154	669	1,178

As baseball dealings go, a young pitcher coming off his Rookie of the Year season in exchange for a clear-cut Hall of Famer offers reasonably good odds for success. Cincinnati's Pat Zachry, the rookie, for veteran Tom Seaver was, indeed, a mutually satisfactory transaction back in 1977.

Mets fans wailed loudly, though, because Seaver had been the team's bellwether for a decade. But, for the short term at least, they grudgingly began rooting for this tall, thin stranger Zachry. And so, for the second half of '77 and over the following two seasons, Zachry rewarded their mild acceptance by posting 22 wins against just 13 defeats.

One embarrassing interruption, however, derailed Pat's progress for a while. Singling off Zachry, Pete Rose extended his hitting streak to 37 games, tying the modern National League record. Angry, Zachry kicked the dugout steps. He went to the disabled list with a seriously injured foot.

The Reds had been reluctant to deal away Zachry, but knew that a quality starter must be part of a Seaver transaction. Cincinnati fans were disappointed too. Not about Seaver's arrival, but because Zachry was not awarded the Rookie of the Year trophy . . . outright . . . the year before. They felt that Pat registered a better season than cowinner Butch Metzger of San Diego.

Zachry's freshman year was outstanding. His 14–7 record with a brilliant 2.74 ERA helped lead the Reds to a perfect postseason: a three-game sweep of

Philadelphia in the NLCS, four in a row versus the Yankees in the World Series. Zachry was 1–0 in each set.

Over the next five years, mostly with the Mets, Pat's career bounced from excellent to mediocre. With New York he was a level 41–41 (ironically, 41 was Seaver's uniform number). He then pitched extremely well in helping the 1983 Dodgers to the League Championship Series. By then he had become a relief pitcher.

Originally Zachry was a front-line starter. But by 1982 his starting and relieving work was about evenly divided. Then, over his final three seasons—two in Los Angeles and one at Philadelphia—he made 108 relief appearances. He started just once.

Pat's overall mark, like that of nearly all Rookie of the Year pitchers, did not match up with his first year's numbers. But at age 33, when his career ended, he looked back on a respectable 69–67 log with a 3.52 earned run average. And to a World Series win against the vaunted Yankees.

The Lone Star State native now resides in Waco, Texas.

BOB HORNER
1978   Atlanta Braves, National League

Personal Data: B. August 6, 1957, at Junction City, KS.
Physical Attributes: 6′ 1″, playing weight 195 lbs. Bats right, throws right.
Rookie Year, 1978:   Primary position third base.
Total Career, 10 years: Braves 1978–86; Cardinals '88.

	BA	G	H	2B	3B	HR	RBI
1978	.266	89	86	17	1	23	63
Lifetime	.277	1,020	1,047	169	8	218	685

"Here was a young man who was unafraid of pitchers. It looked like he had a good, long baseball future." So recalls Bobby Cox from his first tenure as Atlanta manager when 1978 College Player of the Year Bob Horner signed on with the Braves.

When Horner, also the 1978 NL Rookie of the Year, joined Cox's team directly from Arizona State University—with no minor league apprenticeship en route—he immediately worked his way into the starting lineup and gave clear notice that he belonged at the major league level. He arrived in time to play in only 89 games. But they were enough to earn him the votes required to be honored as best NL rookie that year.

Horner homered in his very first game. Twenty-two home runs followed. They helped account for his 63 RBI during his abbreviated freshman summer.

The potential that Cox observed in Horner continued in full flower over the next few seasons. Overall his second year was his career best offensively: lifetime highs in average (.314), hits (153), and RBI (98). He hit 33 home runs that year, and followed with 35 the next.

By 1982, Horner was a National League All-Star, and the Braves won the NL West division title. But injury problems began to plague him, and his career started to decelerate.

A broken wrist suffered while sliding in August 1983 was his first setback. The next May the same wrist was broken again. By 1985 he had basically recovered. Atlanta shifted him to first base, and he turned in solid performances for two years. Although Horner's achievements didn't match his early-career consistency, he still played regularly.

His most notable one-game accomplishment came on July 6, 1986. He became the 11th man in history to belt four home runs in a game.

Horner and the Braves parted company after the '86 campaign. Bob played in Japan for one year, then returned for his final big league season, at St. Louis, in 1988. He appeared in only 60 games. And then, at age 31, he retired.

Now a resident of the Dallas, Texas, area, where he was involved in the oil and gas business for several years, the 1978 Rookie of the Year recently reflected on his career with MLB.com writer Mark Bowman.

"When it's over," he said, "it seems like it went by so fast. But you see pictures on the wall to prove it wasn't a dream. So I look back on my career and am just thankful that I had the opportunity."

LOU WHITAKER
1978   Detroit Tigers, American League

Personal Data: B. May 12, 1957, at Brooklyn, NY.
Physical Attributes: 5' 11", playing weight 160 lbs. Bats left, throws right.
Rookie Year, 1978:   Primary position second base.
Total Career, 19 years: Tigers 1977–95.

	BA	G	H	2B	3B	HR	RBI
1978	.285	139	138	12	7	3	58
Lifetime	.276	2,390	2,369	420	65	244	1,084

When "Sweet Lou" Whitaker earned Rookie of the Year honors for his 1978 achievements, hardly anyone figured him for the durable spark plug he was destined to be. Yes, he clearly earned the rookie trophy. But it was during the ensuing two decades that his enormous value to the Detroit Tigers would be taken for granted.

Teaming with shortstop Alan Trammell, the current Detroit manager, to form the longest-running double-play duo in history, Whitaker was a fixture in the Tigers' lineup for 19 years.

A .300 hitter once, the consistent Whitaker seldom strayed far from the .285 average he posted during his impressive freshman season. Usually a leadoff hitter, he became Detroit's first left-handed batsman to deliver 200 hits (206 in 1983) since Hall of Famer Charlie Gehringer 46 years earlier. Ironically, Gehringer was also a second baseman who played *his* entire 19-year career with Detroit.

Five times over those nearly two full decades Lou was selected to the American League All-Star squad. He hit a virtual cycle. In nine All-Star at bats he had four hits—a single, a double, a two-run triple, and a two-run homer.

He distinguished himself in another spotlight, the 1984 World Series, in which Detroit dispatched San Diego in five games. Lou hit .278, scored six runs, and fielded seamlessly with 15 putouts and 18 assists.

Whitaker was a three-time Gold Glove winner. But he never led the American League in any batting category, a factor that's likely to deny him serious Hall of Fame consideration. However, he is surely an honored member of Detroit's slate of dignitaries for ranking eighth or better in no fewer than nine offensive listings. He's third in Tiger games played (2,390) and fourth behind only Ty Cobb, Gehringer, and Al Kaline in runs scored. Lou's 420 doubles are fifth best in Tigers history.

When he retired after the 1995 season, Whitaker was only the third second baseman of all time to register 2,000 hits, 1,000 runs, 1,000 walks, and 200 home runs. The others in that distinctive trio are Rogers Hornsby and Joe Morgan.

Most of Lou's 244 home runs were slugged during the second half of his career. His batting averages generally finished in the .270 range most of those years, but his run production increased significantly. In 1989, his 12th full season, Whitaker posted career highs in homers (28) and runs batted in (85). He was 32 then.

Remembered now primarily for his partnership in baseball's longest-running double-play combination, Lou Whitaker takes equal pride in his myriad individual accomplishments during those 19 seasons with the Detroit Tigers.

ALFREDO GRIFFIN
1979   Toronto Blue Jays, American League cowinner

Personal Data: B. October 6, 1957, at Santo Domingo, Dominican Republic.
Physical Attributes: 5' 11", playing weight 160 lbs. Bats both, throws right.
Rookie Year, 1979:   Primary position shortstop. 21 stolen bases.
Total Career, 18 years: Indians 1976–78; Blue Jays '79–84; A's '85–87; Dodgers '88–91; Blue Jays '92–93.

	BA	G	H	2B	3B	HR	RBI
1979	.287	153	179	22	10	2	31
Lifetime	.249	1,962	1,688	245	78	24	527

If it weren't for a diligent batting coach and a compassionate teammate, Alfredo Griffin would not have been Rookie of the Year. In fact, he'd probably be merely a dusty footnote in old baseball archives.

Instead, he played 18 years in the major leagues and appeared in three World Series as a player and another as an Anaheim coach, a post he currently holds.

Griffin, who was traded to Toronto by Cleveland, where he had a 31-game trial over three seasons, recalls his good fortune of long ago:

> It was 1979. I was hitting about .170 after the first month. My confidence was shot. Our hitting coach, [Hall of Famer] Bobby Doerr, said, "I'll help you, but you're about down to your last chance to stay in the majors." So before our game in Texas that night, he worked with me on choking up on the bat, and relaxing a bit. Only trouble was, I did not speak English very well then. Or understand it. So he drew some pictures, and asked Rico Carty—one of our veteran Blue Jay players—to help out. Al Oliver, of the Rangers, was also with us. All three of them were very encouraging. I went 2-for-4 that game and all of a sudden I had a 21-game hitting streak. I really appreciated their help. They not only improved my batting; they also built up my confidence.

At season's end Alfredo deadlocked with Minnesota's John Castino for AL rookie honors. Castino suffered severe back problems a few years later. "We congratulated each other that next spring," said Griffin, "but the last time I saw John he was in a wheelchair. Sad."

The rookie award lifted his confidence further. So did the Jays' front office, which gave him a loan to purchase a home for his mother.

> I was so happy for all the help—from the team, and from Rico, Oliver, and Bobby Doerr—that I came back the next season ready to put even more effort into my game. I tried to copy the veterans who set a good example. Coaching now, I try to have patience with our young players, because I know from memory what they're going through.

Even though he never quite matched his first season's .287, and despite recurring hand injuries, Alfredo's steady defensive work and his base-path speed (nearly 200 stolen bases and, in 1980, a switch-hitter record of 15 triples) were key factors in his big league longevity. After a few years out of baseball and two seasons coaching in Toronto, Griffin was invited by his former Dodger teammate Mike Scioscia to be an Angels coach. He cheerfully accepted.

Griffin, his wife Noris, and their two daughters have homes in the Dominican Republic, his birthplace, and in Miami. Alfredo's trophy cases bear proud testimony to his World Series participation at Toronto (2), Los Angeles, and Anaheim.

RICK SUTCLIFFE
1979   Los Angeles Dodgers, National League

Personal Data: B. June 21, 1956, at Independence, MO.
Physical Attributes: 6' 7", playing weight 215 lbs. Throws right, bats left.
Rookie Year, 1979:   Primary position pitcher. Batted .247 with one home run.
Total Career, 18 years: Dodgers 1976, '78–81; Indians '82–84; Cubs '84–91; Orioles '92–93; Cardinals '94.

	Record	ERA	G	GS	SO	IP
1979	17–10	3.46	39	30	117	242
Lifetime	171–139	4.08	457	392	1,679	2,697⅔

Right-hander Rick Sutcliffe has a significant amount of Numbers One surrounding his name. Starting right out of the chute with the 1979 National League Rookie of the Year citation.

Four Los Angeles Dodgers pitchers have won the award. Sutcliffe was the first, followed immediately by Steve Howe and Fernando Valenzuela and eventually by Hideo Nomo. (Dodger hurlers Don Newcombe and Joe Black also were Rookies of the Year, but the team was still operating in Brooklyn then.)

Eventually Sutcliffe would leave Los Angeles and carry the Main Man tag with him to other cities, for he and the Dodgers were soon ready to divorce. Following his excellent 1979 debut with a 17–10 record, it appeared Rick was victimized by the dreaded sophomore jinx. He produced a 5–11 record over the next two years, with high earned run averages. The Dodgers were not happy with his performance. He was dissatisfied with bullpen assignments. Sutcliffe was dealt to Cleveland.

He turned in a 35–25 Indians record in two and a third seasons. In his first Cleveland summer, 1982, he was Number One in AL earned run average—2.96. But little more than a year later Rick would be working elsewhere.

Having compiled a 4–5 Cleveland log in early 1984, Sutcliffe was traded to the Chicago Cubs. His effectiveness suddenly returned. Within four months he won the NL Cy Young Award for his brilliant 16–1 record at Chicago. Combining his Cleveland and Chicago victories, Rick won 20 for the only time in his career. He is the only Cy Young winner to have divided the season by participating in both leagues.

Rick's 16 consecutive wins over two seasons—his 14 in a row in '84 and two more the next year—represent the Cubs' all-time Number One figures. Sutcliffe was greatly responsible for Chicago's advancement to the 1984 NLCS, the Cubs' first postseason games since 1945. He pitched Chicago to victory in Game One, hitting a home run along the way. San Diego, however, won the five-game series.

Sutcliffe still had more Numbers One for his résumé. His 18 Chicago wins in 1987 were tops in the league. As his solid 18-year career entered its home stretch, his 36 games started for Baltimore in 1992 was an American

League–leading number. Rick spent one more year in Baltimore, then a finale with the Cardinals. He was a respectable 16–14 over those final seasons.

An articulate, gregarious man, Sutcliffe went into baseball announcing shortly after leaving the playing field. He is now one of the regular San Diego Padres broadcasters, and is also seen and heard nationally on selected ESPN telecasts.

STEVE HOWE
1980   Los Angeles Dodgers, National League

Personal Data: B. March 10, 1958, at Pontiac, MI.
Physical Attributes: 6′ 1″, playing weight 180 lbs. Throws left, bats left.
Rookie Year, 1980:   Primary position pitcher. 17 saves.
Total Career, 12 years: Dodgers 1980–83, '85; Twins '85; Rangers '87; Yankees '91–96.

	Record	ERA	G	GS	SO	IP
1980	7–9	2.66	59	0	39	84²/₃
Lifetime	47–41	3.03	497	0	328	606

His early baseball career showed exceptional potential. And for a while the 1980 National League Rookie of the Year lived up to that great promise.

Unlike most pitchers, Steve Howe would improve his earned run average three straight years after his impressive 2.65 rookie ERA. Brilliant marks of 2.50, 2.08, and 1.44 followed immediately. The southpaw reliever, who was never assigned to start any of his 497 big league games, was a World Series star in just his second season. He appeared in three games, winning one of them, as Los Angeles came from behind to defeat the 1981 Yankees, four games to two.

Sadly for Howe, his personal and professional lives began a tailspin before a fifth major league season got under way. In May of 1983, his fourth year with the Dodgers, Howe had checked into a rehabilitation center for cocaine addiction treatment. The therapy was unsuccessful.

Three months later the 25-year-old missed a team flight, refused to take a urinalysis test, and was suspended. Over the next dozen years Steve Howe was furloughed a total of seven times. After a second 1983 incident, baseball Commissioner Bowie Kuhn suspended him for the entire 1984 season.

Those days were among baseball's darkest times. Several other players were suspended for failing drug tests. Substance abuse, reflecting large pockets of society, became a widespread problem in all sports. Steve Howe was probably baseball's most prominent personification of addictiveness.

He was permitted to reenter the game in 1985. After 19 appearances with Los Angeles he was sent to Minnesota. His earned run average ballooned there. The Twins released him. Howe was out of organized baseball for all of 1986. He played briefly for independent teams, had a short stay in the Mexican League, then signed with Texas, where he turned in respectable performances in 1987.

Over the next three years, however, drug dependency continued to plague Howe. Baseball issued a lifetime ban. It was soon overthrown, though, by a court arbitrator. The Yankees took him on. His numbers at New York were solid: ERAs well under three. But after a 6.35 earned run average over 17 games in 1996, he was released. For the final time. Two days later airport police arrested him for carrying a concealed gun. He was sentenced to three years probation and assigned 150 hours of community service.

When Steve Howe, who entered baseball with such great promise in 1980, volunteered to coach his daughter's school softball team in 1999, he was turned down by county authorities.

DAVE RIGHETTI
1980   New York Yankees, American League

Personal Data: B. November 28, 1958, at San Jose, CA.
Physical Attributes: 6′ 4″, playing weight 195 lbs. Throws left, bats left.
Rookie Year, 1981:   Primary position pitcher. League-leading 2.06 ERA. Won the two divisional playoff games and the one ALCS game he started.
Total Career, 16 years: Yankees 1979, '81–90; Giants '91–93; A's '94; Blue Jays '94; White Sox '95.

	Record	ERA	G	GS	SO	IP
1981	8–4	2.06	15	15	89	105⅓
Lifetime	82–79	3.46	718	89	1,112	1,403⅔

Until Mariano Rivera eventually overtook him in 2004, Dave Righetti had ranked as the New York Yankees' all-time leader in games pitched.

Righetti's first of 522 mound appearances for the Yanks came early in 1981, his Rookie of the Year season, when he was purely a starting pitcher. In his 15 games during that strike-shortened summer, the tall southpaw posted an 8–4 won-lost record and registered a league-leading 2.06 ERA. An 11–10 record followed in 1982, and a no-hitter—New York's first since Don Larsen's 1956 World Series masterpiece—highlighted Dave's 14–8 1983 season. By then he'd started 76 major league games.

During Righetti's remaining 639 games over 12 seasons, he started only 17 times. He recalls:

The Yanks needed a stopper after Goose Gossage left in 1984. I volunteered. Back then most relievers had been starters at one time or another anyway. I was apprehensive, though, because as a starter I'd led the American League in walks the year before.

My biggest concern was the transition. Starters have a different mind-set. They gear up for every fifth day. Relievers must have the mentality of a position player— be like a regular. I had to relearn how to prepare. Fortunately, the transition came smoothly.

Indeed it did. Dave saved 251 games for the Yankees (through 1990) and San Francisco ('91–93). His 46 saves, then a record, led the AL in 1986. The previous year his 12 victories were a league best for relievers. When Dave signed as a free agent with San Francisco in 1991, he'd returned home. He was born and raised down the road in San Jose.

> Right after my rookie year, the Yankees sent me to Columbus to iron out some control problems while they dealt with some roster adjustment technicalities. For the first time, I thought about the sophomore jinx. My old friend Joe Charboneau was 1980 Rookie of the Year. He got sent out the next year, and never really made a comeback. Would that happen to me? Fortunately, no. The next award-winning rookie put jinx talk to rest for a long time. Fella named Cal Ripken.

Dave chuckles when remembering his rookie award.

> There weren't special ceremonies then. In fact I had a phone call telling me I won, then I read about it in the paper. No testimonials. Nothing like that. Although, come to think of it, I participated in a spaghetti commercial in New York. Must have been something about my Italian heritage . . . and the rhyming!

Righetti later appeared in two All-Star games and pitched in the 1981 World Series. After his active career ended, he joined the Giants as a minor league pitching instructor. Since 2000, Dave's been a Giants coach.

He's also active in his community, having been involved with the Leukemia Society, a school for the deaf, and various cerebral palsy organizations.

Dave and his wife, Kandice, are parents of three teenagers—triplets Nicolette, Natalee, and Wesley. The Righettis live in Los Altos, California.

FERNANDO VALENZUELA
1981   Los Angeles Dodgers, National League

Personal Data: B. November 1, 1960, at Navajoa, Mexico.
Physical Attributes: 5′ 11″, playing weight 180 lbs. Throws left, bats left.
Rookie Year, 1981:   Primary position pitcher. Led league in starts, strikeouts, and innings pitched in strike-shortened season.
Total Career, 17 years: Dodgers 1980–90; Angels '91; Orioles '93; Phillies '94; Padres '95–97; Cardinals '97.

	Record	ERA	G	GS	SO	IP
1981	13–7	2.48	25	25	180	192⅓
Lifetime	173–153	3.54	453	424	2,074	2,930

"Fernandomania" captured the enthusiastic attention of baseball fans in two nations when a chubby, 20-year-old southpaw cut a broad, imposing swath through the tangles of the National League's 1981 season.

Fernando Valenzuela, Los Angeles Dodgers, 1981
Sensational freshman season was responsible for "Fernandomania" craze. Cy Young award winner in rookie year led Dodgers to '81 World Series title.
(Courtesy of Los Angeles Dodgers)

From day one, literally, Fernando Valenzuela made positive headlines as he set sail toward an uncontested Rookie of the Year Award. On opening day the relative unknown was a surprise starter for Los Angeles, substituting for Jerry Reuss, who suffered a leg injury the day before. Fernando pitched a five-hit shutout. It was the first of his myriad heroics that sparked the Dodgers to the strike-shortened '81 season's World Championship. And only the third of Valenzuela's 141 Dodger wins (he was previously 2–0 in a September 1980 call-up) over his 10-year Los Angeles tenure.

Fernando's sensational 1981 featured a 13–7 regular-season record with league-leading marks in games started (25), complete games (11), innings pitched (192), strikeouts (180), and shutouts (9). No wonder he was the All-Star Game starter, and no surprise that he registered a 3–1 postseason record featuring a World Series shutout of the New York Yankees.

As a capper on his 1981 honors, Valenzuela is the only man to win both the Rookie of the Year and Cy Young awards in the same season.

His rookie performance foreshadowed a magnificent career in which he completed nearly 27 percent of the 424 games he started. Valenzuela was a double-digit winner nine times, with a high of 21 victories in 1986. He was a six-time All-Star, and in the 1984 All-Star Game, Fernando, then 23, combined with 19-year-old Dwight Gooden to strike out six consecutive American Leaguers. Before his Dodger days ended, Valenzuela notched a 1990 no-hitter, 6–0 versus St. Louis.

Frequently, as we've seen, several pitchers with Rookie of the Year trophies eventually suffer sore arms. Valenzuela is among them. The Dodgers released him. From 1991 through 1997, mostly as a spot starter, he pitched for five more major league teams and with summer league clubs in his native Mexico. He told *Sports Illustrated* upon his 1997 release by St. Louis, his last big league club, "I didn't want to announce my retirement. I wanted to keep pitching at whatever level I could."

In the 2000s he no longer suits up. Instead he closely follows the progress of Fernando, Jr., a hard-hitting first baseman whom San Diego signed in the 2003 major league draft. Fernando, Sr., is also associated with his wife Linda's real estate business. And he's back where his celebrity began . . . with the Dodgers . . . as a Spanish-language radio analyst and one of the team's community relations representatives.

STEVE SAX

1982   Los Angeles Dodgers, National League

Personal Data: B. January 29, 1969, at Sacramento, CA.
Physical Attributes: 5′ 11″, playing weight 185 lbs. Bats right, throws right.
Rookie Year, 1982:   Primary position second base. 49 stolen bases.
Total Career, 14 years: Dodgers 1981–88; Yankees '89–91; White Sox '92–93; A's '94.

	BA	G	H	2B	3B	HR	RBI
1982	.282	150	180	23	7	4	47
Lifetime	.281	1,769	1,949	278	47	54	550

Admit it. Upon hearing the name Steve Sax you immediately think of the Dodger second baseman whose throws couldn't hit the "broad side of a barn door." He's bunched with "Wrong Way" Riegels, Bill Buckner, Mickey Owen, and Steve Blass in your catalog of sports goats. Whether they deserve to be so categorized or not.

Yes, Sax was indeed tormented with a lengthy spell of wildness. After he'd misfired a few times back in 1983, he soon developed an obsession about his errant throwing. And so the problem worsened. Happily he eventually overcame it en route to a solid 14-year career. Still, it's that unfortunate stretch of misdirected throws that comes to mind when we recall Steve Sax.

Often overlooked is his 1982 Rookie of the Year season. His great promise prompted the Dodgers to break up their long-standing infield of Steve Garvey, Davey Lopes, Bill Russell, and Ron Cey. To make room for Sax, second baseman Lopes was the first to go.

Steve fit in immediately. He set a team rookie record of 49 stolen bases and led LA with 180 hits and 88 runs. He made the first of three National League All-Star teams. His .282 batting average typified his entire career (.281 lifetime). He surpassed .300 three times. His 290 stolen bases are fifth best in all-time Dodger annals.

Steve's most outstanding year was 1986 when he hit .332. That's not all. He led Los Angeles in hits (210), doubles (43), triples (4), total bases (279), and runs (91), and had a 25-game hitting streak that still ranks eighth in Brooklyn/Los Angeles franchise history. Oh, by then his defensive marksmanship was no longer a big issue. Sax committed only 16 errors. He bettered his 1986 fielding average of .980 four more times.

After eight years with the Dodgers, Sax joined the 1989 Yankees as a free agent. He hit over .300 twice in three seasons at New York. When his playing days ended after two seasons with the White Sox and a finale at Oakland, Steve Sax had exemplified consistent productivity. Rarely missing a game, he registered more than 600 at bats eight times. He fell short of a 2,000-hit total by only 51. His stolen bases averaged more than 30 per season. And, after all accounts were closed, he committed only about 15 errors, on average, per year.

A few errant throws in early years are but a minor glitch in Steve Sax's otherwise excellent, productive career. Since his baseball days Steve has earned a karate black belt, and he now works as a financial adviser.

RON KITTLE
1983   Chicago White Sox, American League

Personal Data: B. January 5, 1958, at Gary, IN.
Physical Attributes: 6′ 4″, playing weight 200 lbs. Bats right, throws right.
Rookie Year, 1983:   Primary position outfield. Led league in home runs per times at bat in first two full seasons.
Total Career, 10 years: White Sox 1982–86; Yankees '86–87; Indians '88; White Sox '89–90; Orioles '90; White Sox '91.

	BA	G	H	2B	3B	HR	RBI
1983	.254	145	132	19	3	35	100
Lifetime	.239	843	648	100	3	176	460

Only two Rookie of the Year position players—Ron Hansen and Curt Blefary—completed their careers with lower lifetime batting averages than did big Ron Kittle. But when the lanky outfielder did put his bat on the ball, the result was often a tape-measure home run. Especially during his exciting first season.

A native of Gary, Indiana, which wasn't far from old Comiskey Park, Kittle earned instant popularity from Chicago White Sox fans in that 1983 rookie season. More than one of every four of Ron's hits was a home run. Each, it seemed, was longer than the last one. Better yet, Kittle's long-distance blasts helped the Sox advance to their first postseason since they won the 1959 American League pennant. (Chicago was ultimately defeated by Baltimore in the '83 League

Championship Series.) His early-season exploits earned him a place in the All-Star Game, which happened to be played at Comiskey. To the delight of home-town fans Ron singled and scored a run.

Even though Kittle hit just .254, his 35 home runs and 100 runs batted in clearly merited his Rookie of the Year selection.

Overall, though, concern about his long-term future as a major lea-guer surfaced. The only category in which he led the league that first year was . . . strikeouts. A 150 total. Ron was unable to reduce that number much in his sophomore year when his average dipped to .215. He fanned 137 times. But he continued to deliver the long ball. He stroked 32 homers.

Following those first two seasons, Kittle's playing time was reduced. He became virtually a platoon player. Nevertheless, facing mostly southpaw pitching, he homered in a good percentage of his plate appearances.

An amiable, well-liked teammate, Ron was traded frequently. Each new employer hoped he would regain his rookie year productivity. At one stop, a return to the Sox in 1989, he hit the ball more frequently and, for the only time in his career, Ron surpassed .300. In 51 games he averaged .302. But strikeouts—nearly one per game—continued to haunt him.

By 1990, Ron's career was nearly finished. He went from Chicago to Baltimore that year, then returned to "new" Comiskey Park in '91 for a final shot. It lasted only 17 games and produced but two home runs.

Now, more than a decade after his last game, Ron Kittle and his family continue to reside in his native Indiana. He still closely follows the game that brought him national prominence.

DARRYL STRAWBERRY
1983   New York Mets, National League

Personal Data: B. May 12, 1962, at Los Angeles, CA.
Physical Attributes: 6′ 6″, playing weight 190 lbs. Bats left, throws left.
Rookie Year, 1983:   Primary position outfield. 27 stolen bases in 122 games.
Total Career, 17 years: Mets 1983–90; Dodgers '91–93; Giants '94; Yankees '95–99.

	BA	G	H	2B	3B	HR	RBI
1983	.257	122	108	15	7	26	74
Lifetime	.259	1,583	1,401	256	38	335	1,000

As you'd expect, Rookies of the Year leave the starting gate in winning style. After all, as the award's name implies, they performed very well in their first big league seasons. Some, however, tail off quickly and eventually achieve only "journeyman" status. Others are soon tabbed future Hall of Fame candidates.

New York Met Darryl Strawberry was among the latter.

His power hitting immediately generated headlines. Straw poled 26 home runs en route to 1983 National League Rookie of the Year honors. He duplicated that total the next year, and drove home 97 runs. He was on a roll.

Darryl's 39 home runs in 1988 led the National League. When his Shea Stadium tenure ended in 1990, he had established several Mets slugging standards that still exist: runs scored—662 . . . home runs—252 . . . RBI—733 . . . extra-base hits—469. He remains second to Ed Kranepool in Mets career total bases. The speedy Straw Man was a base thief too, recording 191 steals during his eight Mets seasons.

But soon Strawberry's ticket to Cooperstown would be canceled. Primarily because of self-inflicted derailments.

In November 1990 he signed a five-year pact with Los Angeles, and he registered typical Strawberry-like numbers his first year there. So far, so good. Then serious troubles surfaced, beginning with 1992 injuries limiting him to 43 games. Instead of his accustomed high-ranking appearances on baseball statistics lists, Straw 's name soon became alarmingly associated with medical charts and police reports.

In 1994, after the Dodgers released him, Strawberry was indicted for failing to report autograph income. Earlier that year he entered the Betty Ford Clinic for substance abuse treatment. But upon his discharge, he failed to remain drug free. The Giants, for whom he played briefly after Los Angeles dismissed him, dropped him.

Continuous turmoil, plus one last chance in the baseball spotlight, have characterized Darryl's past 10 years. He was arrested four times and imprisoned or sentenced to house arrest at least three times on drug possession and aftercare-failure charges. Baseball officials suspended him three times. He was imprisoned for parole violations.

During this upheaval Strawberry had successful colon cancer surgery in 1998. Yet between and betwixt Strawberry's travails, Yankee owner George Steinbrenner gave him additional chances.

Darryl delivered important late-season and postseason long balls for the Yankees in 1996 and 1999. But the 1983 NL Rookie of the Year was unable to overcome cocaine addiction. And when more suspensions and arrests occurred in the early 2000s, it was clear that Darryl Strawberry's Hall of Fame hopes had long since been destroyed. Still, the Yankees owner hasn't forsaken him. Prior to the 2004 season Steinbrenner employed Straw again—this time as a player development instructor. But he resigned soon after, saying church work required more of his time.

ALVIN DAVIS
1984   Seattle Mariners, American League

Personal Data: B. September 9, 1960, at Riverside, CA.
Physical Attributes: 6′ 1″, playing weight 190 lbs. Bats left, throws right.
Rookie Year, 1984:   Primary position first base.
Total Career, 9 years: Mariners 1984–91; Angels '92.

	BA	G	H	2B	3B	HR	RBI
1984	.284	152	161	34	3	27	116
Lifetime	.280	1,206	1,189	220	10	160	683

From the very first day he appeared in an official major league game, to his final at bat nine seasons later, Alvin Davis was the personification of productive consistency.

The left-hand-hitting Seattle first baseman, who still holds one big league standard and shares another, hit a home run in each of his first two games—to tie an American League record. Fast-forward to October. Alvin's .284 average, 27 home runs, and 116 RBI in 152 games clearly merited Rookie of the Year honors.

As the statistics show, his lifetime average was .280. And that's where that positive consistency is reflected. He rarely varied more than a dozen or so points from his rookie season's .284. Alvin exceeded .300 only once—.305 in 1989—and he never dropped below .271 until his final two seasons.

After his average dropped to .221 and he had just 12 homers in 1991, the Mariners sent Davis to the California Angels. He played in only 40 games, batted .250, and called it a career.

Before he left, though, Alvin etched his named into Mariners' archives. Fourteen years removed from the Seattle dugout, he still ranked fourth all-time in several key Mariners categories: games played—1,166, at bats—4,136, hits—1,163, doubles—212, total bases—1,875, and runs batted in—667. He's in good company. The three players above him are named Edgar Martinez, Ken Griffey, Jr., and Jay Buhner.

Davis owns five Seattle rookie records, including home runs and RBI. Additionally, he and Ichiro Suzuki each hit 34 doubles in their initial seasons.

The two major league records still attached to his name are most intentional walks in a rookie season (16) and, in a tie with others, most putouts in a nine-inning game (22).

Alvin was only 32 when his baseball career concluded. Since then he has become a proud inductee of the Seattle Mariners Hall of Fame.

Asked about his best day, Alvin gladly answers—with nary a word about baseball. "The biggest day of my life was when I was a 12-year-old kid and, through the ministry of my church, I began to realize I needed God." Today, from his Riverside, California, base, Alvin Davis is associated with Pro Athletes Outreach, which is headquartered in Wisconsin.

"I no longer worry about the future," he says. "I know everything will turn out all right because God has a great track record."

DWIGHT GOODEN
1984   New York Mets, National League

Personal Data: B. November 16, 1964, at Tampa, FL.
Physical Attributes: 6′ 3″, playing weight 210 lbs. Throws right, bats right.
Rookie Year, 1984:   Primary position pitcher. League-leading 276 strikeouts.
Total Career, 16 years: Mets 1984–94; Yankees '96–97; Indians '98–99; Astros 2000; Devil Rays '00; Yankees '00.

	Record	ERA	G	GS	SO	IP
1984	17–9	2.60	31	31	276	218
Lifetime	194–112	3.51	430	410	2,293	2,800²/3

Within the tiny fraternity of rookie pitchers who enjoyed season-long headlines and nationwide adulation, 19-year-old Dwight Gooden ranks among its foremost members. Advancing to the New York Mets directly from a single minor league season in Class A, the tall right-hander set a new strikeout record for rookies (276), posted a 17–6 won-lost mark, and fashioned a brilliant 2.60 earned run average. Clearly, a Rookie of the Year performance.

Then later he teamed up with 1981 Rookie of the Year Fernando Valenzuela to fan six successive batters in the '84 All-Star Game.

Gooden's amazing initial season was merely an appetizer. His sophomore year, when he won the Cy Young trophy at age 20, featured these stratospheric league-leading highlights:

Twenty-four victories (only four losses)... a 1.53 ERA... 16 complete games... 276²/3 innings pitched... 268 strikeouts. He won the mythical Pitcher's Triple Crown (wins, ERA, strikeouts), an NL accomplishment not matched until Randy Johnson achieved a similar feat in 2002. For good measure Gooden delivered 21 hits and a .226 batting average.

After Dwight's sensational start, some close observers felt he was aiming toward... not 300 victories, but shooting for 400. After six seasons, and still only 25, he had already posted 119 wins. Unforeseen detours, however, would spoil his hopes. Pitching off and on for another full decade Gooden won only 75 more times, finishing with 194 victories. In 10 postseason appearances, from 1986 through 2000, he was winless.

Nicknamed Doctor K, to honor his early-career strikeouts, then simply called Doc, the young Gooden fell victim to illegal drugs. Addiction led to several of his eight trips to the disabled list. Another DL visit, in 1989, resulted from a sore shoulder. Later, in 1994 and for the entire 1995 season, Gooden was suspended from baseball by the Office of the Commissioner for repeated violations of the drug aftercare program.

Ever the competitor, Gooden fought hard to resume his baseball career. The Yankees signed him for 1996. In May he pitched a no-hitter, 2–0 over Seattle. Doc was 11–7 in '96, his last double-digit victory season.

A hernia problem limited him to 20 games the following year. After that he bounced from one ailment to another, and from one minor league rehab assignment to another. He pitched briefly for Cleveland, Houston, Tampa Bay, and, again, the Yankees, but won only 17 games and registered comparatively high earned run averages over his final three seasons.

Dwight Gooden, New York Mets, 1984
At age 19 his 276 K's set an all-time rookie record. Then, before reaching 21 in late 1985, "Doc" had led the NL in wins, in ERA, and twice in strikeouts.
(Courtesy of New York Mets)

Since his retirement from active duty, the 1984 Rookie of the Year—who was legitimately dubbed a phenom—has been employed by Yankee owner George Steinbrenner in several advisory and instructional capacities . . . most recently in his Tampa hometown as pitching coach of New York's rookie team in the Gulf Coast League.

VINCE COLEMAN
1985   St. Louis Cardinals, National League

Personal Data: B. September 22, 1961, at Jacksonville, FL.
Physical Attributes: 6′ 0″, playing weight 170 lbs. Bats both, throws right.
Rookie Year, 1985:   Primary position outfield. 110 stolen bases led league in first of six straight seasons.
Total Career, 13 years: Cardinals 1985–90; Mets '91–93; Royals '94–95; Mariners '95; Reds '96; Tigers '97.

	BA	G	H	2B	3B	HR	RBI
1985	.267	151	170	20	10	1	40
Lifetime	.264	1,371	1,425	176	89	28	346

Not surprisingly, the headlines Vince Coleman made as a minor leaguer simply foretold the excitement he would bring to St. Louis and the entire National League in his remarkable Rookie of the Year season of 1985.

Unfortunately, he was also responsible for too many antics outside the white lines. Some of them were harmful to others. Most of them led to his own downfall.

But before his off-diamond escapades occurred, Coleman was a big attraction. During the South Atlantic League's 1983 season, for example, he stole 145 bases even though he was disabled for a month with a broken hand. His accomplishment represented a professional baseball record. It was the second time he had swiped more than 100 bases.

He was equally dazzling in the major leagues. As a unanimous choice for Rookie of the Year, Coleman stole 110 bases, a rookie record. That was just the beginning. Vince would become the first player in big league history to steal 100 bases in each of his first three seasons. In his fifth year he set another record: 50 consecutive successful steals. Back in 1987 he produced oohs and aahs by stealing second and third . . . in the same inning . . . 13 times. When Coleman's sixth season ended, he had led the NL in stolen bases all six years.

By then, though, he was the unofficial leader in accidents and poor judgment. His first national brush with negativity came before Game One of the 1985 World Series. While stretching near the infield, Vince was injured by the automated tarpaulin at Busch Stadium. His leg was trapped for several seconds. He missed the Series.

Rib and hamstring injuries afflicted him frequently after he'd been traded to the Mets in 1991. His New York tenure ended late in '93 following several major incidents. He carelessly swung a golf club in the locker room, injuring pitcher Dwight Gooden. He engaged in an on-field shouting match with manager Jeff Torborg. He was charged with reckless endangerment—and suspended by the team—for setting off a firecracker that injured a woman and two children in the Dodger Stadium parking lot.

Short stints at Kansas City, Seattle, Cincinnati, and Detroit followed. But baseball days were clearly ebbing for this one-time Rookie of the Year. His age, 36, was a factor. Mostly, though, it was his inability to reach base with frequency that signaled an end to a career whose primary value had been the threat and execution of the stolen base. But even though his playing days ended, Vince was not forgotten. He has been a Chicago Cubs employee over the past few seasons—as a baserunning mentor at both the major and minor league levels.

TODD WORRELL
1986   St. Louis Cardinals, National League

Personal Data: B. September 28, 1959, at Arcadia, CA.
Physical Attributes: 6' 5", playing weight 215 lbs. Throws right, bats right.
Rookie Year, 1986:   Primary position pitcher. Led league in saves with 36.
Total Career, 11 years: Cardinals 1985–89, '92; Dodgers '93–97.

	Record	ERA	G	GS	SO	IP
1986	9–10	2.08	74	0	73	103⅔
Lifetime	50–52	3.09	617	0	628	693⅔

A World Series hero one year. Rookie of the Year the next!

No, that's not a misprint even though it seems illogical. Credit Todd Worrell, then with the St. Louis Cardinals, with those two exceptional feats.

When the big right-hander was elevated from the minors in late 1985, his brilliant relief pitching helped St. Louis win the National League East and advance to the World Series. Todd posted three wins and saved five other Cardinals victories from late August through September. And if that wasn't enough from a newcomer, Worrell then tied a World Series record by striking out six straight Royals in Game Five.

His major contribution to the Cardinals' regular season cause was accomplished in only 21 2/3 innings over just 17 games—few enough games and innings to keep him eligible for Rookie status in the future.

The future, it seems, followed immediately. Todd was expected to produce again. And quickly. He did. In addition to posting nine 1986 wins, all in relief, Worrell saved 36 games—a league-leading figure and a rookie saves record at the time.

Todd continued to impress. Over six St. Louis seasons—he sat out '90 and '91 with arm injuries—his earned run average never exceeded 3.00. He totaled 129 saves. And then he departed, as a free agent, for Los Angeles, where he virtually duplicated his St. Louis performances.

During his five Dodger years, before arm ailments ended his major league career, Todd saved 127 games to rank number two all-time among Dodger relievers. His won-lost log at St. Louis had been 33–33; he went 17–19 for LA. He was the Dodgers' saves leader four years in a row and represented them in the 1995 and '96 All-Star games. Worrell's 44 saves in 1996 were an all-time best Dodger single-season standard until Eric Gagne surpassed it in 2002.

Whether Todd's statistics will continue to be his *family's* all-time best is another matter. Brother Tim, another right-hander also over 6' 4", has been a big league reliever for more than a decade, working for eight teams. As a Giants reliever in 2002, Tim recorded a pair of NLCS wins and a World Series victory.

Older brother Todd (by eight years) claims he taught Tim everything he knows.

CHRIS SABO
1988   Cincinnati Reds, National League

Personal Data: B. January 19, 1962, at Detroit, MI.
Physical Attributes: 5′ 11″, playing weight 185 lbs. Bats right, throws right.
Rookie Year, 1988:   Primary position third base. 46 stolen bases.
Total Career, 9 years: Reds 1988–93; Orioles '94; White Sox '95; Cardinals '95; Reds '96.

	BA	G	H	2B	3B	HR	RBI
1988	.271	137	146	40	2	11	44
Lifetime	.268	911	898	214	17	116	426

Chris Sabo's comings and goings were, well . . . surprising.

He was already 26 when he brought a minor league journeyman's résumé to Cincinnati's big league camp in the early spring of 1988. Unheralded, the newcomer Sabo would soon be a celebrity. Rookie of the Year.

Several years later, his myriad skills would suddenly disappear.

Veteran Buddy Bell had been slotted as the Reds' 1988 third baseman. When Bell was placed on the disabled list for opening day, Chris Sabo was chosen to substitute. Fill in he did. Big time. During the season's first week he tied a record for third basemen with 11 assists in a nine-inning game. Before the year ended, he led NL third sackers in double plays. He stole a base in the '88 All-Star Game, and swiped 46 bases in the regular season. His .271 batting average included a career-high 40 doubles.

It was a spectacular big league entrance. Especially from a "journeyman" whose realistic expectations had him playing a utility role. When Rookie of the Year balloting was tabulated, Sabo was the honoree. Chicago's Mark Grace was runner-up.

Chris's sophomore year was jinxed by knee injuries that resulted in September surgery and appearances in only 82 games. But he bounced back quickly to produce his best overall seasons in 1990 and '91.

Cincinnati won the 1990 World Series. Sabo displayed long-ball power that season and the next, hitting 25 home runs and then 26. As the Reds swept Oakland in the '90 Series, Chris sparkled by hitting .563, including two homers in Game Three. The next year, 1991, he posted his best batting average, a .301 mark. It was his last fully productive season.

Injuries limited him to 96 games in 1992. He hit 21 homers the following year, but his speed had diminished noticeably, and his strikeouts increased alarmingly. Sabo spent the next three years trying, unsuccessfully, to return to early-career form. He served short stints with Baltimore, Chicago's White Sox, and St. Louis before a 1996 return to Cincinnati for his big league goodbye. It was typically Sabo dramatic, but not very appealing.

On July 29 his bat shattered. Pieces of cork sprayed out. Sabo was suspended for seven games. That season was the last for the feisty, goggle-wearing Rookie of the Year who had helped bring championship-level excitement to Riverfront Stadium just a few seasons earlier.

Eight years after his playing career ended, Chris returned to the Reds' fold in good graces as the organization's newest minor league hitting instructor.

WALT WEISS
1988   Oakland Athletics, American League

Personal Data: B. November 28, 1963, at Tuxedo, NY.
Physical Attributes: 6' 0", playing weight 175 lbs. Bats both, throws right.
Rookie Year, 1988:   Primary position shortstop. Hit .333 with two doubles in four-game ALCS.
Total Career, 14 years: Athletics 1987–92; Marlins '93; Rockies '94–97; Braves '98–2000.

	BA	G	H	2B	3B	HR	RBI
1988	.250	147	113	17	3	3	39
Lifetime	.258	1,495	1,207	182	31	25	386

The late 1980s offered a great opportunity to Oakland Athletics newcomers— a good chance to be Rookie of the Year. Jose Canseco started the trend in 1986. The next year Mark McGwire was the American League's foremost freshman.

Classy shortstop Walter Weiss completed the A's' "trifecta" when he was saluted as 1988 Rookie of the Year.

The young switch-hitter got the attention of Oakland brass during a late 1987 call-up. In just 26 at bats he registered a .462 average, with four doubles, to set the stage for a full-time post in '88.

So impressive was Weiss's promise that, to make room for him in the starting infield, the A's traded veteran shortstop Alfredo Griffin to the Dodgers. Ironically, Griffin had also been a Rookie of the Year when, as a Blue Jay, he deadlocked for the 1979 honor with John Castino.

Obviously Weiss could not maintain his brief 1987 batting pace over a full season. In fact, as an official rookie in '88, he finished at .250 . . . which allowed ample room for improvement. Better figures, however, would not be achieved immediately.

Walt Weiss, Oakland Athletics, 1988
This stylish shortstop was Oakland's third consecutive Rookie of the Year. During Walt's four-club career his teams advanced to the postseason eight times.
(Michael Zagaris, Oakland Athletics)

An injury limited him to 84 games and a .233 average in 1989. He returned in 1990, hitting .265 in 138 games. But after that Weiss was frequently disabled again or on rehab assignments.

"Of the three great rookies we had in Oakland, Walt had those tough breaks early on, missing a lot of games due to injuries," recalls Tony LaRussa, his manager then.

After six seasons his Oakland career was finished. He was dealt to Florida for the Marlins' initial expansion campaign, then went to Colorado where he enjoyed a successful four-year stretch. He exceeded his rookie season's .250 each year in Denver, and hit a career high .282 in 1996.

Atlanta signed Walt off the free-agent list following the 1997 season. He continued to be an injury victim, though, and after he played in more than 100 games only once in three years with the Braves, his career ended.

Known primarily as a defensive specialist, his skill at shortstop enabled Walt, now a Colorado resident, to help lead his teams into eight different postseason appearances—four in Oakland, one with the 1995 Rockies, and three more at Atlanta.

GREGG OLSON
1989   Baltimore Orioles, American League

Personal Data: B. October 11, 1966, at Scribner, NE.
Physical Attributes: 6′ 4″, playing weight 210 lbs. Throws right, bats right.
Rookie Year, 1989:   Primary position pitcher.
Total Career, 14 years: Orioles 1988–93; Braves '94; Indians '95; Royals '95; Tigers '96; Astros '96; Twins '97; Royals '97; Diamondbacks '98–99; Dodgers 2001–02.

	Record	ERA	G	GS	SO	IP
1989	5–2	1.69	64	0	90	85
Lifetime	40–39	3.46	622	0	588	672

After more than a dozen baseball seasons, and a résumé that lists almost as many employers as his years in the business, 1989 American League Rookie of the Year Gregg Olson still holds some impressive pitching records from his first big league stop, Baltimore.

The big right-hander never once started a game in the majors. Over 14 seasons he relieved in all 622 of his outings for nine different teams—one club twice.

Olson's lengthiest one-team tenure coincided directly with his career's best run of success. In his six consecutive seasons with the Orioles several of Olson's achievements continue to rank among the team's most distinguished. They include these:

First in career saves, 160. Fifty-five more than runner-up Tippy
Martinez.

Led team in saves first five full seasons in majors. Most saves by a
rookie, 27.

Most consecutive shutout innings, 41 from August 1989 to May 1990.

Most consecutive scoreless appearances, 29, same period.

Most games finished, 62 in 1991.

A rocketlike fastball and a snappish curve were Olson's trademark pitches.
But in August 1993 the man who had set the AL rookie record of 27 saves in
1989 feared for his baseball future. A severely torn elbow ligament put him on
the shelf.

The Orioles, believing that he was finished, did not re-sign Olson. Atlanta
took a chance, but he was unable to pitch more than 14 2/3 innings. Over the
next three years Cleveland, Kansas City twice, Detroit, Houston, and Minnesota
took him on. But only briefly.

Gregg's persistence seemed finally to have paid off after he joined the expansion Arizona Diamondbacks in 1998. By then 10 years had passed since his
Orioles debut. Now, both his change-up and sinker were effective again. Working in long relief and as a closer, Olson finished '98 with 30 saves. That impressive
1998 season, though, proved to be his last hurrah.

Back spasms and only sporadic effectiveness the next year were discourage-
ments. He seemed to be finished as a big leaguer and did not pitch in 2000. But
that off-season the Dodgers signed him to . . . his final contract. He appeared in
28 games for Los Angeles, all in middle relief, where he was 0–1 with an 8.03
ERA.

Yes, he experienced many disappointments along the way. But Gregg Olson
still maintains a lofty prominence in the Baltimore Orioles archives, especially
his Rookie of the Year exploits.

JEROME WALTON
1989   Chicago Cubs, National League

Personal Data: B. July 8, 1965, at Newman, GA.
Physical Attributes: 6' 1", playing weight 175 lbs. Bats right, throws right.
Rookie Year, 1989:   Primary position outfield. 24 stolen bases.
Total Career, 10 years: Cubs 1989–92; Angels '93; Reds '94–95; Braves '96; Orioles '97; Devil Rays '98.

	BA	G	H	2B	3B	HR	RBI
1989	.293	116	139	23	3	5	46
Lifetime	.269	598	423	77	8	25	132

For the first time in 32 years, teammates ranked one-two in the National League Rookie of the Year voting when Chicago Cub Jerome Walton won out over fellow newcomer Dwight Smith.

The two rookies joined veteran Andre Dawson (a previous Rookie of the Year) to complete a formidable outfield trio. Along with Mark Grace (1B), Ryne Sandberg (2B), and pitchers Rick Sutcliffe and a youngster named Greg Maddux, they led manager Don Zimmer's Cubs to the 1989 NL East title.

With the passage of time, Smith and Walton have become probably the least remembered of those particular Cubs. Those who do recall Walton usually say he's a guy with one of the shortest careers of all Rookies of the Year.

Right. And not exactly right. Yes, decent longevity in terms of years played. A short timer, though, in games played—with six different teams—during 10 big league seasons.

Jerome made national headlines during his debut season when he hit safely in 30 consecutive games. That accomplishment remains a Cubs record. Neither Walton nor Smith was a long-ball hitter. Between them they totaled only 14 home runs in their rookie year. Walton, the flashier of the two, stole 24 bases, hit .293, and committed only three outfield errors to convince writers that he deserved their Rookie of the Year votes. He seemed headed to a solid career.

But early the following season he began to nosedive. The spiral continued for nearly a decade. He never recovered. Hand and wrist injuries cut into his playing time in his sophomore year. Jerome responded medically, but his on-field performance continued to fizzle. His average dropped to .263, .219, then .127. After 370 games in four years the Cubs released Walton.

He traveled to five more teams during the next six summers, appearing in a total of only 228 games over that span. That promising rookie season spark never returned. Zimmer, his manager, suggests a reason.

Jerome did a lot of great things to help us win in '89, but at spring training the next year he wasn't the same guy. Wasn't bouncing around like he did before. I called him in, asked him what's wrong. He said he was disappointed in how the front office treated him financially. I said, "Look, you signed a contract that you agreed to. Now go out there and put two good years back to back and you'll make all the money you'll want." Well, he said, they weren't right with me. He was really down. I hated to see that happen to a young guy, dejection like that hurting a promising career. He just never got untracked after that.

DAVID JUSTICE
1990   Atlanta Braves, National League

Personal Data: B. April 14, 1966, at Cincinnati, OH.
Physical Attributes: 6′ 3″, playing weight 200 lbs. Bats left, throws left.
Rookie Year, 1990:   Primary position first base/outfield.
Total Career, 14 years: Braves 1989–96; Indians '97–2000; Yankees '00–01; A's '02.

	BA	G	H	2B	3B	HR	RBI
1990	.282	127	124	23	2	28	78
Lifetime	.279	1,610	1,571	280	24	305	1,017

When Bobby Cox returned to Atlanta as manager in 1990, he inherited a roster that included a young man who would be that season's National League Rookie of the Year. Cox was delighted.

"David Justice was one of the good guys," he says. "And he always had that smooth swing like Ted Williams."

Justice's 14-year career didn't quite produce Williams-like statistics. But he was always a welcomed teammate. Because every year from 1991 forward (except for 1994's work stoppage) the teams David played for advanced to the postseason. He was annually a major contributor.

David Justice, Atlanta Braves, 1990
He played in the postseason for all four of his major league teams during a 14-year career—the Braves, Indians, Yankees, and Athletics.
(Courtesy of Atlanta National Baseball Club, Inc.
© *2003. All rights reserved.)*

Some highlights: career-best 120 RBI in 1993 at Atlanta . . . career-high .329, with 33 home runs for AL champ Cleveland in 1997 following a trade with Marquis Grissom for Kenny Lofton and Alan Embree . . . a combined .286, 41 homers, and 118 RBI for Cleveland and the Yankees in 2000 . . . five hits, including a three-run triple, and four RBI for Oakland in 2002 AL Division Series versus Minnesota.

David Justice is the all-time record holder for postseason games played. He appeared in 112 of them—for the Braves, Indians, Yankees, and Athletics. Six of his teams proceeded on to the World Series—Atlanta 1991–93, Cleveland 1997, New York 2000–01. Until Yankee Bernie Williams surpassed him in 2003, Justice, with 63, had been the all-time postseason runs-batted-in record holder.

Clearly with pride of accomplishment over a 14-season career, David recently reflected on his Rookie of the Year season:

> The award is special because there's only one chance to win it. Every year new-comers make explosive entries, but only one in each league is honored. I was fortunate to win a close battle with Delino DeShields and Todd Zeile back in 1990. At first I was platooned with Francisco Cabrera at first base. But after the Braves traded Dale Murphy, I played the outfield full-time. For me the award was special because it gave me the satisfaction of having a good first year. Later it was hard to avoid hearing about the sophomore jinx. I guess it caught up with me because I missed over two months on the disabled list. Fortunately I bounced back and was relatively injury free for the next couple of years.

During his widely respected career the Cincinnati native had been married to actress Halle Berry. Retired since 2002 as an active player, David is remarried, resides in the San Diego area, and is a member of the ESPN telecasting unit.

CHUCK KNOBLAUCH
1991   Minnesota Twins, American League

Personal Data: B. July 7, 1968, at Houston, TX.
Physical Attributes: 5′ 9″, playing weight 180 lbs. Bats right, throws right.
Rookie Year, 1991:   Primary position second base. Hit .350 in ALCS, .308 in World Series.
Total Career, 12 years: Twins 1991–97; Yankees '98–2001; Royals '02.

	BA	G	H	2B	3B	HR	RBI
1991	.281	151	159	24	6	1	50
Lifetime	.289	1,632	1,839	322	64	98	615

Exploding from "worst to first," the 1991 Minnesota Twins, featuring Kirby Puckett, Kent Hrbek, Jack Morris, and Scott Erickson, were seven-game World Series victors over Atlanta. Arguably, they might not have reached that pinnacle had it not been for their new second baseman.

Chuck Knoblauch's contributions were considerable. They included a .281 batting average along with 50 RBI and 25 stolen bases en route to his selection as American League Rookie of the Year. But he wasn't finished yet. In October he totaled 15 hits in the ALCS and World Series, hit over .300 in each series, and stole four bases against Atlanta.

Knoblauch's initial season was a preview of a successful 12-year career. Chuck's batting average climbed to .297 his sophomore year. From 1994 through '96 he hit .312, .333, and a career-high .341. With 45 doubles he was on a pace to break the all-time single-season two-base-hit record when the infamous work stoppage ended the '94 season in mid-August.

His speed was another major asset. He sprinted to a league-high 14 triples in 1996; 10 in '97. Chuck's 25 stolen bases tied a team rookie record, and his 62 in '97 were a personal high among his 407 career steals.

But 1997 was Knoblauch's final Minnesota season. His on-field aggressiveness was combined with a feistiness that sometimes irritated teammates. Often he and longtime Twins pilot Tom Kelly differed with each other. Knoblauch was especially disappointed with Minnesota's front office that, in his opinion, failed to snare top-rate personnel because of budgetary limitations. So he campaigned loudly for a trade to a contender. The Twins complied. Chuck became a Yankee in 1998.

Although he hit .292 at New York in 1999 and had totaled 35 home runs his first two years there, he was unable to regain his early Minnesota form. And in 1998 he suddenly began making wild throws after fielding ground balls. Chuck had been a Gold Glove second baseman. Now he'd hesitate before firing to first. The psychological problem would not completely disappear. Eventually the Yankees moved Knoblauch to left field, a position he played reasonably well. But after his 2001 batting dropped to .250, he opted for free agency.

A full-time outfielder by then, Chuck signed on with Kansas City. But the 1991 Rookie of the Year was unable to muster his old-time consistency, and after 300 at bats and a .210 batting average in 2002, the Royals did not re-sign him.

Knoblauch reflects on his career with pride. "I appreciate it when people comment on our hustle and spirit. I was brought up to put complete effort into the game. If you don't go all out you cheat everybody—fans, teammates, yourself."

7
Ready for 21st-Century Action

Rookies of the Year Still Active in the Major Leagues

Y ou see a good many of them in the postseason these autumns. The prime-time headliners. Jeter and Pujols. Furcal, Beltran, Rolen. Recently Willis, Wood, and Salmon, too.

All of them Rookies of the Year.

Perhaps the likes of Hinske and Grieve and Garciaparra and Piazza will star as Misters October some year. All of them Rookies of the Year.

Not every Rookie of the Year has reached old-timer status yet. Benito Santiago, still going strong at 40 and now with his ninth franchise, is the eldest of the active players who were rookie-year honorees. During the 2004 season, 27 Rookies of the Year—including '04 selections Bobby Crosby and Jason Bay— were on current rosters. You've read about two of the 27, Jeff Bagwell and Ichiro Suzuki, in Chapter 3.

Surely you won't be surprised if some of these active associates of theirs join them at MVP reunions someday.

BENITO SANTIAGO
1987   San Diego Padres, National League

Personal Data: B. March 9, 1965, at Ponce, Puerto Rico.
Physical Attributes: 6' 1", playing weight 185 lbs. Bats right, throws right.
Rookie Year, 1987:   Primary position catcher. Set rookie record by hitting in 34 consecutive games.
Career to Date, 19 years: Padres 1986–92; Marlins '93–94; Reds '95; Phillies '96; Blue Jays '97–98; Cubs '99; Reds 2000; Giants '01–03; Royals '04.

	BA	G	H	2B	3B	HR	RBI
1987	.300	146	164	33	2	18	79
Career to date	.263	1,972	1,824	322	40	217	920

Benito Santiago leads all active Rookies of the Year in big league seniority. The 2004 campaign was Benny's 19th season—with his eighth different team.

Only eight Rookies of the Year have surpassed Santiago's 19 seasons. Six of them—Carlton Fisk, Willie Mays, Willie McCovey, Eddie Murray, Frank Robinson, and Tom Seaver—are Hall of Famers. Another, Cal Ripken, soon will be. Pete Rose, a 24-year player, is the eighth.

After Benito's 11th season, grave doubts surfaced. "He might never play again." Maybe not even walk comfortably. Involved in a major January 1998 auto accident in Florida, Santiago suffered multiple serious injuries. He soon recovered from many of them. But due to severely strained right knee ligaments, he was not activated until August. He rehabilitated in 16 minor league games. Then Toronto, his fifth big league club, recalled him for 15 late-season outings. All he did was hit .310. The gloomy outlook of six months earlier was transformed into modest hopes for 1999.

Benito Santiago, San Diego Padres, 1987
In terms of age and years of service, Benny was the eldest Rookie of the Year still active during the 2004 season.
(Courtesy of San Diego Padres)

His rapid comeback reminded some onlookers of Benny's freshman performance, which remains a San Diego hallmark. In addition to his solid .300 batting average, 18 homers, and 79 RBI, Santiago fashioned a 34-game hitting streak that still stands as a record for the Padres, for catchers, and for rookies. To this day he ranks among the top eight all-time Padres in five offensive categories.

"A lot of good things have happened to me in baseball," he recently recalled. "That hitting streak, at the beginning, put some attention on me right away. I was in the right place at the right time. When the second year started, though, I realized that baseball doesn't get easier. The opposition knows you better, and adjusts."

Evidently Benny also adjusted. For years his defensive ability was judged to be his game's strong point. On entering the National League in 1993, the expansion Marlins drafted him primarily to handle their pitching staff and for his catching skills.

Once considered a contentious competitor, Santiago has softened somewhat over the years. At his recent outpost, for example, he was basically a mentor and pitching stabilizer for manager and old friend Tony Pena's Kansas City Royals. Pena and Benny hope the results mirror San Francisco's success during Santiago's recent three years there.

The Giants advanced to postseason play in 2002 and 2003. Leading them toward the '02 World Series, Benito was the NLCS MVP. It seemed each of his six safeties was a clutch hit. He batted .300, collected two walks, smacked a pair of home runs, and delivered six RBI.

Santiago leveled off a bit the following year, but, at age 38, he still hit .279—16 points above his lifetime average.

Joining Kansas City as a free agent, he appeared eager for another baseball semester to commence. "Sure, you have your ups and downs when you play as long as I have," he reflected. "But it's really been very satisfying to stay this long. In fact, I'm not even thinking about a post-baseball career yet. I hope I can play for maybe another two or three years." Shortly after he commented, Benny suffered a broken left hand and was limited to 49 Royals games in 2004.

SANDY ALOMAR, JR.

1990   Cleveland Indians, American League

Personal Data: B. June 18, 1966, at Salinas, Puerto Rico.
Physical Attributes: 6′ 5″, playing weight 215 lbs. Bats right, throws right.
Rookie Year, 1990:   Primary position catcher.
Career to Date, 17 years: Padres 1988–89; Indians '90–2000; White Sox '01–02; Rockies '02; White Sox '03–04.

	BA	G	H	2B	3B	HR	RBI
1990	.290	132	129	26	2	9	66
Career to date	.273	1,277	1,168	233	10	111	557

Mention Cleveland's Central Division dynasty of the 1990s and such names as Lofton, Baerga, Belle, Ramirez, Vizquel, and Thome come to mind. Many analysts, however, credit catcher Sandy Alomar, Jr., as the team's key ingredient.

Beginning in 1995, Cleveland captured its division flag five straight years and advanced to the '95 and '97 World Series. Victory totals might have been even greater had injuries not forced Alomar onto the disabled list nearly every year.

The popular 1990 AL Rookie of the Year was traded to Cleveland by San Diego, where he auditioned briefly in 1988 and '89. Sandy's .290 batting average, along with his obvious ability to handle Cleveland's pitching staff, quickly established his considerable promise.

But that promise was soon accompanied by the first of numerous injuries. For four straight seasons, beginning in '91, he missed an average of 83 games per year . . . roughly half of his team's outings. Most injuries involved leg, back, or arm ailments.

Sandy's lengthiest run of good health was from 1996 through 1998. He was brilliant during the 1997 pennant-winning season. In July, at his home ballpark, he was the All-Star MVP. Sandy posted career highs that season in batting (.324), home runs (21), and runs batted in (83). Basically injury free, he played in 125 games. Although Sandy homered twice and batted .367 in the 1997 World Series, his team suffered a heartbreaking loss to Florida in Game Seven.

Alomar's offensive numbers fell off in 1998. More DL visits followed. Later, trades to the White Sox and Rockies kept him on the move. At both Chicago (twice) and Denver he was hired primarily to stabilize pitching staffs. Now in his late 30s and recently released by the White Sox again, Sandy thinks instructor opportunities might be in his future when his playing days are over. After his active career, though, he'd like a one- or two-year break. In the meantime, he reflects on his rookie award . . . and on his famous baseball family.

"I had little chance to advance in San Diego, because Benito Santiago was already catching there. So I was happy to go to Cleveland. I was gratified, of course, but surprised to be a unanimous MVP choice. John Olerud, Kevin Maas, and Robin Ventura had good rookie years, too. Those guys were stars. I just wanted to play."

Sandy's father, now coaching with the Mets, enjoyed a 15-year career as an infielder. Sandy's younger brother Roberto was also with Sandy in Cleveland for two seasons and on the White Sox briefly. Even though the Alomar brothers are well-seasoned veterans, they still get tutoring and advice from their dad. "He's a great student of the game," says Sandy, Jr.

Sandy, with a wink and a grin, said, "Sometimes people get my brother and me mixed up. They ask me, 'Are you Robby's brother?' Hey, wait a minute. I went to the All-Star Game and got Gold Gloves before he did. What are you talking about," he laughs. "You think I was an All-Star by accident?"

Sandy's actually very fond and proud of his sibling. And he's modest and realistic about those winning seasons at Cleveland.

"You know, we didn't have the greatest pitching staff in the world, but it was pitching that took us to the World Series. As for me, I'm just happy for the good years between the injuries."

Eric Karros
1992   Los Angeles Dodgers, National League

Personal Data: B. November 4, 1967, at Hackensack, NJ.
Physical Attributes: 6′ 4″, playing weight 216 lbs. Bats right, throws right.
Rookie Year, 1992:   Primary position first base.
Career to Date, 14 years: Dodgers 1991–2002; Cubs '03; A's '04.

	BA	G	H	2B	3B	HR	RBI
1992	.257	149	140	30	1	20	88
Career to date	.268	1,755	1,724	324	11	284	1,027

Eric Karros is the answer to a pretty good trivia question.

In the storied history of the Brooklyn/Los Angeles Dodgers, only two players—Duke Snider and Gil Hodges—hit more home runs than the 270 delivered by Karros, the National League's 1992 Rookie of the Year.

Seldom earning elite billing among a cast of annual All-Stars, Karros quietly lifted himself to all-time top-10 status in six of the franchise's key offensive categories. He exceeded 100 RBI five times, including three consistent consecutive seasons—1995–97—with 105, 111, and 104. His homers over that stretch: 32, 34, 31.

Karros was an underpublicized newcomer in 1992. Twenty home runs and 88 RBI later he was duly recognized as Rookie of the Year. Eric started that season in the same role he filled in his later career. Platoon player.

"When training in '92 ended," he remembers, "I didn't know if I'd make the team. But after a decent spring and an unfortunate injury to Jay Howell, I was

The Dodgers' Unprecedented Five in a Row
Los Angeles established a record unlikely to be matched: five consecutive Rookies of the Year, beginning
in 1992. In order of their arrivals, and from left to right, are Eric Karros, Mike Piazza, Raul Mondesi,
Hideo Nomo, and Todd Hollandsworth. In 2004 all continued to be active major league players.
(Courtesy of Los Angeles Dodgers)

placed on the roster. Tommy Lasorda kidded about sending me out, but it was
tongue-in-cheek.

"Tommy platooned me at first base with Todd Benzinger and Kal Daniels,
but after a hot run in late May, I was pretty much the regular."

Eric credits Dodger organization instructors Kevin Kennedy, Reggie Smith,
and Tim Johnson with preparing him for advancement. "Brett Butler and pitchers
Kevin Gross and Roger McDowell also took me under their wings.

"By my second year I just tried to prove I belonged. I learned quickly, though,
that you must carefully study pitchers' tendencies . . . even those pitchers you've
already faced."

Karros echoes one of this book's continuing themes. "To stay productive in
the big leagues you adjust constantly. Not only early, but throughout your career."

When his 11-full-season tenure with the Dodgers ended, Eric was traded to
the Cubs, where he primarily platooned—déjà vu—at first base. He recorded
several key hits as Chicago won the 2003 NL Central title. His 40 runs batted in
vaulted him past the 1,000-career-RBI level.

Karros reflects on that career. "I was born in New Jersey, where my dad was a Brooklyn fan. We moved to California when I was very young. When the Dodgers signed me, Dad was more excited than I was! My parents always encouraged me to pursue opportunities of interest. I try to do that with my children." Eric and his wife Trish, parents of three boys, live in California's Manhattan Beach.

After that 2003 season in the Midwest, Eric filed for free agency and was signed by Oakland to platoon again in 2004. Not exactly Southern California, but closer to home than Chicago was. However, at midseason the A's chose to release him.

With his active career winding down, Karros said he'd probably like to stay involved with the game. "But first, I want to be with my family to see the kids grow up. Baseball requires a lot of travel. I want to cut down on that. For a while, anyway."

When asked about a future in broadcasting, the well-spoken Karros didn't rule out the possibility. In fact, he did some midseason studio work in 2004. He recalled his early Dodger days. "I had fun doing a car commercial with Lasorda after my rookie season. Had some camera stints on television dramas, too. Being Rookie of the Year and playing in Los Angeles gives a player a great opportunity to do some of those things."

MIKE PIAZZA
1993   Los Angeles Dodgers, National League

Personal Data: B. September 4, 1968, at Norristown, PA.
Physical Attributes: 6' 3", playing weight 197 lbs. Bats right, throws right.
Rookie Year, 1993:   Primary position catcher.
Career to Date, 13 years: Dodgers 1992–98; Marlins '98; Mets '98–2004.

	BA	G	H	2B	3B	HR	RBI
1993	.318	149	174	24	2	35	112
Career to date	.315	1,590	1,829	385	6	378	1,161

When a player registers a brilliant rookie season, it's usually followed by a decade or more of excellence before Hall of Fame likelihood is preordained.

Here's betting that Mike Piazza's Cooperstown trip was assured long before his career reached the 10-year mark.

Now entering his late 30s, the 1993 National League Rookie of the Year has established numerous offensive standards that won't soon be matched. Among them, on May 5, 2004, he set the all-time major league home run mark by a catcher—352. Carlton Fisk, another Rookie of the Year, held the previous record.

Mike's .315 lifetime average through 2004 is among the best of all active players. He hit over .300 in each of his first eight full seasons. Six times during that span he drove home more than 100 runs. He came close again in 2001 (98 RBI) and the next year (94). His totals fell significantly in 2003 and 2004 when he was limited by injuries.

One wonders who baseball scouts were watching back in the late 1980s. Piazza was completely overlooked. As has been well documented, he was drafted only as a favor. Tom Lasorda, a Piazza family friend, persuaded the Dodgers to select Mike in 1988. He was the draft's 1,390th—and final—pick.

Not until his third minor league season, 1991, did Piazza began to deliver offense with consistency and power. In 1992 the Dodgers elevated him for a late-season trial. They saw enough to roster him for 1993. It was a mutually gratifying decision.

"I wasn't particularly shooting for Rookie of the Year," Piazza remembers. "I just wanted to show that I belonged in the majors. When the award followed, my immediate thoughts were about showing improvement the next year. I confess, though, that it was an honor to carry on the Dodgers' long tradition of Rookies of the Year."

Mike did, indeed, improve the next year. And the years after that. His batting average rose in each of his five full Los Angeles seasons, reaching a career high of .362 in 1997. As for power, he generally blasted between 32 and 40 home runs. As the game's MVP, Mike homered to lead the 1996 National League All-Stars to victory.

Piazza and the Dodgers parted company in early 1998. The team determined it couldn't afford Mike's free-agency salary demands that likely would follow at season's end. He was traded to Florida with Todd Zeile for four top-level veterans. And for . . . just one week.

The rebuilding Marlins couldn't afford him either. Mike was promptly dealt to the Mets.

Over the next two and a half campaigns he sparked New York to two post-season appearances, including the 2000 World Series. He led the Mets with a .412 average in the 2000 NLCS, then homered twice and drove in four Series runs in a losing effort against the World Champion Yankees.

In five-plus Dodger years, and nearly seven as a Met, Piazza remains among lifetime leaders with both teams. His 124 RBI in single seasons at each city are team records for catchers. Mike's .331 batting average is fourth best of all Brooklyn and Los Angeles Dodgers. He ranks fourth in RBI and extra-base hits with the Mets, for whom he's the all-time leader in career batting average and third in home runs.

Whether or not he lines up defensively at first base, catcher, or somewhere else over his final big league seasons, or with other teams, Mike Piazza will continue to build on his totals en route to an eventual Cooperstown welcome.

Presumably he'll continue to be nationally visible after his baseball curtain finally drops. An affable fellow with an engaging personality, Mike has already appeared in television guest roles and been seen as a spokesman for various commercial products.

"Right now I'll still concentrate on baseball," he says. "But after that, yes, maybe I'll have a chance to pursue some camera and microphone opportunities."

TIM SALMON
1993   California Angels, American League

Personal Data: B. August 24, 1968, at Long Beach, CA.
Physical Attributes: 6′ 3″, playing weight 220 lbs. Bats right, throws right.
Rookie Year, 1993:   Primary position outfield.
Career to Date, 13 years: Angels 1992–2004.

	BA	G	H	2B	3B	HR	RBI
1993	.283	142	146	35	1	31	95
Career to date	.283	1,596	1,618	331	22	290	989

Tim Salmon, California Angels, 1993
Starring for the franchise's only World Series entry, the 2002 champions, Salmon is the team's lone Rookie of the Year to date.
(The Lovero Group)

It's been more than a dozen seasons now. Still, Tim Salmon, 1993 Rookie of the Year, continues to produce at the same outpost where he started.

Salmon is the Angels' all-time leader in home runs (290), runs batted in (989), and extra-base hits (643). Along the way he's been a model of consistency, seldom far from his rookie-season numbers. One notable exception, 1995; he hit a career high .330.

Salmon is a role model off the field, too. He and his wife Marci (parents of four children) established the Tim Salmon Foundation benefiting Family Solutions. Tim is active in other programs focusing on family solidarity— Kids Helping Kids, Rod Carew's Friends of Kiley Benefit, and California's Responsible Fatherhood Campaign among them. Twice he was the Angels' Roberto Clemente "Man of the Year." In 2002, Salmon was the American League Comeback Player of the Year. He wonders if that's an honor.

"It emphasizes how bad your previous year must have been," he chuckled. "Seriously, though, I was disabled three weeks with a sprained upper left cervical shoulder strain in 2001. Hit just .227, by far my worst season. Drove in only 49 runs."

His comeback award resulted from a .286 average, 22 homers, and 88 RBI as the underdog, wild-card Angels won the World Series. Tim batted .346 with nine hits, including a four-hit, two-homer performance in Game Two. According to Tim, that title-winning campaign was "a magical season, the highlight of my career. It put to rest some of the old ghosts of heartbreaking Angels' seasons past."

Although 12 seasons removed now, Salmon still has clear recollections from his Rookie of the Year summer.

> I always seem to start slow. And I did that season. But it was a rebuilding year, and manager Buck Rodgers stuck with me. Chili Davis, our veteran outfielder, took me under his wing and was a great influence. After feeling my way through the first half, I soon felt like I belonged, because I'd moved through the minor league levels in a timely manner and was able to finish strong that first year. Then came the rookie award, and that, of course, was something special after a season of thrills playing with guys I'd admired and seen on TV.
>
> The award's biggest impact for me, ironically, came from the Dodgers. Mike Piazza was the National League rookie winner that same year, and the Dodgers gave him a multiyear contract. So when I was named Rookie of the Year, it was a big deal for the Angels, who always compete with the Dodgers for fan support. Piazza got the big contract, so the Angels gave me a multiyear deal, too. Truly, it enabled me to concentrate on baseball instead of business. I've never enjoyed the business side of the game. So, in a way, I thank Piazza and the Dodgers for my Rookie of the Year benefits!

The entertainment industry, centered nearby, has often made offers to Salmon. He's declined most of them. He had planned to concentrate on baseball for a few more years, then stay home with his family and complete his final year of studies at Grand Canyon College. "My time at home's important," he says. "Getting out of the limelight when the time comes will be just fine."

Injuries, however, may have hastened his career's completion. Tim joined the 2004 disabled list after only 60 games and a .253 batting average. Knee and shoulder surgery followed, and it's been speculated that Salmon will retire when his 2005 contract expires.

RAUL MONDESI
1994   Los Angeles Dodgers, National League

Personal Data: B. March 12, 1971, at San Cristóbal, Dominican Republic.
Physical Attributes: 5′ 11″, playing weight 202 lbs. Bats right, throws right.
Rookie Year, 1994:   Primary position outfield.
Career to Date, 12 years: Dodgers 1993–99; Blue Jays 2000–02; Yankees '02–03; Diamondbacks '03; Pirates '04; Angels '04.

	BA	G	H	2B	3B	HR	RBI
1994	.306	112	133	27	8	16	56
Career to date	.275	1,484	1,559	312	48	267	843

By the time Raul Mondesi was anointed as his league's top 1994 newcomer, it seemed almost automatic that a Los Angeles player would be Rookie of the Year. Mondesi was the third in an unprecedented string of five consecutive Dodgers who won the award from 1992 through 1996.

The Dominican Republic native had arrived in Los Angeles for 42 games in late 1993 to hit .291 with long-ball power in 86 at bats. He also demonstrated an exceptionally strong arm during his September audition. Over the next decade he would annually rank among major league outfield assist leaders.

After Raul's batting average slipped to .253 in 1999—when he delivered a career-high 99 runs batted in—the Dodgers traded him to Toronto as part of a transaction that brought perennial All-Star candidate Shawn Green to the West Coast. Mondesi did not find American League pitching much to his liking. He hit just .243 in two and a half Blue Jay summers before a 2002 midyear trade to the Yankees.

His New York tenure was short-lived. Frequently displaying a sour locker room disposition throughout his career, Raul angrily left the Yankee clubhouse during a late July 2003 game. AWOL. Within hours he was dispatched to the Arizona Diamondbacks.

The sudden return to the National League appeared to rejuvenate Mondesi, who hit over .300 and drove in 22 runs during the 2003 season's final 45 games.

Sadly, his "comeback" was an abbreviated one. Signed by Pittsburgh for the 2004 campaign, Raul was soon in the doghouse again. He left the team, first with permission, to deal with a civil matter back in the Dominican Republic (a court there ruled he owed $640,000). Later he threatened to leave the team because the Pirates withheld salary after Mondesi had left again and failed to return as expected. Pittsburgh cited breach of contract and terminated Mondesi. A few weeks later Anaheim took a chance on the veteran outfielder, despite his headlined run-ins with front offices and field managers. Soon, for the second time during the 2004 season, Mondesi's contract was terminated, this time for his continued failure to keep physical therapy appointments following a quadriceps injury that occurred a few days after he joined the Angels. It seems highly questionable that the controversial Mondesi—once an esteemed Rookie of the Year—will ever regain big league eminence.

MARTY CORDOVA
1995   Minnesota Twins, American League

Personal Data: B. July 10, 1969, at Las Vegas, NV.
Physical Attributes: 6′ 0″, playing weight 207 lbs. Bats right, throws right.
Rookie Year, 1995:   Primary position outfield. Career highs in home runs (24) and stolen bases (20). Tied for second in AL outfield assists. Homered in five consecutive games.
Career to Date, 9 years: Twins 1995–99; Blue Jays 2000; Indians '01; Orioles '02–03 (disabled list throughout '04).

	BA	G	H	2B	3B	HR	RBI
1995	.277	137	142	27	4	24	84
Career to date	.274	952	938	192	18	122	540

In extremely close 1995 voting for Rookie of the Year, Minnesota outfielder Marty Cordova edged California's Garret Anderson. Each player collected 13 first-place BBWAA ballots, but Cordova's runner-up votes made the difference. Andy Pettitte finished third.

Marty Cordova, Minnesota Twins, 1995
Enjoyed career-high 24 home runs and 20 stolen bases during Rookie of the Year season. As 2003 Oriole, Cordova underwent Tommy John surgery.
(Courtesy of Minnesota Twins)

Less than a decade after his excellent debut, injuries placed Marty Cordova's baseball future in serious doubt.

He was prophetic during an interview for this book before the 2003 season. "Don't worry or get caught up with what's happened in the past," he said. "Prepare for today's game, the game at hand. Don't worry about the next game either. You never know what'll happen tomorrow."

After a productive 2001 season with Cleveland and a solid performance in 131 games for the 2002 Orioles, Marty was eager to start the next campaign.

His 2003 season was only nine games and 30 at bats old before he went on the disabled list. A severe elbow injury required Tommy John surgery. He was out for the season. He'd been a prominent athlete for 20 years. Now he wondered about the future.

Cordova was an honored three-sport athlete at Bishop Gorman High in Las Vegas, where he still resides. He later focused on baseball at the University of Nevada–Las Vegas. Drafted in 1989, Marty moved through Minnesota's minor league system for five summers before his breakout 1995 season. His rookie year's 24 home runs are a career high.

He performed even more impressively the following season. His motto? "Last year's over. Time to focus on now." Cordova delivered career bests in average (.309), doubles (46, still a Twins record), and RBI (111). But in 1997 the first of several injuries victimized him, reducing his playing time and batting average over the following two years.

Marty rebounded to .285 in 1999, then opted for free agency. After a spring trial with Boston, Cordova signed with Toronto. But the Jays benched him for much of the second half. A free agent again, Marty joined Cleveland for 2001.

It was his best season since '96 at Minnesota. He averaged .301, drove home 69 runs, hit 20 homers, fashioned a 22-game hitting streak, and entered the postseason for the first time. Cleveland lost to Seattle in the Division Series.

Another free-agent opportunity enabled him to sign a three-year contract with the Orioles in 2002. He ranked fourth on the team with 18 home runs and tied for third with 64 RBI. He hit safely in 19 of his first 22 Baltimore games.

Then came the 2003 elbow surgery, the disappointment connected with it, and the slow recovery that kept him on the disabled list for his Baltimore contract's entire final year. Yet, as the optimistic 1995 Rookie of the Year says, "Don't dwell on tomorrow. Focus on doing your best today."

HIDEO NOMO
1995   Los Angeles Dodgers, National League

Personal Data: B. August 31, 1968, at Osaka, Japan.
Physical Attributes: 6′ 2″, playing weight 210 lbs. Throws right, bats right.
Rookie Year, 1995:   Primary position pitcher. Led league with 236 strikeouts.
Career to Date, 10 years: Dodgers 1995–98; Mets '98; Brewers '99; Tigers 2000; Red Sox '01; Dodgers '02–04.

	Record	ERA	G	GS	SO	IP
1995	13–6	2.54	28	28	236	191⅓
Career to date	118–101	4.05	301	289	1,856	1,871⅓

Hideo Nomo has many "firsts" to his credit. Some of them relate to his nationality. Many are A1 accomplishments on the baseball field.

Yes, he was indeed the first native of Japan to make significant marks in American big league baseball. The first Rookie of the Year from Japan, for example. And he was the first Japan-born player selected to an All-Star Game, in which, by the way, he started and pitched two scoreless innings during his 1995 rookie season.

However, aside from being his country's pathfinder, Nomo has achieved several more baseball "firsts." Such as the Dodgers' rookie record of 16 strikeouts in a game. Or leading the NL with a .192 opponents' batting average his first year. He's one of only four men to pitch no-hitters in both major leagues. He has recorded nearly as many strikeout as innings pitched. And, as a rookie, his career-high 236 strikeouts in only 28 games led the National League.

Having joined the Dodgers a week after the 1995 season opener, Hideo quickly became a box office hit. Not only in Los Angeles, but throughout the National League. By midseason, walk-up ticket sales hit all-time highs at many ballparks when it was announced that Nomo would pitch. He was only 26, and a long, bright future seemed assured.

Fate, along with a touch of déjà vu, suddenly surfaced. Back in 1957, as we saw in Chapter 6, Gil McDougald's line drive severely injured pitcher Herb Score's eye, effectively ending young Score's brilliant career. Both men had been Rookies of the Year. Now, 40 summers later, Rookie of the Year Scott Rolen's liner smashed into Rookie of the Year Nomo's right elbow in 1997. Surgery was later successful, but Hideo's career began to skid.

His ERA soared over the next few seasons. From mid-1998, with a 2–7 record and 5.05 earned run average, he went from Los Angeles to four other teams in four years. Nomo's strikeouts per inning remained high, but he continued to allow too many earned runs. However, at Boston in 2001, his overall effectiveness had clearly returned.

Opting for free agency, Nomo signed on with Los Angeles again. His 2002 return to Dodger Stadium was a success. His strikeout totals remained strong, and his ERA dipped to 3.09 in 2003. Seemingly fully returned to early-career form, he started 67 games his first two years back. Sixteen wins each season were career highs.

Hideo ultimately would slump to a 4–11 record in 2004. Nevertheless, of the 29 pitchers who've been Rookies of the Year, Hideo Nomo resuscitated a sagging career at least as well as, and arguably better than, any of the others.

TODD HOLLANDSWORTH
1996   Los Angeles Dodgers, National League

Personal Data: B. April 20, 1973, at Dayton, OH.
Physical Attributes: 6′ 2″, playing weight 195 lbs. Bats left, throws left.
Rookie Year, 1996:   Primary position outfield.
Career to Date, 10 years: Dodgers 1995–2000; Rockies '00–02; Rangers '02; Marlins '03; Cubs '04.

	BA	G	H	2B	3B	HR	RBI
1996	.291	149	139	26	4	12	59
Career to date	.279	897	742	157	19	85	330

Rare, indeed, is the young man who appears in a postseason lineup before his rookie year. Todd Hollandsworth is one of the few who fit that description.

Elevated by the Dodgers in late 1995—just in time to qualify for the post-season roster—Hollandsworth recorded 103 regular season at bats. But they weren't enough to disqualify him from official rookie status in the future. So in 1996, when he became a regular in the Los Angeles outfield and turned in the best offensive performance of his career, he was crowned National League Rookie of the Year.

Todd was the Dodgers' fifth consecutive Rookie of the Year, a streak no other franchise has come close to matching. As this is written, he is the team's most recent.

Although a series of injuries soon began to interrupt his progress, Todd looks back on his rookie year with pride and satisfaction:

> That '96 season was very exciting. It enabled me to see how God worked in wonderful ways, especially after I had several injuries in the minors during 1995. In '96, I was blessed to be on a good team. When you're with a contender a rookie gets more visibility. I guess I helped the team, and I know the team helped me. We got into the playoffs [losing to Atlanta in the opening round]. The Rookie of the Year notoriety can never be taken away. It was a tremendous honor.

Injuries from minor league days resurfaced in 1997. Todd missed nearly 60 games that season, and more than 100 the following year. He rebounded in 1999 with a solid .284 average in 92 games. Then the traveling started.

Midway through 2000, Hollandsworth was traded to Colorado. With good health restored, he played in 137 games for both the Dodgers and Rockies, and smacked a career-high 19 home runs. But the disabled list beckoned again, limiting him to only 33 games in '01. It was his ninth visit to the DL.

Colorado traded Todd to the Rangers for the second half of 2002. Then he was sent to Florida for the 2003 season. It was a fortuitous transaction for Hollandsworth, who finally, in his ninth big league season, played for a pennant winner.

Todd was primarily a utility player that summer, and a valuable contributor in the League Championship Series with three hits, including a double in three at bats, two RBI, and two runs scored against Chicago.

Evidently the Cubs liked what they saw, because they signed free agent Hollandsworth after the 2003 season. A good '04 start was negated when—again—Todd went to the DL. A serious shin injury limited him to 57 games.

Currently an off-season resident of Castle Rock, Colorado, Hollandsworth proudly displays a Rookie of the Year trophy on the mantle . . . and a World Series ring on his finger.

DEREK JETER
1996   New York Yankees, American League

Personal Data: B. June 26, 1974, at Pequannock, NJ.
Physical Attributes: 6' 3", playing weight 175 lbs. Bats right, throws right.
Rookie Year, 1996:   Primary position shortstop.
Career to Date, 10 years: Yankees 1995–2004.

	BA	G	H	2B	3B	HR	RBI
1996	.314	157	183	25	6	10	78
Career to date	.315	1,366	1,734	283	42	150	693

Someday the New York Yankees will retire Frank Crosetti's uniform number.

Crow, as he was nicknamed, broke in with the 1932 Bronx Bombers. Eventually sharing his shortstop post with Phil Rizzuto, he played 17 seasons. Then Crosetti coached at third base for another couple of decades. His on-field tenure was longer than any Yankee in history.

It's unlikely, however, that Crosetti's name will headline his retired number's plaque. Because that numeral—2—now belongs to Derek Jeter. Unless a startling turn of events occurs, Jeter will continue his All-Star-caliber journey to the Hall of Fame.

After a 15-game late-season trial in 1995, Jeter's Cooperstown trip started auspiciously when he hammered a home run against Cleveland on opening day, 1996. Six months later he was named American League Rookie of the Year.

Is it a coincidence that Jeter's rookie season was also Joe Torre's first year as New York manager? And that the Yankees won six pennants and four World Series in the next nine years? Most of the team's flag-winning All-Stars came or went during those nine seasons. Except for Jeter, Bernie Williams, Mariano Rivera, and Jorge Posada. They're the only key players continually together with Torre from '96 through 2004.

Along the way Jeter was selected team captain, the Yankees' first since another Rookie of the Year, Thurman Munson. That captaincy is a testament to his on-field leadership and his solid standing among the troops.

The Rookie of the Year honor, coming as it did in a championship season, revives pleasant memories for Jeter.

"That was a special October," he recalls.

> Winning the Series, and then the rookie award. It [Rookie of the Year] was something I hadn't thought much about until maybe September. My mind was on the pennant race first.
>
> We had a veteran team that year, and the guys made it easy for me to fit in. Tim Raines and Wade Boggs were among the players who gave me a lot of encouragement. When the next season came along I just concentrated on making adjustments. Didn't think about a sophomore jinx because I knew pitchers had already seen me for the first time, so they were making adjustments for me. Of course by then I was familiar with most of them, too.

In addition to Raines, Boggs, and others, Derek gives a nod to his father. "A big reason that I play shortstop is because that was my dad's position at Fisk University. I've always wanted to be like him."

Former player and long-time manager and coach Don Zimmer also came to the Yankees in 1996. He was Torre's bench coach throughout Jeter's first eight full seasons. In 2003, Zim said:

> I've seen a lot of rookies come and go. Some were Rookies of the Year. But Jeter stands out. He's had some great years. He does everything the same way, the right way, and is the same kind of individual as he was eight years ago. Some people have a big year, then they don't even know you anymore. Not Jeter. It's really a pleasure to be around this guy. Despite the New York press, and the pressures here, he never changes. Has the same level head as eight years ago.

Sidelined briefly with various sprains and strains over the years, Derek sustained a dislocated shoulder while sliding into third base at Toronto in the 2003 season opener. "It was my first major injury," said Jeter. The team's offense, which had been inconsistent, solidified when Jeter returned after seven weeks on the disabled list.

Jeter's brilliant play continually dazzles Yankee fans. They've watched him perform, as Zimmer said, at a consistently high level. He followed his rookie year's .314 finish with averages of .291, .324, .349 in 1999 with a career-high 102 RBI, .339, .311, .297, and .324 again. Never a noted long-ball hitter—but a highly regarded clutch hitter—Derek averages about 15 home runs per season.

He illuminates the postseason, as nationwide televiewers know—.302 in 32 World Series starts and a .300-plus average over 78 division series and LCS games. Jeter was the 2000 World Series MVP and the All-Star Game MVP that year. He hit .571 in his first five All-Star Games.

Jeter was born in New Jersey but grew up in Kalamazoo, Michigan. Kalamazoo is the headquarters of Turn 2 Foundation, an organization established by Derek in 1996 to promote healthy lifestyles. Youngsters are encouraged to "turn to" it for guidance in avoiding drugs and alcohol. Derek's mother, Dot Jeter, is the foundation's executive director.

Derek has become something of a media celebrity. He once hosted NBC-TV's "Saturday Night Live." Jeter teamed with another Rookie of the Year, Nomar Garciaparra, on an electronics company's television commercial. And he appears with Yankee owner George Steinbrenner in humorous spots for a credit card company.

Don't expect him, though, to be a full-time broadcasting personality quite yet. He recently signed a long-term contract to play with the Yankees through 2010. Some years after that number 2 will be added to Yankee Stadium's Monument Park. Frank Crosetti's name should appear in a prominent footnote. But the plaque's spotlight will focus directly on Derek Jeter.

NOMAR GARCIAPARRA
1997   Boston Red Sox, American League

Personal Data: B. July 23, 1973, at Whittier, CA.
Physical Attributes: 6' 0", playing weight 167 lbs. Bats right, throws right.
Rookie Year, 1997:   Primary position shortstop. Led league in hits (209), triples (11), and at bats (684).
Career to Date, 9 years: Red Sox 1996–2004; Cubs '04.

	BA	G	H	2B	3B	HR	RBI
1997	.306	153	209	44	11	30	98
Career to date	.322	1,009	1,330	293	50	182	710

Nomar Garciaparra, born Anthony Nomar Garciaparra, registered one of history's very best rookie seasons. Ever.

Of course one remarkable season does not a potential Hall of Fame career make. But what followed clearly has Nomar targeted for a probable trip to Cooperstown.

First though, review his 1997 Rookie of the Year performance. Garciaparra's 684 at bats were a Boston Red Sox single-season record. His 11 triples and 209 hits led the league. Nomar was Boston's first rookie in 22 years to make the All-Star team. He established the AL rookie consecutive-game hit streak record (30). It tied Tris Speaker for the second-best Boston skein behind Dom DiMaggio's 34.

Nomar Garciaparra, Boston Red Sox, 1997
The first right-handed hitter to win two
straight American League batting titles
(.357 in 1999 and .372 in 2000) since Joe
DiMaggio 60 years earlier.
(Courtesy of Boston Red Sox)

Overall he led AL rookies in 13 offensive categories en route to his unanimous
Rookie of the Year selection.

All that was just the appetizer. He continued to create headlines. Here are
some of his encore accomplishments:

A career-high 122 RBI highlighted his sophomore year when his batting
average rose to .323. He ranked second in MVP balloting.

A 10-RBI game in 1999, the season he won his first of two successive
batting titles with a .357 average. Was starting shortstop in All-Star
Game.

Won second straight batting championship in 2000, with a .372 average.
First right-handed AL hitter with consecutive crowns since Joe
DiMaggio 60 years earlier. Only third right-hand-hitting shortstop to
capture AL batting title (after Luke Appling and Alex Rodriguez).
His .372 performance was fourth best in Red Sox annals, trailing
only Ted Williams and Speaker.

After only eight seasons, Nomar ranked ninth in Boston home runs
(173), 13th in RBI (669), fourth among hitters with 1,500 or more

at bats (.323 average), seventh in extra-base hits (492). The 56 doubles he delivered in 2002, a league-leading figure, represent the second-best single-season mark in Red Sox history.

Garciaparra was a key performer in Boston's advancement to three postseason appearances since his 1997 arrival. He hit .417 in the 1999 five-game Division Series triumph over Cleveland. He drove home a team-leading 105 runs, hit an AL second-best 13 triples, and batted .301 in the 2003 regular season before Boston's loss to New York in the ALCS.

Nomar confesses to two major disappointments. Being limited to 21 games in 2001 because of right wrist surgery to repair a tendon. And failing, so far, to reach the World Series.

"The records have been personally satisfying, of course," he said recently. "And, in looking back to 1997, the Rookie of the Year selection was a very nice honor. But I'd substitute them for a World Series ring if I could make the switch."

In reflecting on his rookie season, Nomar credits teammates:

> I owe a lot to the other people on our team. I learned so much from them. Mo Vaughn and John Valentin are among the men who were there to support me. It's been gratifying to see the way so many Red Sox hand down encouragement to the new guys who come along. Some of the veterans have gone elsewhere, but their presence is still felt in our clubhouse.
>
> People ask if I knew I had a shot at Rookie of the Year. Very honestly, I didn't think much about it. My focus was on our battle for a playoff spot. The biggest benefit I received, from the rookie honor, was the long-term contract negotiated afterward. It showed me that the Red Sox had confidence in my long-term ability.

That contract officially concluded after 2003, with an option year for '04. Speculation had Garciaparra possibly traded from Boston before becoming a free agent at the end of the 2004 campaign—and in late July a major transaction did, indeed, transpire. In a four-team, eight-player deal Nomar—who might have been Boston's most popular player since Ted Williams—went to the Chicago Cubs. The season ended as it began for Garciaparra: in disappointment. With Boston, at the start of '04, he missed the first 56 games because of Achilles tendinitis. Then, at the end, a late-season collapse prevented the Cubs from going to the postseason. Thus, no World Series—again—for Nomar. Boston, of course, without him, finally shattered the Bambino Curse.

A free agent after the 2004 season, Garciaparra wasn't certain about which suitor's uniforms he'd wear in the near future. The Cubs seemed a strong possibility. Perhaps a club in his native California would land him. It's been suggested that he and his wife, Olympic soccer star Mia Hamm, would like to live on the West Coast. Ultimately, Nomar re-signed with Chicago for 2005.

SCOTT ROLEN
1997   Philadelphia Phillies, National League

Personal Data: B. April 4, 1975, at Evansville, IN.
Physical Attributes: 6′ 4″, playing weight 195 lbs. Bats right, throws right.
Rookie Year, 1997:   Primary position third base.
Career to Date, 9 years: Phillies 1996–2002; Cardinals '02–04.

	BA	G	H	2B	3B	HR	RBI
1997	.283	156	159	35	3	21	92
Career to date	.286	1,195	1,254	296	28	226	831

Painful though it was, an errant pitch shared some responsibility for Scott Rolen's Rookie of the Year selection.

A loudly heralded prospect in the Phillies system, Rolen raced through Class-AA Reading's first half, advanced to Triple-A Scranton/Wilkes-Barre for 45 games, and was then elevated to Philadelphia on August 1, 1996.

After a creditable showing of four home runs and 18 RBI in 38 National League games, Rolen stepped to the plate September 7 against Chicago's Steve Trachsel. Seconds later a Trachsel delivery fractured the ulna bone in Scott's right arm.

Scott Rolen, Philadelphia Phillies, 1997
Smooth-fielding, hard-hitting third baseman was NL Rookie of the Year during the 50-year anniversary celebration of Jackie Robinson's major league debut. *(The Rich Westcott Collection)*

Rolen's season was over. After 130 at bats. Ironically, just one more at bat in 1996 would have categorized Scott as a veteran. Instead, when he came to 1997 spring training with his arm fully healed, he was still technically a rookie in the eyes of the Baseball Writers' Association of America. Eight months later the writers named him National League Rookie of the Year.

The honor was well deserved. All he did was lead all NL rookies in batting (.283), home runs (21), RBI (92), runs (93), hits (159), doubles (35), and total bases (263). He was also the league's top rookie in on-base percentage, slugging percentage, and extra-base hits.

Rolen continued to improve as his second full season unfolded. His average rose to .290, home runs increased to 31, and he registered 110 runs batted in. He has equaled or exceeded 100 RBI five times, including four years in a row (2001–04). His career high 124 RBI helped spark St. Louis to the 2004 National League title.

"I had no thoughts about a sophomore jinx back in '98," Scott recalled. "But I knew that my rookie year's performance required me to work doubly hard to improve and to show that I truly belonged in the big leagues."

He's hardly missed an offensive beat. And despite lower-back injuries, he's been a perennial Gold Glove winner and NL All-Star. The back problems first surfaced in 1999, limiting Scott to 112 games.

Another kind of problem would develop. One Philadelphia front office veteran accused Rolen of lack of hustle, a widely disputed charge. And manager Larry Bowa was alleged to have questioned Scott's clutch hitting. By mid-2002 a mutual discomfort zone had reached combustible levels. Rolen was traded to St. Louis in a transaction that pleased all parties involved.

Since arriving in Missouri, Rolen has continued to play All-Star caliber baseball. The Indiana native also seems comfortable playing regularly back in the Midwest where he grew up.

Yet who can blame him if he occasionally thinks back to Philadelphia days and Chicago pitcher Steve Trachsel's fortuitous role in that 1997 Rookie of the Year matter.

BEN GRIEVE
1998   Oakland Athletics, American League

Personal Data: B. May 4, 1976, at Arlington, TX.
Physical Attributes: 6' 4", playing weight 220 lbs. Bats left, throws right.
Rookie Year, 1998:   Primary position outfield.
Career to Date, 8 years: A's 1997–2000; Devil Rays '01–03; Brewers '04; Cubs '04.

	BA	G	H	2B	3B	HR	RBI
1998	.288	155	168	41	2	18	89
Career to date	.269	953	859	192	7	118	491

Taking a mammoth salary reduction, probably among the deepest in baseball history, the 1998 American League Rookie of the Year hoped that new scenery and a major medical repair would combine to resuscitate a sagging career.

Ben Grieve was eager to "start over." During Christmas week of 2003 he signed a reported $700,000 contract with his third big league team, Milwaukee. It was his first venture into the National League after three full seasons with Oakland and another three at Tampa Bay. His 2003 Devil Rays salary was said to be $5.5 million.

As the 2003 campaign entered its second half, there was far more concern about Grieve's health than his income. Blood clots formed in his right arm. His

Ben Grieve, Oakland Athletics, 1998
Ben posted a career-high 104 RBI for Oakland in the 2000 season. Was later signed by Tampa Bay, Milwaukee, and Cubs.
(Michael Zagaris, Oakland Athletics)

condition worsened. On July 31, in Dallas, Ben's top right rib was removed to eliminate an impingement that might have been responsible for the clot. Clearly, his season was over and his baseball future in doubt.

The Brewers were betting that Ben, then only 27, would rebound toward the form that led to his 1998 Rookie of the Year award based on a .288 batting average with a strong power performance. His average dropped into the .260s and .270s during the following two summers, but he ripped 55 homers over those seasons with a career-high 104 RBI in 2000. When Devil Rays pitchers Cory Lidle and Roberto Hernandez became available, Oakland traded Grieve to Tampa Bay for them.

His overall output went into a decline. Batting dropped from .264 in 2001 to .251 the next year. Home runs improved from 11 to 19, but RBI totals continued to fall. When Ben hit only .230 with but four homers and 17 RBI over 55 games in 2003, something more than his batting reflexes needed help. Eventually the rib surgery was performed.

Friends and baseball foes alike have been rooting for Ben's return to full health. He's a respected competitor, a trait he learned from his father Tom. Tom Grieve is a former outfielder primarily with Texas, then an executive there, and now a Rangers television announcer. Young Ben spent several seasons shagging Rangers flies before games. He credits his dad with preparing him for professional baseball.

"After the rookie award I put too much pressure on myself. Dad reminded me to stay calm. And humble. It took a month and a half before I turned the second year around. But it's tough to turn that pressure off. First at Tampa, [then] at Milwaukee, [and eventually with the Cubs for 2004's final month] you're starting all over again."

With revitalized health, it might be easier this time.

KERRY WOOD
1998   Chicago Cubs, National League

Personal Data: B. June 16, 1977, at Irving, TX.
Physical Attributes: 6′ 5″, playing weight 225 lbs. Throws right, bats right.
Rookie Year, 1998:   Primary position pitcher.
Career to Date, 6 years: Cubs 1998, 2000–04.

	Record	ERA	G	GS	SO	IP
1998	13–6	3.40	26	26	233	166⅔
Career to date	67–50	3.63	164	164	1,209	1,043

As this book goes to press, Kerry Wood is 27 years old. If his right arm is healthy for another decade or more, he'll challenge several all-time strikeout records.

He's already in the Chicago Cubs archives for K's. Strikeouts, in fact, led to his celebrity as 1998 National League Rookie of the Year. Not yet 21, Wood set a major league rookie mark of 20 strikeouts in shutting out Houston on May 6, 1998. No rookie, until then, had ever fanned more than 18 batters; no Cub—rookie nor veteran—had exceeded 17 until then. By the way, the 2–0 victory was a one-hitter.

Wood finished his marvelous rookie season with 233 strikeouts. Typically, the Texas native, who now resides in Scottsdale, Arizona with his wife Sarah, fanned significantly more batters than innings pitched. His single-season strikeouts-to-innings-hurled ratio was Chicago's 20th-century best.

The 20-strikeout performance was just Kerry's fifth big league start. With additional successes during the rest of the season—and a Rookie of the Year award that Wood candidly felt Colorado's Todd Helton would likely win—a brilliant career seemed assured. Suddenly a detour sign loomed.

"As the '99 season started," Wood remembers, "I was determined that the

Kerry Wood, Chicago Cubs, 1998
Hard-throwing right-hander set an all-time rookie record by registering 20 strikeouts in his fifth major league start. His first-year strikeout total was 233.
(Steve Green, Chicago Cubs)

sophomore jinx wouldn't affect me. Guess what? In my very first spring training start I blew out my arm. I didn't pitch again all year."

Kerry tore a right-elbow ligament that was surgically repaired with a graft from his right forearm. He was unable to pitch for 15 months. After three minor league rehab starts, he joined the 2000 Cubs in time for 23 games.

"Getting back on the mound was pretty shaky for a while," he admits. "Things got better, though, the next year. But it really wasn't until 2002 that I felt all the way back—throwing like I used to."

Kerry fanned 217 opponents in '02, then added a league-leading 266 K's as he and teammate Mark Prior delivered a one-two mound punch that helped propel the 2003 Cubs to the NL Central title. They were nosed out, four games to three, in the League Championship Series by eventual World Series champ Florida. During '03 he reached the 1,000-strikeout mark in his 134th game—faster than any other major leaguer in history.

Convinced that Chicago is a solid pennant contender, Kerry and the ball club agreed to a three-year multimillion-dollar contract through 2006, with a mutual option for '07. Cubs pitching is considered by many as the NL's strongest.

Relying more on a slider than before his elbow surgery, and confident that his arm was fully recovered, Wood developed tendinitis in a lower right triceps during May 2004, then recovered well enough to pitch 141 innings. "But I figure whenever the career's done, it's done. Who knows? Hopefully that's a long way off. By then I'll probably want to give something back to the game."

Maybe that means showing youngsters how to pitch. Or to adjust to big-time baseball life. Then again, don't be surprised to see handsome, articulate Kerry Wood in a baseball telecaster's booth in 15 years or so.

CARLOS BELTRAN
1999   Kansas City Royals, American League

Personal Data: B. April 24, 1977, at Manatí, Puerto Rico.
Physical Attributes: 6' 0", playing weight 175 lbs. Bats both, throws right.
Rookie Year, 1999:   Primary position outfield.
Career to Date, 7 years: Royals 1998–2004; Astros '04.

	BA	G	H	2B	3B	HR	RBI
1999	.293	156	194	27	7	22	108
Career to date	.284	885	985	173	52	146	569

Outside of Kansas and Missouri, until 2004, Carlos Beltran was probably the least-known heavyweight baseball player in America. If you had asked casual fans to name the last dozen American League Rookies of the Year, chances are they would have been hard put to include Beltran.

The Royals seldom appear on national television and, until 2003, were usually a second-division club in recent years. Little opportunity existed for Beltran to be prominently visible. He couldn't help but feel slighted, you figure, but disappointment doesn't surface when he talks about his Rookie of the Year experience.

Carlos Beltran, Kansas City Royals, 1999
Drove in 100 or more runs in four of first five seasons. Eighty extra-base hits in 2002 broke Mickey Mantle's one-season record for switch-hitters.
(Photo Courtesy of Kansas City Royals)

I was just very happy to have made the ball club in 1999. Not until midseason, when reporters began talking about it, did I think about the rookie award. Then I began working even harder. From that year on I knew I was capable of playing well, but I put too much pressure on myself the second season. I tried too hard, and started slow. I was sent to the minors, and later a bone bruise put me on the disabled list. [Carlos was suspended briefly when he refused to report for rehab assignments.] I learned valuable lessons. I realized I'd been blessed from God with ability to play baseball, and also realized it's not how you start, but how well you finish. So I looked back and recognized that I was capable of playing well. My approach since then has been positive. Stay healthy, take good times with the bad ones that are inevitable in baseball. Concentrate on playing the game correctly.

He smilingly reflected on the rookie year's high notes—both professionally and personally. Just three days after Carlos and his wife Jessica were married they attended the 1999 Rookie of the Year award presentation in New York. These were some of his accomplishments cited there: first AL rookie with 100 RBI since Mark McGwire in '87, eighth rookie in history and only third Royal with 100 runs scored and 100 RBI, had hitting streaks of 10 and 12 games, hit safely in 22 of a 23-game stretch.

His second season, as we've seen, was disappointing. He hit just .247 in only 98 Kansas City games. But with a positive outlook he bounced back in 2001. Later his .307 was a career high in 2003 when he surpassed 100 RBI for the third successive year and joined with Joe Randa, Mike Sweeney, Angel Berroa, and their teammates to lift Kansas City to its first winning season in 10 years. Carlos became the only Royal to hit 20 home runs (26) and steal 20 bases (41) in four different seasons. A reported $9 million one-year contract for 2004 resulted.

Had his impressive accomplishments been more widely publicized, fans everywhere would have been aware that Beltran, in 2002, broke Mickey Mantle's American League switch-hitting extra-base hits record. In 1956, Mantle had 79. Beltran posted 80 extra-base hits—44 doubles, seven triples, 29 homers—in 2002.

Suddenly, after the Royals' winning 2003 season, Beltran, that frequently overlooked 1999 Rookie of the Year, attracted the All-Star-caliber attention he deserves. By midyear 2004, contending teams in both leagues discussed trading for him. Houston won out from two standpoints. One, the Astros signed him. Two, he was a major contributor in Houston's advancement to the National League Championship Series.

After the season Carlos Beltran was the foremost position player among all big league free agents, with an extremely promising future.

SCOTT WILLIAMSON
1999   Cincinnati Reds, National League

Personal Data: B. February 17, 1976, at Fort Polk, LA.
Physical Attributes: 6' 0", playing weight 185 lbs. Throws right, bats right.
Rookie Year, 1999:   Primary position pitcher. Recorded 19 saves.
Career to Date, 6 years: Reds 1999–2003; Red Sox '03–04.

	Record	ERA	G	GS	SO	IP
1999	12–7	2.41	62	0	107	93⅓
Career to date	25–24	2.98	269	10	429	371⅓

It's doubtful that any franchise will soon, if ever, match the Dodgers' Rookie of the Year total. Sixteen. The Cincinnati Reds, however, moved into second place among National League teams when relief pitcher Scott Williamson was the only player listed on all 32 first-place ballots in 1999.

Williamson, just the 14th rookie pitcher ever named to the NL All-Star team, became Cincinnati's seventh Rookie of the Year and its first since Chris Sabo 11 years earlier.

His standout summer was something of a surprise. Scott's previous season, 1998, was spent largely at Double-A Chattanooga prior to a late-season trial at Indianapolis. He was reliable at both minor league stops, yet not especially sensational. But at Cincinnati in '99 he quickly blossomed.

Scott set Reds records for relief wins (12)—and losses, too (7)—led all major league relievers in victories, and registered the year's longest scoreless streak by NL pitchers, 23⅔ innings. At age 23 his future appeared to be very promising.

Suddenly every pitcher's dreaded nightmare, injuries, surfaced. A strained back disabled Williamson after 48 appearances, 10 of them starts, in 2000. The season's bright spot was his impressive strikeouts-to-innings-pitched ratio. He fanned 136 batters in 112 innings. However, worse news was yet to come.

Right-elbow surgery shelved Scott for the full 2001 campaign—except for two-thirds of an inning.

It was a devastating situation. But good news followed in 2002. The elbow operation was successful. Scott pitched in 63 games, and was nearly as effective as back in his luminous Rookie of the Year season. He saved eight wins and posted a strong 2.92 ERA. That year ended happily on a personal note, too. Scott and Lisa McWilliams were married right after the baseball season closed.

His arm was healthy again in 2003. But during that summer, Cincinnati, with a lackluster record, dealt away nearly a dozen veterans. Scott was one of them. He went to Boston, improved its bullpen, and appeared in the ALCS versus New York against other erstwhile Reds Gabe White and Aaron Boone.

Scott saved all three Red Sox wins in that historic League Championship Series, which New York won. Again. But whether or not the team was "cursed," Williamson headed into the 2004 campaign confident that his arm had fully returned to midcareer form.

He was effective—at first. But elbow tendinitis sidelined Scott again. He totaled only 29 innings with a solid 1.26 ERA. And was disappointingly left off Boston's successful postseason roster.

RAFAEL FURCAL
2000   Atlanta Braves, National League

Personal Data: B. August 24, 1980, at Loma de Cabrera, Dominican Republic.
Physical Attributes: 5' 10", playing weight 150 lbs. Bats both, throws right.
Rookie Year, 2000:   Primary position shortstop. 40 stolen bases.
Career to Date, 5 years: Braves 2000–04.

	BA	G	H	2B	3B	HR	RBI
2000	.295	131	134	20	4	4	37
Career to date	.283	663	749	129	27	45	234

With death and taxes, add an annual Braves' postseason appearance to your list of sure things. You'd be mistaken, though, to call Atlanta skipper Bobby Cox a "push-button manager."

Other than personnel stability in center field and for the most part behind the plate, Cox has been forced to mix and match Atlanta's position players into a virtually new lineup almost every year. Oh, one other exception: shortstop Rafael Furcal's name is automatically printed on Cox's lineup card.

Rafael Furcal, Atlanta Braves, 2000
Single-A minor leaguer one season; National League Rookie of the Year the next. Has given Braves stability at key shortstop position for over five years.
(Courtesy of Atlanta National Baseball Club, Inc. © 2003. All rights reserved.)

At first many onlookers were surprised to see the 21-year-old listed there as the 2000 season got under way. Because, even though Furcal excelled in minor league ball the previous year, it was, after all, at the Class-A level. He stole 96 bases and hit .322, but Single-A is normally a long way from the big leagues.

Not so for Furcal, who switched from second base to shortstop during that 1999 minor league season in Macon and Myrtle Beach. His rapid maturation propelled him to Rookie of the Year, Atlanta's first since David Justice 10 seasons earlier.

"That's really a special honor," he smiles, "because you have only the one chance to win it. When that season began I decided to take advantage of the opportunity [to make the Braves roster] and try to do well." As his .295 average and career-high 40 steals attest, he did.

The only extended period during which Cox played someone else at shortstop was the second half of Furcal's sophomore year. A major injury sidelined him for 83 games. Rafael suffered a dislocated left shoulder while sliding in a game at Boston. Healthy again for 2002 (.275 average) and '03, Furcal returned full-time to his post as the Braves' leadoff catalyst.

As Atlanta won its 13th consecutive division crown in 2004, Rafael's combination of speed (5 triples) and newfound power—14 home runs—were key elements in the team's success. For a while Rafael's name regularly appeared among MVP candidates. Even though he awaited incarceration for a DUI violation, he excelled in the division series.

Annually gaining more baseball recognition nationally, Furcal is extremely popular in Atlanta. The Dominican Republic native is now a full-time resident of Douglasville, Georgia. His popularity carries into the workplace, too. According to his manager, "Raffie's a great kid; a real delight to have in our dugout."

Furcal also enjoys continuing to play winter ball in Latin America. "It helps me to be ready for spring training."

ALBERT PUJOLS
2001   St. Louis Cardinals, National League

Personal Data: B. January 16, 1980, at Santo Domingo, Dominican Republic.
Physical Attributes: 6′ 3″, playing weight 210 lbs. Bats right, throws right.
Rookie Year, 2001:   Primary positions outfield, third base, first base. Missed only one game all season.
Career to Date, 4 years: Cardinals 2001–04.

	BA	G	H	2B	3B	HR	RBI
2001	.329	161	194	47	4	37	130
Career to date	.333	629	787	189	9	160	504

They might have to rewrite and update *The Natural* soon. This time, though, the story won't center on a fictional character. Albert Pujols, by all accounts, seems to be a real-life incarnation of the fabled Roy Hobbs.

It matters little if this 2001 National League Rookie of the Year is 25 now, as he reports, or older, as some suspect. His baseball future, barring injury or illness, seems bright, profitable, exciting, and very likely heading in a straight path toward Cooperstown.

Albert's St. Louis manager, Tony LaRussa, has managed six men in their Rookie of the Year seasons. He's skippered other All-Stars, too. Pujols, he proclaims, is the best player he's ever managed. Period.

This "best player" was a 13th round draft selection in 1999 after he and his father had emigrated from Santo Domingo to New York City and then to Independence, Missouri. Thirteenth round! That translates into embarrassed, red-faced talent scouts.

Bounding out of the 2001 big league gate after only 14 at bats beyond Class A, Pujols was the NL's undisputed, unanimous Rookie of the Year choice. Philadelphia shortstop Jimmy Rollins, who ranked a distant third in the voting, offers this testimonial to Pujols:

"That man just took off. He absolutely ran away with it [the award]. He really showed what can be done with speed, power, and adaptability."

As if Pujols' rookie year accomplishments were not brilliant enough, he improved many of them over the ensuing seasons. The chart that follows might be the best way to emphasize this, yes, phenom's, achievements:

	2001	2002	2003	2004
Batting	.329	.314	.359	.331
Hits	194	185	212	196
Runs	112	118	137	133
Doubles	47	40	51	51
Home runs	37	34	43	46
Runs batted in	130	127	124	123

The Pujols résumé already includes other notable exploits. In contending for the 2003 Triple Crown he was the Cardinals' first batting champ since Willie McGee in 1990. He is history's eighth player with 50 doubles and 40 homers in a season. Albert is the first man to surpass 30 homers, and drive in and score 100 runs in his first three seasons. Then his fourth. In fact, after 2002, he was the first to accomplish that feat in his first two years.

All that is aside from his defensive contributions. Albert may fall short of winning Gold Gloves, but his versatility has permitted LaRussa to play him, with confidence, in the outfield, at third base, and at first. His manager and teammates are also confident that Pujols will usually put the ball in play. He's averaged only about 65 strikeouts a season over his first four years in the National League. That's just one K every two and a half games or so.

For the record, and for the numerous plaques and citations that will surely follow, Albert's full name is Jose Alberto Pujols. He, his wife Dee Dee, and their two children live full-time in St. Louis. Their daughter, Bella, is afflicted with Down's syndrome. Albert actively supports the Make-a-Wish Foundation, a Down's organization.

Baseball fans and media have strongly supported Albert for MVP from his Rookie of the Year season forward. A fella named Barry Bonds has always blocked his way. Pujols does not seem obsessed with the award. Not yet, anyway.

"If it comes, great," he told USA Today. "Barry Bonds is probably the best player right now. Something like the MVP award—hopefully my time will come. If I play 10 or 15 more years, hopefully I can do that. But I don't live for it. I just try to get ready [for the game]—physically and mentally."

All evidence suggests that he prepares effectively.

ERIC HINSKE
2002   Toronto Blue Jays, American League

Personal Data: B. August 5, 1977, at Menasha, WI.
Physical Attributes: 6′ 2″, playing weight 225 lbs. Bats left, throws right.
Rookie Year, 2002:   Primary position third base.
Career to Date, 3 years: Blue Jays 2002–04.

	BA	G	H	2B	3B	HR	RBI
2002	.279	151	158	38	2	24	84
Career to date	.257	430	407	106	8	51	216

Eric Hinske, a relatively unheralded newcomer, played his first major league game on April 1, 2002.

Ten months later, decked out in formal dress tuxedo and holding the Jackie Robinson Rookie of the Year plaque, he appeared in full color on the cover of the Toronto Blue Jays' 2003 official information guide. If ever a ball club publicly put its faith in a young man's future, this was surely among the foremost examples.

In his sophomore year that followed, and despite an early-season injury, Eric gave the Jays no reason to discard their high hopes for him.

A modest four-year minor league background offered little indication that Hinske would turn in a superb big league rookie season. He'd been a low-round draft pick, by the Chicago Cubs in 1998, and was traded to the Oakland organization three years later. Oakland dealt him to Toronto with Justin Miller for reliever Billy Koch prior to 2002.

Consistent all season, he established Toronto rookie records in runs scored (99), doubles (38), homers (24), RBI (84), extra-base hits (64), total bases (272), and walks (77). No wonder the Jays gave him "poster boy" treatment.

He describes his rookie year this way:

> At first, I hadn't thought much about Rookie of the Year. But by midseason teammates and media people talked about it. I figured that Baltimore pitchers Rodrigo Lopez, Jorge Julio, and Travis Driskill had good chances, too. A lot of people kept cheering me on, though. Afterward a trip to New York for the Rookie of the Year award presentation was exciting. There were autograph sessions, too, and some contracts from equipment and apparel suppliers. And it was especially satisfying to have a five-year contract from the Blue Jays, who told me right from the start that I was their third baseman.

Eric admits he gave little thought to a sophomore jinx. However, after he struggled for a month or more in '03, fans and media reminded him of it. By mid-May his ability to hit with power was virtually nonexistent. Eventual diagnoses determined that his problem stemmed from a broken hamate bone in his right hand. It was successfully repaired surgically, but he spent five weeks on the disabled list.

Upon returning to the active roster, his hitting, and power, improved immediately. Even though he missed 38 games, Eric totaled 45 doubles by season's finish, fifth best in the American League. His batting average, down to .220 in May, was raised to .243 by the end of 2003.

Toronto finished 10 games over .500 in 2003, a 16-game bump from '02. Pitching and offense were significantly improved. The Blue Jays slumped to 67–94 in '04, with their third baseman playing at his sophomore-season level. All parties involved expect he'll soon return to his rookie-year standards.

JASON JENNINGS
2002   Colorado Rockies, National League

Personal Data: B. July 17, 1978, at Dallas, TX.
Physical Attributes: 6′ 2″, playing weight 242 lbs. Throws right, bats left.
Rookie Year, 2002:   Primary position pitcher.
Career to Date, 4 years: Rockies 2001–04.

	Record	ERA	G	GS	SO	IP
2002	16–8	4.52	32	32	127	185⅓
Career to date	43–34	5.03	104	104	405	607

Winning a Golden Spikes Award as America's top college player for his pitching excellence at Baylor University in 1999 had been the most cherished baseball honor to come his way. That is, until the big right-hander was named the 2002 National League Rookie of the Year.

Jason Jennings will forever hold the distinction of being the Colorado Rockies' first Rookie of the Year. So far he is Colorado's only player so honored. (His teammate Todd Helton finished second to Kerry Wood in 1998 balloting.)

Jennings' strong performance in 2002 included a 16–8 won-lost record and a 4.52 earned run average. That ERA, while not nearly record setting, is noteworthy because Jennings' home ballpark is the notoriously hitter-friendly Coors Field.

Even though he failed to complete any of his 32 starts, Jennings pitched 185⅓ innings during his rookie season after an audition in late 2001 when he registered a creditable 4–1 record.

No sophomore jinx was apparent during 2003, although Jason's numbers didn't quite match up to his Rookie of the Year achievements. Still, he turned in a 12–13 record with 119 strikeouts before a viral infection hospitalized him. It forced Jennings to miss out on his final scheduled start that year.

Recalling his rookie season, Jennings told the Associated Press, "Over the first two months of that season I wasn't even sure I'd be there the whole year, since I had all my options [possible minor league assignments] left. But things worked out well for me."

He started 17 games at Coors Field, posting a 9–4 record there. "Everybody knows it's an offensive park," he said. "So I just kind of expect the worst and hope for the best. If you give up five runs and win 7–5, you have to be happy. You can't worry about your ERA, your stats, your hits or anything like that."

Evidently, with an outlook like that, Jennings, with 104 consecutive starts to his credit since his September 2001 call-up, has the kind of mind-set required for finding pitching success on Coors' mile-high mound in Denver.

ANGEL BERROA
2003   Kansas City Royals, American League

Personal Data: B. January 27, 1978, at Santo Domingo, Dominican Republic.
Physical Attributes: 6′ 0″, playing weight 175 lbs. Bats right, throws right.
Rookie Year, 2003:   Primary position shortstop. 21 stolen bases.
Career to Date, 4 years: Royals 2001–04.

	BA	G	H	2B	3B	HR	RBI
2003	.287	158	163	28	7	17	73
Career to date	.273	327	330	64	14	25	125

Every professional sport has its one-year phenoms. The so-called flash in the pan. It also has its occasional pleasant surprise, an athlete who matures at a slow but steady pace. Angel Berroa ranks among this latter group—players who eventually perform at a grade-A level after years of preparation.

He ultimately rose to prominence as the 2003 American League Rookie of the Year. But just barely. On two counts.

First, in a razor-thin ballot victory, he nosed out highly regarded Japanese star Hidecki Matsui of the pennant-winning Yankees. Tampa Bay's Rocco Baldelli and Cleveland's Jody Gerut also challenged.

Second, except for attracting a couple of bases on balls in earlier years' call-ups, Angel would not have qualified as a 2003 rookie. The Royals promoted him for a total of 35 games over the two preceding seasons, during which he accumulated 128 at bats. Just three more—131—and he would have officially relinquished rookie status.

Berroa stepped into Kansas City's starting shortstop post on opening day of 2003. And as the Royals played undefeated baseball for nearly two weeks, he was clearly one of the team's spark plugs. He never let up . . . offensively or defensively. Coming off a 2002 season in which he hit only .215 for AAA Omaha, Angel was among Kansas City's top hitters all year. He finished at .287. And his 17 home runs and 73 RBI were stronger power figures than Royals' brass had probably expected.

Shaky defensively from time to time early in the year, Berroa settled down by early June. From then on, over the year's final 100 games or so, his error total never surpassed single digits. His 473 assists ranked in the top half dozen among major league shortstops in '03.

Berroa originally signed with the Oakland organization. After three mediocre seasons in the low minors, he was part of a five-player trade. Disappointed to see Johnny Damon and Mark Ellis traded, Royals' fans in 2003 were delighted with the previously unheralded Berroa.

Enthusiasm soon turned to despair, however, in Kansas City. The team finished in last place in 2004, never having contended for the AL Central title. Berroa also slumped badly, to the point that he was demoted to Omaha in July. He was hitting only .249 with little power and was already charged with 23 errors. Happily for Angel, his month-long trip to Triple A seemed to rejuvenate him. Upon his return to Kansas City, his hitting perked up to a final .262 mark, and his defense was considerably tighter. Whether Berroa can return to 2003 Rookie of the Year form in '05 is a big question confronting the Royals and their fans.

DONTRELLE WILLIS
2003   Florida Marlins, National League

Personal Data: B. January 12, 1982, at Oakland, CA.
Physical Attributes: 6′ 4″, playing weight 200 lbs. Throws left, bats left.
Rookie Year, 2003:   Primary position pitcher. Nearly a 3-to-1 strikeout/walk ratio. Pitched in All-Star Game after only two months in NL.
Career to Date, 2 years: Marlins 2003–04.

	Record	ERA	G	GS	SO	IP
2003	14–6	3.30	27	27	142	160⅔
Career to date	24–17	3.70	59	59	281	357⅔

If you had to select one "feel good" story from the 2003 baseball season, Dontrelle Willis just might be the central character. He's the guy with the herky-jerky motion, the long-billed cap drawn close to his eyes, and a Valenzuela-style skyward look before delivering his pitch.

The 21-year-old southpaw was unheralded nationally when he emerged from the minors on May 9, 2003. His arrival in South Florida closely coincided with Jack McKeon's coming on board as Marlins manager. Two weeks later Florida began the surprising run toward its World Series title.

Willis's fast start was a major ingredient as Florida posted the best record in baseball over the season's final two-thirds. He won his first seven decisions. And just six weeks after entering the major leagues he was selected to the National League All-Star team.

A mere three years earlier, at Alameda, California's Encinal High, the tall left-hander was posting a 10–1 record with a 0.70 ERA. Dontrelle was the state's high school Player of the Year. The Chicago Cubs drafted him.

Following the 2001 minor league season, Willis was traded to the Marlins' organization when Chicago acquired Matt Clement, an accomplished, effective starter. Meanwhile, even though America's casual fans weren't paying close attention, Willis turned in strong performances for Marlin farm clubs at Class A and AA levels. Evaluating personnel at the end of 2002, Marlin officials rated Willis their minor league system's fourth best pitcher.

Seven months later many fans and some media considered him the *best* pitcher at the team's *major league* level.

After Willis's first trip around the National League, opposing hitters began to familiarize themselves with the newcomer's flamboyant style. Toward season's end he, too, adjusted to the adjustments. Featuring sharp control, Dontrelle finished the regular season with a nifty 14–6 record and a 3.30 earned run average. He walked only about three batters per nine innings, and fanned an average of nearly one man per inning. His solid performance earned him freshman honors over worthy challengers Scott Podsednik and Brandon Webb.

A starter in the regular season and during both NL playoff rounds, Dontrelle was used exclusively in relief against New York during the World Series. Then, just three years past high school graduation—and with a World Championship ring and Rookie of the Year trophy in tow—he returned home to Alameda as a national celebrity.

Dontrelle's second-year figures dropped only slightly from 2003, and the Marlins are counting on him to remain a stable starter.

JASON BAY
2004   Pittsburgh Pirates, National League

Personal Data: B. September 20, 1978, at Trail, BC, Canada.
Physical Attributes: 6' 2", playing weight 200 lbs. Bats right, throws right.
Rookie Year, 2004:   Primary position outfield. Led team with a .550 slugging average.
Career to Date, 2 years: Padres 2003; Pirates '03–04.

	BA	G	H	2B	3B	HR	RBI
2004	.282	120	116	24	4	26	82
Career to date	.283	150	141	31	8	30	96

When the National League's Rookie of the Year winner was announced in early November 2004, Jason Bay said he couldn't believe that he was the first Pittsburgh Pirate, ever, to win that honor. "How about Clemente or Stargell," he wondered. "Or Barry Bonds?"

No Jason, incredibly Pittsburgh had been shut out of RoY laurels during the 47 seasons since Jackie Robinson became the Baseball Writers' Association of America's first honoree in 1947. All of the other 15 existing franchises that were in business back then have welcomed multiple Rookies of the Year to their honor rolls in the meantime.

Jason Bay clearly merits the honor as Pittsburgh's first. He was a yearlong spark plug as the struggling Bucs played at roughly the .500 level over the season's first half. Bay was a model of consistency. He rarely veered far away from the .282 batting average with which he finished the year. His 26 home runs were just three shy of team leader Craig Wilson's total, and his 82 runs batted in tied Wilson for the Pittsburgh leadership. Jason turned in a solid defensive performance, too. Playing mostly in left field, he committed only two errors in 120 games.

Clearly a fixture in Pittsburgh, Bay began his career in the San Diego organization before a 2003 trade in which then-Pirate Brian Giles was the most prominent name at the time. He played in only 30 games during the '03 campaign, thus maintaining his RoY eligibility.

As the Pirates' initial Rookie of the Year, Bay accomplished yet another "first." A native of Trail, British Columbia, Jason is the first Canadian-born player among baseball's 116 specially honored rookies.

BOBBY CROSBY
2004   Oakland Athletics, American League

Personal Data: B. January 12, 1980, at Lakewood, CA.
Physical Attributes: 6′ 3″, playing weight 200 lbs. Bats right, throws right.
Rookie Year, 2004:   Primary position shortstop. Only 19 errors at shortstop in 1,356 innings.
Career to Date, 2 years: Athletics 2003–04.

	BA	G	H	2B	3B	HR	RBI
2004	.239	151	130	34	1	22	64
Career to date	.233	162	130	34	1	22	64

Occasionally a "horse race" develops in the balloting for baseball's Rookie of the Year. Not so, though, when BBWAA voters filed their American League selections in 2004.

Oakland shortstop Bobby Crosby was their clear-cut choice. In fact, he failed to be a unanimous selection by just a single first-place vote. That nod went to White Sox relief pitcher Shingo Takatsu.

Crosby's election had been something of a foregone conclusion. Even early in the year, if not before the official start of the '04 season. Many observers had named him their preseason choice as the AL's top rookie. He did not disappoint them. Nor his employer, the Oakland A's. Manager Ken Macha penned Bobby's name onto his lineup card from Day One, and the newcomer—who had auditioned with 12 at bats for Oakland in late 2003—was the regular shortstop throughout 2004.

Although his offensive output lost steam late in the regular year—Crosby finished at .239, the lowest batting average ever for any Rookie of the Year position player—he was a consistently solid clutch hitter for most of the season and again during the final week's showdown against Anaheim. Bobby ranked second among the Athletics in doubles (34), home runs (22), and games played (151).

Defensively the 24-year-old ranked among the American League's elite short-stops. He covered ground with speed and style, accounting for a whopping 505 assists and committing only 19 errors in a team high of 1,356 innings.

Veteran baseball scouts expect 2004 Rookie of the Year Bobby Crosby to contend for additional individual honors over the next decade or more.

List of *The Sporting News* Rookies of the Year (1946–2004)

One Major League Rookie of the Year

1946	Del Ennis, OF, Phillies
1947	Jackie Robinson, 1B, Dodgers
1948	Rich Ashburn, OF, Phillies
1950	Whitey Ford, P, Yankees

One Player from Each Major League

	American	National
1949	Roy Sievers, OF, Browns	Don Newcombe, P, Dodgers
1951	Minnie Minoso, OF, White Sox	Willie Mays, OF, Giants
1952	Clint Courtney, C, Browns	Joe Black, P, Dodgers
1953	Harvey Kuenn, SS, Tigers	Jim Gilliam, 2B, Dodgers
1954	Bob Grim, P, Yankees	Wally Moon, OF, Cardinals
1955	Herb Score, P, Indians	Bill Virdon, OF, Cardinals
1956	Luis Aparicio, SS, White Sox	Frank Robinson, OF, Reds
1957	Tony Kubek, IF-OF, Yankees	(tie) Ed Bouchee, 1B, Phillies Jack Sanford, P, Phillies
1958	(tie) Albie Pearson, OF, Senators Ryne Duren, P, Yankees	(tie) Orlando Cepeda, 1B, Giants Carlton Willey, P, Braves
1959	Bob Allison, OF, Senators	Willie McCovey, 1B-OF, Giants
1960	Ron Hansen, SS, Orioles	Frank Howard, OF, Dodgers
1962	Tom Tresh, SS-OF, Yankees	Ken Hubbs, 2B, Cubs
2004	Bobby Crosby, SS, Athletics	Jason Bay, OF, Pirates

List of *The Sporting News* Rookies of the Year (1946–2004) (continued)

One Position Player and One Pitcher from Each Major League

	American	National
1961	(tie) Dick Howser, SS, Athletics Don Schwall, P, Red Sox	Billy Williams, OF, Cubs Ken Hunt, P, Reds
1963	Pete Ward, 3B, White Sox Gary Peters, P, White Sox	Pete Rose, 2B, Reds Ray Culp, P, Phillies
1964	Tony Oliva, OF, Twins Wally Bunker, P, Orioles	Dick Allen, 3B, Phillies Billy McCool, P, Reds
1965	Curt Blefary, OF, Orioles Marcelino Lopez, P, Angels	Joe Morgan, 2B, Astros Frank Linzy, P, Giants
1966	Tommie Agee, OF, White Sox Jim Nash, P, Athletics	Tommy Helms, 3B, Reds Don Sutton, P, Dodgers
1967	Rod Carew, 2B, Twins Tom Phoebus, P, Orioles	Lee May, 1B, Reds Dick Hughes, P, Cardinals
1968	Del Unser, OF, Senators Stan Bahnsen, P, Yankees	Johnny Bench, C, Reds Jerry Koosman, P, Mets
1969	Carlos May, OF, White Sox Mike Nagy, P, Red Sox	Coco Laboy, 3B, Expos Tom Griffin, P, Astros
1970	Roy Foster, OF, Indians Bert Blyleven, P, Twins	Bernie Carbo, OF, Reds Carl Morton, P, Expos
1971	Chris Chambliss, 1B, Indians Bill Parsons, P, Brewers	Earl Williams, C, Braves Reggie Cleveland, P, Cardinals
1972	Carlton Fisk, C, Red Sox Dick Tidrow, P, Indians	Dave Rader, C, Giants Jon Matlack, P, Mets
1973	Al Bumbry, OF, Orioles Steve Busby, P, Royals	Gary Matthews, OF, Giants Steve Rogers, P, Expos
1974	Mike Hargrove, 1B, Rangers Frank Tanana, P, Angels	Greg Gross, OF, Astros John D'Acquisto, P, Giants
1975	Fred Lynn, OF, Red Sox Dennis Eckersley, P, Indians	Gary Carter, OF-C, Expos John Montefusco, P, Giants

List of *The Sporting News* Rookies of the Year (1946–2004) (continued)

One Position Player and One Pitcher from Each Major League (continued)

	American	National
1976	Butch Wynegar, C, Twins Mark Fidrych, P, Tigers	Larry Herndon, OF, Giants Butch Metzger, P, Padres
1977	Mitchell Page, OF, Athletics Dave Rozema, P, Tigers	Andre Dawson, OF, Expos Bob Owchinko, P, Padres
1978	Paul Molitor, 2B, Brewers Rich Gale, P, Royals	Bob Horner, 3B, Braves Don Robinson, P, Pirates
1979	Pat Putnam, 1B, Rangers Mark Clear, P, Angels	Jeff Leonard, OF, Astros Rick Sutcliffe, P, Dodgers
1980	Joe Charboneau, OF, Indians Britt Burns, P, White Sox	Lonnie Smith, OF, Phillies Bill Gullickson, P, Expos
1981	Rich Gedman, C, Red Sox Dave Righetti, P, Yankees	Tim Raines, OF, Expos Fernando Valenzuela, P, Dodgers
1982	Cal Ripken, Jr., SS-3B, Orioles Ed Vande Berg, P, Mariners	Johnny Ray, 2B, Pirates Steve Bedrosian, P, Braves
1983	Ron Kittle, OF, White Sox Mike Boddicker, P, Orioles	Darryl Strawberry, OF, Mets Craig McMurtry, P, Braves
1984	Alvin Davis, 1B, Mariners Mark Langston, P, Mariners	Juan Samuel, 2B, Phillies Dwight Gooden, P, Mets
1985	Ozzie Guillen, SS, White Sox Teddy Higuera, P, Brewers	Vince Coleman, OF, Cardinals Tom Browning, P, Reds
1986	Jose Canseco, OF, Athletics Mark Eichorn, P, Blue Jays	Robby Thompson, 2B, Giants Todd Worrell, P, Cardinals
1987	Mark McGwire, 1B, Athletics Mike Henneman, P, Tigers	Benito Santiago, C, Padres Mike Dunne, P, Pirates
1988	Walt Weiss, SS, Athletics Bryan Harvey, P, Angels	Mark Grace, 1B, Cubs Tim Belcher, P, Dodgers
1989	Craig Worthington, 3B, Orioles Tom Gordon, P, Royals	Jerome Walton, OF, Cubs Andy Benes, P, Padres

One Position Player and One Pitcher
from Each Major League (continued)

	American	National
1990	Sandy Alomar, Jr., C, Indians Kevin Appier, P, Royals	David Justice, OF, Braves Mike Harkey, P, Cubs
1991	Chuck Knoblauch, 2B, Twins Juan Guzman, P, Blue Jays	Jeff Bagwell, 1B, Astros Al Osuna, P, Astros
1992	Pat Listach, SS, Brewers Cal Eldred, P, Brewers	Eric Karros, 1B, Dodgers Tim Wakefield, P, Pirates
1993	Tim Salmon, OF, Angels Aaron Sele, P, Red Sox	Mike Piazza, C, Dodgers Kirk Rueter, P, Expos
1994	Bob Hamelin, 1B, Royals Brian Anderson, P, Angels	Raul Mondesi, OF, Dodgers Steve Trachsel, P, Cubs
1995	Garrett Anderson, OF Angels Julian Tavarez, P, Indians	Chipper Jones, 3B, Braves Hideo Nomo, P, Dodgers
1996	Derek Jeter, SS, Yankees James Baldwin, P, White Sox	Jason Kendall, C, Pirates Alan Benes, P, Cardinals
1997	Nomar Garciaparra, SS, Red Sox Jason Dickson, P, Angels	Scott Rolen, 3B, Phillies Matt Morris, P, Cardinals
1998	Ben Grieve, OF, Athletics Rolando Arrojo, P, Devil Rays	Todd Helton, 1B, Rockies Kerry Wood, P, Cubs
1999	Carlos Beltran, OF, Royals Tim Hudson, P, Athletics	Preston Wilson, OF, Marlins Scott Williamson, P, Reds
2000	Mark Quinn, OF, Royals Kazuhiro Sasaki, P, Mariners	Rafael Furcal, SS, Braves Rick Ankiel, P, Cardinals
2001	Ichiro Suzuki, OF, Mariners C. C. Sabathia, P, Indians	Albert Pujols, 3B, Cardinals Roy Oswalt, P, Astros
2002	Eric Hinske, 3B, Blue Jays Rodrigo Lopez, P, Orioles	Brad Wilkerson, OF, Expos Jason Jennings, P, Rockies
2003	Jody Gerut, OF, Indians Rafael Soriano, P, Mariners	Scott Podsednik, OF, Brewers Dontrelle Willis, P, Marlins

Summary

Saluting So Few

Long Odds

From opening day every spring until September 1st, 750 baseball players are members of Major League Baseball's 30 active rosters. A maximum of 25 men per team.

All of them were rookies once. Talented enough to overcome challenges from their fellow aspirants at Florida and Arizona training camps. Good enough then to fill a roster spot, usually as a utility man or, if a pitcher, perhaps as a long reliever or spot starter.

They've achieved a major goal. "Making it to the show!" Their next target? Simply fitting in, feeling comfortable, effectively contributing in whatever their assigned roles. In their own phrasing throughout this book, the 116 honored rookies repeated that very theme—". . . and our major objective is to feel that we belong in the big leagues."

Very seldom did they focus on winning Rookie of the Year laurels. First things first. Make the club. Hope for increased playing time. Be productive. Maybe, by late season, dare to think about Rookie of the Year. Then, if chosen, recognize that you've beaten long odds.

On any typical day during baseball season (prior to September call-ups), normally no more than 70 or so rookies are rostered among the 750 big leaguers in uniform. On average, a little more than two per team.

Only two rookies, one in each major league, are judged to be worthy of the Jackie Robinson Award. As we heard, in another of the book's continuing themes, winners are especially proud of this honor. Because it's available only once a career.

WHO'S A ROOKIE? OR NOT

From the late 1990s forward a controversy's been brewing about one particular Rookie of the Year eligibility requirement. The matter of allowing players with considerable longevity in Japanese professional leagues to be eligible for the award.

Some members of the Baseball Writers' Association of America have voiced an unofficial opinion that the issue should be formally addressed. As of this writing the BBWAA officially continues its eligibility parameters described in this book's introduction. In effect, a first-year player in the American or National League is designated a *rookie*. Regardless of his age, place of birth, or time spent as a participant in a league outside the purview of America's organized baseball.

Hideo Nomo of the 1995 Dodgers was the first Japanese league player to be named a Rookie of the Year. Since then, two Seattle Mariners, Kaz Sasaki and Ichiro Suzuki, were similarly honored. All three had lengthy careers in Japan before coming to the United States. Sasaki, as we've seen, is officially the eldest Rookie of the Year—32 in 2000. He's since returned to Japan to finish his professional career there. Suzuki was 27 in his brilliant 2001 Rookie-of-the-Year-and-MVP season. Nomo made his National League debut at 26.

Hideki Matsui, a 10-season Japanese league veteran of unquestioned ability, turned 29 midway through his rookie year with the 2003 New York Yankees. He was an offensive leader throughout the season. Many felt he was New York's most consistent, productive position player as his team advanced to the World Series. He was clearly a Rookie of the Year contender, although Royals shortstop Angel Berroa—whose performance also merited accolades—was the American League RoY winner. It is believed that two or three writers omitted Matsui from their ballots. They allegedly protested against the eligibility requirements, not Matsui personally.

The subject is not new. More than 50 years earlier a similar situation existed. Back in Jackie Robinson's time.

Veterans of Negro leagues were finally given a chance to play major league baseball. Some of them were experienced Negro League standouts. Robinson himself, an ex–Kansas City Monarch, was 28 when presented with the BBWAA's first Rookie of the Year award in 1947. Three years later Sam Jethroe, the Boston Braves speedster, was the National League's premier rookie. He had at least six years of Negro league experience by then, and was a reported 28. As we've seen, Jethroe might have been three or four years older than that. That same year eventual Hall of Famer Monte Irvin came to the Giants from Negro league background. Irvin was a 30-year-old rookie by then, and unfortunately his prime career was behind him.

Legendary pitcher Satchel Paige signed with the Cleveland Indians in 1948. He was at least 43, and by some accounts had already played professionally in Negro leagues for 20 years. Paige expressed disappointment that Alvin Dark, instead, was named '48 Rookie of the Year.

So, from more than a half century ago to now, when a player first shows up in the major leagues—regardless of his age or background—he is a rookie. That's the BBWAA's firm and official stance. At the moment.

ROLLER COASTER CAREERS

From the instant they stepped onto the big league stage some players delivered headlined performances all season. And of course they deservedly won Rookie of the Year honors. A few of them would never again match their freshman performances. Others who debuted with solid accomplishments built on them as their careers accelerated. Rod Carew is the best example among the 116 RoY.

Research for this book turned up few statistical surprises. But this might be one. Only one in approximately four position players finished his career with a batting average higher than his rookie year's output.

Several others were lower by just a few percentage points while consistently batting in the same range year after year. A very few fell markedly off their fine first season's performance, and soon departed the big leagues.

There was another surprise—at first glance. Of the 29 pitchers who won Rookie of the Year laurels, only one—just one single pitcher—wound up his career with an earned run average lower than his rookie season's figure. Kazuhiro Sasaki, four seasons a Seattle relief pitcher before returning to play in Japan, fashioned a 3.16 ERA in 2000. When he bowed out after the 2003 season Kaz's lifetime ERA was 3.14.

No other pitcher finished as strong as he started . . . in terms of earned run average.

Former hurler Larry Andersen, long-time pitching coach Joe Kerrigan, and manager Bobby Cox all point to three factors for the decrease in ERA effectiveness. One, over time batters familiarize themselves with pitchers' styles and tendencies. Two, with few exceptions pitchers develop sore arms or other physical ailments of varying degrees. In looking at the list of the 29 pitchers, analysts found very few who had not experienced one or more injuries. And three, everybody winds down eventually. If not, careers would continue on and on. Whether he be pitcher or hitter, a player invariably suffers statistically as his career phases out.

THEY ALSO PLAYED

We have seen that Hideki Matsui was nosed out by Angel Berroa in 2003 balloting. You assume he was disappointed. But he displayed only gentlemanly class in offering sincere congratulations to Berroa.

Montreal Expos outfielder Brad Wilkerson missed out on the BBWAA honor but was *The Sporting News* position player RoY choice in 2002. Midway through his rookie season he discussed his chances.

"Yes, people are talking about the rookie award. But that can't be your major goal. Otherwise you put too much pressure on yourself. My goal is to just get better every day. Play hard, and awards will take care of themselves. Naturally I'm aware of the rookie award, and would be honored to win it. But if I don't I wouldn't mind seeing Josh Fogg (Pittsburgh pitcher) get it. We're old pals . . . same age and went to the same school, University of Florida."

Phillies shortstop Jimmy Rollins finished third in the 2001 balloting.

"How could I be disappointed in not winning," he said. "Albert Pujols had just a magnificent season. He took off and absolutely ran away with it (RoY). I look back on my rookie year with great pleasure. It was fun breaking in. Made the All-Star team (first of two consecutive years). Really enjoyed my rookie year. You know, everybody's a rookie once. Many veterans remember that. In my case our third baseman (1997 Rookie of the Year) Scott Rolen gave me a lot of help and built my confidence. My advice to rookies is know yourself, know what you can do, and show the manager and coaches you're capable of playing big league ball."

Former Baltimore pitcher Travis Driskill started the 2002 season with five straight victories. However, he was ineffective after midseason, spent much of the following year in the minors, but later pitched briefly for Colorado.

Nevertheless, during his good run in '02, he said his goal was to make the Orioles staff. "Truly, Rookie of the Year was the farthest thing from my mind. I'm a 30-year-old rookie. Spent several years in the Cleveland and Houston systems. Of course I hope to have a successful season, but just being here is the biggest thrill of my life. You know, until I walked out here for pregame drills, I'd never stepped onto a big league field before. Been in the stands at various ballparks, but never on the field.

"I don't know how long I'll be in the big leagues. But I would hope that any young guy who aspires to it can get a big league chance sometime. I suppose I'll try to stay in baseball as a coach or something. Be a lifer. Baseball got hold of me as a youngster, and won't let go. I'd like to be responsible for helping another young player realize a big league dream."

Ultimately there was no trophy for Travis Driskill. But his enthusiastic outlook is an inspiration for any young ballplayer. Whether or not he becomes Rookie of the Year.

... AND THESE FORGETTABLE LAST WORDS

Four decades ago a 21-year-old basketball player in a regional professional weekend league was asked what winning the Rookie of the Year award meant to him. His serious but not particularly well-considered reply: "I'm really thrilled. Especially since this is only my first year in the league!"

Index

Note: Italicized page numbers denote table entries.

Aaron, Henry (Hank), 4, 23, 29, 30, 44, 55, 106, 123, 124
Aberdeen IronBirds, 33. *See also* Cal Ripkin, Jr.
Aberdeen Project, 33
Agee, Tommy, *11*, *75*, 118, *197*
Alexander, Grover Cleveland, 108
Allen, Richie (Dick), *11*, *40*, 41–43, *77*, 120, *197*
Allison, Bob, *11*, *75*, 110–11, *196*
Alomar, Roberto, 162
Alomar, Sandy, Jr., *12*, *75*, 161–62, *198*
Alomar, Sandy, Sr., 162
Alston, Walt, 9
Alvin Dark Foundation, 62
Andersen, Larry, 44, 202
Anderson, Brady, 126
Anderson, Brian, *199*
Anderson, Garrett, 169, *199*
Anderson, Sparky, 16
Ankiel, Rick, *199*
Aparicio, Luis, *11*, *13*, 14–15, 35, 57, 63, *75*, 117, *196*
Appier, Kevin, *198*
Appling, Luke, 63, 176
Arrojo, Rolando, *199*
Ashburn, Rich, 61, *196*

Baerga, Carlos, 161
Bagwell, Jeff, *12*, *40*, 43–44, *76*, 158, *199*; daughter Bryce Alicia, 44; wife Erica, 44
Bahnsen, Stan, *11*, *75*, 119–20, *197*

Baker, Dusty, 104, 128
Baldelli, Rocco, 191
Baldwin, James, *199*
Baltimore Elite Giants, 103
Banks, Ernie, 4, 23, 39, 106
Baseball Assistance Team, 81
Battey, Earl, 111
Bauer, Hank, 101
Bay, Jason, *12*, *77*, 158, 193–94, *196*
Bearden, Gene, 61
Beazley, Johnny, 2
Bedrossian, Steve, *198*
Belcher, Tim, *198*
Bell, Buddy, 150
Bell, "Cool Papa," 7
Bell, David, 58
Belle, Albert, 161
Beltran, Carlos, *12*, *75*, 158, 182–84, *199*; wife Jessica, 183
Bench, Johnny, *11*, *13*, 15–17, 21, 35, *40*, 40, *76*, *197*
Benes, Alan, *199*
Benes, Andy, *198*
Benzinger, Todd, 163
Berra, Yogi, 101
Berroa, Angel, *12*, *75*, 183, 191–92, 201, 203
Berry, Halle, 156
Betty Ford Clinic, 144
Bilko, Steve, 53
Black, Joe, *11*, 51, *77*, 78, 81–82, 136, *196*

Blair, Paul, 117
Blass, Steve, 141
Blefary, Curt, *11*, *75*, 117, 142, *197*
Blyleven, Bert, *197*
Boddicker, Mike, *198*
Boggs, Wade, 174
Bonds, Barry, 4, 15, 29, 188, 193
Bones, Ricky, 92
Boone, Aaron, 185
Boone, Bob, 93, 121, 129
Bouchee, Ed, *196*
Boudreau, Lou, 2
Bowa, Larry, 121, 129, 179
Bowman, Mark, 133
Branca, Ralph, 52, 99
Braves Field, 80
Brock, Lou, 120–21
Browning, Tom, *198*
Buckner, Bill, 141
Buhner, Jay, 145
Bumbry, Al, *11*, *75*, 126–27, *197*
Bunker, Wally, *197*
Burns, Britt, *198*
Burroughs, Jeff, 122
Busby, Steve, *197*
Busch Stadium, 148
Butler, Brett, 163
Byrd, Harry, *11*, *76*, 82–83

Cabrera, Francisco, 156
Cal Ripken, Jr., Foundation, 33
Cal Ripken, Sr., Foundation, 33
Candlestick Park, 26
Canseco, Jose, *12*, 28, *40*, 45–46, *76*, 151, *198*
Canseco, Ozzie, 45
Canton-Akron team, 91
Carbo, Bernie, 121, *197*
Carew, Rod, *11*, *13*, 17–19, 40, *41*, 57, *75*, 116, 166, *197*, 202
Carlton, Steve, 4, 121, 129
Carreon, Camilo, 118
Carter, Gary, *197*
Carty, Rico, 135
Castino, John, *12*, *75*, 88–89, 135, 151
Cepeda, Orlando, *11*, *13*, 19–21, 40, *41*, 77, *196;* sons Ali Manuel, Hector, Malcolm, and Orlando, Jr., 21; wife Miriam, 21
Cey, Ron, 141
Chambliss, Chris, *11*, *75*, 122–23, *197*
Chance, Frank, 84
Charboneau, Joe, 3, *12*, 66, *75*, 78, 79, 90–91, 139, *198*
Chunichi Dragons, 53
Cimoli, Gino, 73, 106

Clear, Mark, *198*
Clement, Matt, 193
Clemente, Roberto, 4, 74, 125, 166, 193
Cleveland, Reggie, *197*
Cleveland Buckeyes, 80
Cleveland Stadium, 64, 100
Cobb, Ty, 18, 134
Colavito, Rocky, 69, 73, 118
Coleman, Vince, *12*, 77, 147–48, *198*
Comiskey Park, 49, 98, 142–43
Concepcion, Dave, 16
Coors Field, 190–91
Cordova, Marty, *12*, 66, *75*, 169–70
Courtney, Clint, *196*
Cox, Bobby, 132, 155, 185–86, 202
Crohn's and Colitis Foundation of America, 21
Cromartie, Warren, 46
Crosby, Bobby, *12*, *76*, 158, 194–95, *196*
Crosetti, Frank, 173, 175
Cuellar, Mike, 117
Cullen, Tim, 112
Culp, Ray, *197*
Czerwinski, Kevin, 125

Damon, Johnny, 192
Dandridge, Ray, 7
Daniels, Kal, 163
D'Aquisto, John, *197*
Dark, Alvin, *11*, 59, *60*, 61–62, *76*, 97, 124, 202; wife Jackie, 62
Davis, Alvin, *12*, *76*, 145–46, *198*
Davis, Chili, 167
Davis, Tommy, 118
Dawson, Andre, *12*, *41*, 46–47, 77, 154, *198*
Dean, Dizzy, 1, 108, 130
Dedeaux, Rod, 28
Del Greco, Bobby, 73
Dent, Bucky, 118
DeShields, Delino, 156
Dickson, Jason, *199*
DiHigo, Martin, 7
Dillinger, Bob, 96
DiMaggio, Dom, 175
DiMaggio, Joe, 15, 25, 44, 176
Dobson, Pat, 124
Dodger Stadium, 148, 171
Doerr, Bobby, 135
Dorsey, Jim, 49
Dressen, Chuck, 52
Driskill, Travis, 189, 203
Dropo, Walt, *11*, *75*, 98–99
Duncan, Taylor, 124
Dunne, Mike, *198*
Duren, Ryne, *196*

Durocher, Leo, 24
Dyer, Duffy, 97
Dykes, Jimmie, 82

Ebbets Field, 8, 53
Eckersley, Dennis, *197*
Eichorn, Mark, *198*
Eldred, Cal, *199*
Ellis, Mark, 192
Embree, Alan, 156
Ennis, Del, 2, *196*
Erickson, Scott, 156
Estrada, Chuck, 112
Evers, Johnny, 84

Fain, Ferris, 7, 82
Farrell, Kerby, 101
Fenway Park, 22, 49, 83
Ferriss, Boo, 2
Fidrych, Mark, *12*, *75*, 85–86, 130, *197*
Fielder, Cecil, 45
Fisher, Jack, 118
Fisk, Carlton, *11*, *13*, 21–22, *75*, 90, 159, 164, *197*
Flynn, Doug, 37
Fogg, Josh, 203
Forbes Field, 107
Ford, Whitey, *196*
Fosse, Ray, 55
Foster, George, 16
Foster, Roy, *197*
Fox, Nelson, 14
Frick, Ford, 8
Fuentes, Tito, 88
Furcal, Rafael, *12*, *76*, 158, 185–87, *199*

Gaetti, Gary, 89
Gagne, Eric, 149
Gale, Rich, *198*
Garciaparra, Nomar, *12*, *75*, 158, 175–77, *199*
Garner, Phil, 71
Garver, Ned, 96
Garvey, Steve, 141
Gedman, Rich, *198*
Gehrig, Lou, 27, 31, 32, 38, 51
Gehringer, Charlie, 15, 134
Gentile, Jim, 112
Gerut, Jody, 191, *199*
Giamatti, A. Bartlett, 56
Gibson, Bob, 4, 119
Gibson, Josh, 7
Giles, Brian, 194
Gilliam, Jim, *11*, 51, 70, *77*, 103–04, 120, *196*
Gomez, Ruben, 108

Gooden, Dwight, *12*, 77, 101, 125, 140, 146–47, 148, *198*
Gordon, Joe, 71
Gordon, Tom, *198*
Gossage, Goose, 138
Grace, Mark, 150, 154, *198*
Green, Lenny, 110
Green, Pumpsie, 80
Green, Shawn, 168
Grieve, Ben, *12*, *76*, 158, 179–80, *199*
Grieve, Tom, 180
Griffey, Ken, Jr., 145
Griffin, Alfredo, *12*, *76*, 88–89, 134–35, 151; wife Noris, 135
Griffin, Tom, *197*
Griffith, Calvin, 18
Grim, Bob, 3, *11*, *75*, 104–05, 119, *196*
Grissom, Marquis, 156
Gross, Greg, *197*
Gross, Kevin, 163
Groth, Johnny, 97
Guillen, Ozzie, *12*, 59, *60*, 62–64, *75*, *198*
Gullickson, Bill, *198*
Guzman, Juan, *199*

Hamelin, Bob, *12*, *75*, 78, 92–93, *199*
Hamm, Mia, 177
Hansen, Ron, *11*, *75*, 111–12, 142, *196*
Hargrove, Mike, *11*, 59, *60*, 64–66, *76*, 90, *197*; wife Sharon, 66
Harkey, Mike, *198*
Harrelson, Bud, 55
Harvey, Brian, *198*
Harwell, Ernie, 25
Helms, Tommy, *11*, *60*, 66–67, *76*, *197*
Helton, Todd, 181, 190, *199*
Henderson, Steve, 37
Hendrick, George, 97
Henneman, Mike, *198*
Henrich, Tommy, 38, 52, 113
Herman, Billy, 84
Hernandez, Roberto, 180
Herndon, Larry, *197*
Higuera, Teddy, *198*
Hinske, Eric, 3, *12*, *76*, 158, 189–90, *199*
Hodges, Gil, 162
Hollandsworth, Todd, *12*, 77, 172–73
Horner, Bob, *12*, *76*, 132–33, *198*
Hornsby, Rogers, 84, 134
Howard, Frank, *11*, *60*, 67–68, 77, *196*
Howe, Steve, *12*, 77, 136, 137–38
Howell, Jay, 162
Howser, Dick, *197*
Hrbek, Kent, 156

Hubbs, Ken, *11*, 50, *76*, 78, 79, 84–85, *196*
Hudson, Tim, *199*
Hughes, Dick, *197*
Hunt, Ken, *197*

Irvin, Monte, 23, 80, 81, 201

Jackie Robinson Award, 2, 5, 6, 10, 200
Jackie Robinson Foundation, 9
Jackson, Reggie, 50, 127
Jackson, Reverend Jesse, 10
Jansen, Larry, 7
Jennings, Jason, *12*, *76*, 190–91, *199*
Jeter, Derek, *12*, *75*, 158, 173–75, *199*; mother
    Dot, 175
Jethroe, Sam, *11*, 23, 51, *76*, 78, 79–80, 81, 94,
    124, 201; granddaughter Carla, 80; wife
    Elsie, 80
Joe Black Trophy, 82
John, Tommy, 118, 170
Johnson, Billy, 2
Johnson, Davey, 124
Johnson, Judy, 7
Johnson, Randy, 146
Johnson, Tim, 163
Jones, Chipper, *199*
Joost, Eddie, 83
Julio, Jorge, 3, 189
Justice, David, *12*, *76*, 155–56, 186, *198*

Kahn, Roger, 9
Kaline, Al, 4, 134
Kansas City Monarchs, 7, 201
Karros, Eric, *12*, *77*, 162–64, *199*; wife Trish,
    164
Kell, George, 98
Keller, Hal, 65
Kelly, Tom, 157
Kendall, Jason, *199*
Kennedy, Kevin, 163
Kerrigan, Joe, 202
Kiersh, Edward, 99
Killebrew, Harmon, 111, 116
Kimm, Bruce, 92
Kirkland, Willie, 69
Kittle, Ron, *12*, *75*, 142–43, *198*
Klippstein, Johnny, 53
Knoblauch, Chuck, *12*, *75*, 156–57, *199*
Koch, Billy, 189
Koosman, Jerry, *197*
Koufax, Sandy, 4
Kranepool, Ed, 144
Kubek, Tony, *11*, 73, *75*, 107–08, 113, *196*
Kuenn, Harvey, *11*, 59, *60*, 68–70, 73, *75*, *196*
Kuhn, Bowie, 137

Laboy, Coco, *197*
Landreaux, Ken, 18
Lane, Frank, 69, 73
Langston, Mark, *198*
Larsen, Don, 138
LaRussa, Tony, 152, 187–88
Lasorda, Tom, 71, 163–64, 165
Lefebvre, Jim, *11*, *60*, 70–71, *77*, 104, 120
Leonard, Buck, 7
Leonard, Jeff, *198*
Lidle, Cory, 180
Linzy, Frank, *197*
Listach, Pat, *12*, 66, *75*, 91–92; wife Lisa, 92
Littlefield, Dick, 73
Lloyd, Graeme, 92
Lofton, Kenny, 66, 91–92, 156, 161
Long, Terrence, 95
Lopes, Davey, 120, 141
Lopez, Al, 101
Lopez, Marcelino, *197*
Lopez, Rodrigo, 3, 189, *199*
Los Angeles Memorial Coliseum, 106
Luzinski, Greg, 121, 129
Lynn, Fred, *12*, 40, *41*, 47–49, 57, *75*, *197*
Lyons, Steve, 37

Maas, Kevin, 161
Macha, Ken, 194
Mack, Connie, 82
Maddox, Garry, 121, 129
Maddux, Greg, 4, 154
Madlock, Bill, 125
Make-A-Wish-Foundation, 188
Mantle, Mickey, 4, 23, 25, 30, 101–02, 184
Martin, Billy, 74
Martinez, Edgar, 145
Martinez, Tippy, 153
Mathewson, Christy, 108
Matlack, Jon, *11*, *77*, 125–26, *197*; wife Dee,
    126
Matsui, Hideki, 191, 201, 203
Matthews, Gary, *11*, *77*, 127–28, *197*; sons
    Delvon and Gary, Jr., 128; wife Sandra, 128
May, Carlos, 72, *197*
May, Lee, 30, 67, *197*
Mayo Clinic, 108
Mays, Willie, *11*, *13*, 17, 21, 23–25, 30, 40, *41*,
    55, *77*, 104, 159, *196*; wife Mae, 25
Mazeroski, Bill, 73, 107
McBride, Bake, *11*, *77*, 128–29
McCool, Billy, *197*
McCovey, Willie, *11*, *13*, 20, 21, 26–27, 40, *41*,
    77, 159, *196*; and McCovey Cove, 27
McDougald, Gil, *11*, 23, *75*, 99–103, 171; wife
    Lucille, 102

McDowell, Roger, 163
McGee, Willie, 188
McGraw, Tug, 121, 129
McGwire, Mark, *12*, 13, 27–29, 31, 45–46, *76*, 151, 183, *198*
McKeon, Jack, 192
McLain, Denny, 119
McLendon, Lloyd, 74
McMurtry, Craig, *198*
McNamara, John, 65
Memorial Stadium, 33
Merkle, Fred, 118
Metzger, Butch, *12*, *77*, 87–88, 131, *197*
Miller, Justin, 189
Minoso, Minnie, *196*
Molitor, Paul, *198*
Mondesi, Raul, *12*, *77*, 168–69, *199*
Montanez, Willie, 124
Montefusco, John, *12*, *77*, 130–31, *197*
Montreal Royals, 8
Moon, Wally, *11*, 73, *77*, 106, 128, *196*
Morgan, Joe, 16, 67, 134, *197*
Morris, Jack, 156
Morris, Matt, *199*
Morton, Carl, *11*, *77*, 121–22, *197*
Munson, Thurman, *11*, *41*, 50–51, *75*, 113, 122, 174
Murphy, Dale, 156
Murray, Eddie, *12*, *13*, 17, 29–31, *75*, 127, 159; daughters Jessica and Jordan, 31; wife Janice, 31
Murtaugh, Danny, 74
Musial, Stan, 55, 84
Myers, Dave, 58

Nagy, Mike, *197*
Nash, Jim, *197*
Neal, Charlie, 35
Newark Eagles, 52
Newcombe, Don, *11*, 35, *41*, 51–53, 62, *77*, 105, 125, 136, *196*
Nixon, Richard M., 9
Nomo, Hideo, *12*, *77*, 95, 136, 171–72, *199*, 201
Norman, Dan, 37

Oates, Johnny, 124
O'Brien, Dan, 65
Olerud, John, 161
Oliva, Tony, *11*, *75*, 115–16, *197*
Oliver, Al, 135
Olson, Gregg, *12*, *75*, 152–53
Oriole Park at Camden Yards, 32
Osteen, Claude, 68
Osuna, Al, *199*

Oswalt, Roy, *199*
Owchinko, Bob, *198*
Owen, Mickey, 118, 141

Page, Mitchell, *198*
Paige, Satchel, 7, 23, 80, 81, 202
Paine, Phil, 106
Palmer, Jim, 127
Parker, Wes, 70, 104
Parsons, Bill, *197*
Patek, Freddie, 109
Pearson, Albie, *11*, *75*, 109–10, *196*
Pena, Tony, 160
Perez, Marty, 125
Perez, Tony, 16
Perry, Jim, 111
Pesky, Johnny, 84, 98
Peters, Gary, *11*, *75*, 114–15
Pettitte, Andy, 169
Philadelphia Sports Writers Association, 101
Phoebus, Tom, *197*
Piazza, Mike, *12*, *77*, 158, 164–66, 167, *199*
Piniella, Lou, *11*, 59, *60*, 71–72, *75*
Podsednik, Scott, 193, *199*
Polo Grounds, 19, 23
Posada, Jorge, 174
Powell, Boog, 117
Priddy, Gerry, 96
Prior, Mark, 182
Pro Athletes Outreach, 146
Puckett, Kirby, 19, 156
Pujols, Albert, *12*, 57, *77*, 158, 187–88, *199*; daughter Bella, 188; wife Dee Dee, 188
Putnam, Pat, *198*

Quinn, Mark, *199*

Rader, Dave, *197*
Raines, Tim, 46, 174, *198*
Ramirez, Manny, 93
Randa, Joe, 183
Ray, Johnny, *198*
Reese, Pee Wee, 70, 80
Reinsdorf, Jerry, 22
Reiser, Pete, 2
Reuss, Jerry, 140
Reynolds, Harold, 58
Rice, Jim, 48
Richardson, Bobby, 26
Rickey, Branch, 7
Riegels, "Wrong Way," 141
Righetti, Dave, *12*, *75*, 86, 138–39, *198*; daughters Natalee, Nicolette, Wesley, 139; wife Kandace, 139
Ripken, Bill, 33

Ripken, Cal, Jr., *12*, 13, 17, 31–34, 39, 40, *41*, 66, *75*, 139, 159, *198*; wife Kelly, 33
Ripken, Cal, Sr., 33
Ripken Stadium, 33
Ripken Youth Baseball Academy, 33–34
Rivera, Mariano, 138, 174
Riverfront Stadium, 67, 151
Rizzuto, Phil, 173
Roberto Clemente Award, 25
Roberts, Robin, 26, 27, 108
Robinson, Brooks, 4, 15, 33, 117, 127
Robinson, Don, *198*
Robinson, Frank, *11*, *13*, 15, 34–36, 40, *41*, 44, 57, 59, *60*, *76*, 117, 159, *196*
Robinson, Jackie, 5–10, *11*, *13*, 15, 40, *41*, 51, 57, 62, 70, 77, 80, 81, 94, 97, 104, 120, 193, *196*, 201; daughter Sharon, 9; sons David and Jackie, Jr., 9; wife Rachel, 9, 10
Rockefeller, Nelson, 9
Rodgers, Buck, 167
Rodriguez, Alex, 176
Rogers, Steve, *197*
Rolen, Scott, 2, *12*, 77, 158, 171, 178–79, *199*, 203
Rollins, Jimmy, 187, 203
Rose, Pete, *11*, 15–16, 17, *41*, 54–56, 59, *60*, 67, 76, 90, 129, 131, *197*
Rozema, Dave, *198*
Rudi, Joe, 49
Rueter, Kirk, *199*
Russell, Bill, 141
Ruth, George (Babe), 1, 15, 29

Sabathia, C. C., *199*
Sabo, Chris, *12*, *76*, 150–51, 184
Sadecki, Ray, 20
Salmon, Tim, *12*, *75*, 158, 159–60, 161, *199*; wife Marci, 166
Samuel, Juan, *198*
Sandberg, Ryne, 84, 154
Sanford, Jack, *11*, 77, 108–09, *196*
Santiago, Benito, *12*, 77, 158, 159–60, 161, *198*
Santo, Ron, 39
Sasaki, Kazuhiro, *12*, 58, *76*, 80, 94–95, *199*, 201, 202; daughter Reina, 95; son Shogo, 95; wife Kaori, 95
Sax, Steve, *12*, 77, 120, 141–42
SBC Park, 25, 27
Schmidt, Mike, 4, 120, 129
Schwall, Don, *11*, *75*, 83–84, *197*
Scioscia, Mike, 135
Score, Herb, *11*, *75*, 99–103, 125, 171, *196*; wife Nancy, 103
Seals Stadium, 26

Seaver, Tom, *11*, *13*, 36–38, 57, 77, 105, 125, 131–32, 159
Seitzer, Kevin, 28
Sele, Aaron, *199*
Selig, Bud, 31, 56
Shantz, Bobby, 82
Shapiro, Mark, 66
Shea, Frank, 7
Shea Stadium, 55, 144
Sievers, Roy, *11*, 62, *75*, 96–97, *196*
Simmons, Curt, 108
Sisler, George, 1, 58
Sizemore, Ted, *11*, 77, 120–21
Skowron, Bill, 101
Smith, Dwight, 154
Smith, Lonnie, *198*
Smith, Reggie, 163
Snider, Duke, 162
Soriano, Rafael, *199*
Spahn, Warren, 24
Speaker, Tris, 175–76
Stargell, Willie, 193
Steinbrenner, George, 74, 119, 144, 175
Stengel, Casey, 100, 102, 105, 107
Stephens, Vern, 98
Stewart, Jimmy, 67
Strawberry, Darryl, *12*, 77, 143–44, 147, *198*
Stuart, Dick, 84
Sutcliffe, Rick, *12*, 77, 136–37, 154, *198*
Sutton, Don, *197*
Suzuki, Ichiro, *12*, 40, *41*, 48, 56–58, *76*, 145, 158, *199*, 201
Sweeney, Mike, 183

Takatsu, Shingo, 194
Tanana, Frank, 49, *197*
Tanner, Chuck, 42
Tavarez, Julian, *199*
Tebbetts, Birdie, 35
Terry, Ralph, 26
Thomas, Derrel, 88
Thomas, Frank, 42–43
Thomas, Valmy, 108
Thome, Jim, 161
Thompson, Robby, *198*
Thomson, Bobby, 7, 24, 52, 99
Tidrow, Dick, *197*
Tim Salmon Foundation, 166
Tinker, Joe, 84
Topps, 35
Torborg, Jeff, 64, 148
Torgeson, Earl, 7
Torre, Joe, 20, 123, 173–74
Trachsel, Steve, 178–79, *199*

Trammell, Alan, 123
Tresh, Mike, 113
Tresh, Tom, *11, 75,* 113–14, *196*
Trillo, Manny, 121
Trout, Dizzy, 98
Turner, Allen, 95
Turn 2 Foundation, 175

Ueberroth, Peter, 5
Unser, Del, *197*

Valentin, John, 177
Valentine, Ellis, 46
Valenzuela, Fernando, *12, 77,* 125, 136,
    139–41, 146, *198*; son Fernando, Jr., 141;
    wife Linda,141
Valo, Elmer, 83
Vande Berg, Ed, *198*
Vaughan, Arky, 1
Vaughn, Mo, 177
Ventura, Robin, 161
Veterans Stadium, 129
Virdon, Bill, *11,* 59, *60,* 73–74, 77, 128, *196*
Vizquel, Omar, 161
Voiselle, Bill, 2

Waitkus, Eddie, 2
Wakefield, Tim, *199*
Walton, Jerome, *12, 76,* 153–54, *198*
Ward, Pete, 115, *197*
Wealth Enhancement Group, 89
Weaver, Earl, 127
Webb, Brandon, 193
Weis, Al, 118

Weiss, Walt, *12,* 28, 45, *76,* 151–52, *198*
Whitaker, Lou, *12, 75,* 133–34
White, Gabe, 185
Wilkerson, Brad, *199,* 203
Willey, Carlton, *196*
Williams, Bernie, 156, 174
Williams, Billy, *11, 13,* 38–39, *76, 197;* wife
    Shirley, 39
Williams, Earl, *11, 76,* 123–24, *197*
Williams, Ted, 15, 26, 44, 99, 155, 176–77
Williamson, Scott, *12, 76,* 184–85, *199*; wife
    Lisa, 185
Willis, Dontrelle, *12, 76,* 158, 192–93,
    199
Wills, Maury, 70, 104
Wilson, Craig, 194
Wilson, Preston, *199*
Wiltse, Hooks, 88
Wood, Kerry, *12, 76,* 125, 158, 181–82, 190,
    199; wife Sarah, 181
Worrell, Tim, 149
Worrell, Todd, *12, 77,* 149, *198*
Worthington, Craig, *198*
Wrigley Field, 38, 39, 46
Wynegar, Butch, *197*

Yankee Stadium, 37, 51, 52, 102, 112, 113, 114,
    175
Yastrzemski, Carl, 119

Zachry, Pat, *12,* 37, *76,* 88, 131–32
Zeile, Todd, 156, 165
Zernial, Gus, 83, 97
Zimmer, Don, 49, 154, 174